NEW JERUSALEM

NEW JERUSALEM

The Portable New Century Edition

EMANUEL SWEDENBORG

Translated from the Latin by George F. Dole
and Jonathan S. Rose

SWEDENBORG FOUNDATION
West Chester, Pennsylvania

Originally published in Latin as *De Nova Hierosolyma et Ejus Doctrina Coelesti: Ex Auditis e Coelo: Quibus Praemittitur Aliquid de Novo Coelo et Nova Terra,* London, 1758.

Second printing, 2023

Printed in the United States of America

ISBN   978-0-87785-415-9
This text is also included in the hardcover library edition of *The Shorter Works of 1758,* ISBN 978-0-87785-482-1.

Library of Congress Cataloging-in-Publication Data

Swedenborg, Emanuel, 1688–1772.
    [De Nova Hierosolyma et ejus doctrina coelesti. English]
    New Jerusalem / Emanuel Swedenborg ; translated by George F. Dole.
        pages cm
    Summary: "Emanuel Swedenborg understood the city of New Jerusalem—as described in the book of Revelation—to mean not a physical city but an epoch of history, a new spiritual age that was just beginning to take shape during his lifetime in the eighteenth century. This short work, presented as a series of teachings that characterize this spiritual age to come, is also one of Swedenborg's most concise and readable summaries of his own theology. Building on fundamental concepts such as good, truth, will, and understanding, he describes the importance of love and usefulness in spiritual growth. In the second half of the volume he focuses on how this new theology relates to the church of his day and to church teachings about the Bible, the Lord's incarnation on earth, and rites such as baptism and the Holy Supper. Each short chapter is followed by extensive references back to his theological magnum opus, Secrets of Heaven.This volume is an excellent starting point for those who want an overview of Swedenborg's theology presented in his own words."— Provided by publisher.
    Summary: "Swedenborg's brief summary of his teachings about the New Jerusalem, the new spiritual age that he said began in the eighteenth century, with extensive references to his multi-volume Secrets of Heaven for further reading"— Provided by publisher.
        ISBN 978-0-87785-415-9 (paperback) — ISBN 978-0-87785-482-1
    1. New Jerusalem Church—Doctrines—Early works to 1800. I. Dole, George F., translator. II. Title.

BX8712.H7 2016
230'.94—dc23

                                                                                    2014048739

Senior copy editor, Alicia L. Dole
Text designed by Joanna V. Hill
Ornaments from Swedenborg's Latin editions
Typesetting by Alicia L. Dole
Cover designed by Karen Connor

For information contact:
Swedenborg Foundation
320 North Church Street
West Chester, PA 19380 USA
Telephone: (610) 430-3222
Web: www.swedenborg.com
E-mail: info@swedenborg.com

Contents

v

Conventions Used in This Work

MOST of the following conventions apply generally to the translations in the New Century Edition Portable series. For introductory material on the content and history of *New Jerusalem,* and for annotations on the subject matter, including obscure or problematic content, and extensive indexes, the reader is referred to the Deluxe New Century Edition volume *The Shorter Works of 1758.*

Section numbers Following a practice common in his time, Swedenborg divided his published theological works into sections numbered in sequence from beginning to end. His original section numbers have been preserved in this edition, they appear in boxes in the outside margins. Traditionally, these sections have been referred to as "numbers" and designated by the abbreviation "n." In this edition, however, the more common section symbol (§) is used to designate the section numbers, and the sections are referred to as such.

Subsection numbers Because many sections throughout Swedenborg's works are too long for precise cross-referencing, Swedenborgian scholar John Faulkner Potts (1838–1923) further divided them into subsections; these have since become standard, though minor variations occur from one edition to another. These subsections are indicated by bracketed numbers that appear in the text itself: [2], [3], and so on. Because the beginning of the first *subsection* always coincides with the beginning of the *section* proper, it is not labeled in the text.

Citations of Swedenborg's text As is common in Swedenborgian studies, text citations of Swedenborg's works refer not to page numbers but to section numbers, which unlike page numbers are uniform in most editions. In citations the section symbol (§) is generally omitted after the title of a work by Swedenborg. Thus "*Heaven and Hell* 239" would refer to section 239 (§239) of Swedenborg's *Heaven and Hell,* not to page 239 of any edition. Subsection numbers are given after a colon; a reference such as "239:2" indicates subsection 2 of section 239. The reference "239:1" would indicate the first subsection of section 239, though that subsection is not in fact labeled in the text. Where section numbers stand alone without titles, their function is indicated by the prefixed section symbol; for example, "§239:2". However, section marks are generally omitted in Swedenborg's indexlike references to *Secrets of Heaven.*

Citations of the Bible Biblical citations in this edition follow the accepted standard: a semicolon is used between book references and between chapter references, and a comma between verse references. Therefore "Matthew 5:11, 12; 6:1; 10:41, 42; Luke 6:23, 35" refers to Matthew chapter 5, verses 11 and 12; Matthew chapter 6, verse 1; Matthew chapter 10, verses 41 and 42; and Luke chapter 6, verses 23 and 35. Swedenborg often incorporated the numbers of verses not actually represented in his text when listing verse numbers for a passage he quoted; these apparently constitute a kind of "see also" reference to other material he felt was relevant, and are generally retained in this edition. This edition also follows Swedenborg where he cites contiguous verses individually (for example, John 14:8, 9, 10, 11), rather than as a range (John 14:8–11). Occasionally this edition supplies a full, conventional Bible reference where Swedenborg omits one after a quotation.

Quotations in Swedenborg's works Some features of the original Latin text of *New Jerusalem* have been modernized in this edition. For example, Swedenborg's first edition generally relies on context or italics rather than on quotation marks to indicate passages taken from the Bible or from other works. The manner in which these conventions are used in the original suggests that Swedenborg did not feel it necessary to belabor the distinction between direct quotation and paraphrase of the Bible; neither did he mark his omissions from or changes to material he quoted, a practice in which this edition generally follows him. One exception consists of instances in which Swedenborg did not include a complete sentence in a Bible quotation. The omission in such cases has been marked in this edition with added points of ellipsis.

Italicized terms Any words in indented scriptural extracts that are here set in italics reflect a similar emphasis in the first edition.

Special use of vertical rule The prologue of *New Jerusalem* (§§8–10) is set in continuous italics in the first edition. For this edition, the heavy use of italic text was felt to be antithetical to modern tastes, as well as difficult to read, and so these passages are instead marked by a vertical rule in the margin.

Changes to and insertions in the text This translation is based on the first Latin edition, published by Swedenborg himself. It incorporates the silent emendation of minor errors, not only in the text proper but in Bible verse references and in section references to Swedenborg's other published theological works. The text has also been changed without notice where the verse numbering of the Latin Bible cited by Swedenborg differs from that of modern English Bibles. Throughout the translation, references or cross-references that are implied but not stated have been inserted in square brackets []; for example, [Matthew 25:29]. By contrast, biblical references that occur in parentheses reflect references in the first edition.

Chapter numbering Swedenborg did not number the chapters of *New Jerusalem*. His decision not to do so seems to have been deliberate, and in accord with it chapter numbers are not included in the text. However, because some studies of this work make reference to chapter numbers, the table of contents provides them.

Biblical titles Swedenborg refers to the Hebrew Scriptures as the Old Testament and to the Greek Scriptures as the New Testament; his terminology has been adopted in this edition. As was the custom in his day, he refers in *New Jerusalem* 266 to the Pentateuch (Genesis, Exodus, Leviticus, Numbers, and Deuteronomy) as "the five books of Moses."

Problematic content Occasionally Swedenborg makes statements that, although mild by the standards of eighteenth-century theological discourse, now read as harsh, dismissive, or insensitive. The most problematic are assertions about or criticisms of various religious traditions and their adherents—including Judaism, ancient or contemporary; Roman Catholicism; Islam; and the Protestantism in which Swedenborg himself grew up. These statements are far outweighed in size and importance by other passages in Swedenborg's works earnestly maintaining the value of every individual and of all religions. This wider context is discussed in the introductions and annotations of the Deluxe edition mentioned above. In the present format, however, problematic statements must be retained without comment. The other option—to omit them—would obscure some aspects of Swedenborg's presentation and in any case compromise its historicity.

THE NEW JERUSALEM
AND
ITS HEAVENLY TEACHINGS

Seek first the kingdom of God,
and all things will be added to you.

—Matthew 6:33

The New Jerusalem
and Its Heavenly Teachings

The New Heaven and the New Earth,
and What Is Meant by "the New Jerusalem"

IT says in the Book of Revelation,

I saw a new heaven and a new earth, because the first heaven and the first earth had passed away. And I saw the holy city, the New Jerusalem, coming down from God out of heaven, prepared as a bride adorned for her husband. The city had a great and high wall with twelve gates, and on the gates were twelve angels, and names written that are the names of the twelve tribes of Israel.

And the wall of the city had twelve foundations, and on them were the names of the twelve apostles of the Lamb.

The city was laid out as a square; its length was as great as its breadth.

And [the angel who talked with me] measured the city with a reed: twelve thousand stadia. Its length, breadth, and height were equal.

Then he measured its wall: one hundred and forty-four cubits, which is the measure of a human being, that is, of an angel.

Its wall was made of jasper; and the city was pure gold, like clear glass. The foundations of the wall of the city were made of precious stones of every kind.

The twelve gates were twelve pearls. And the street of the city was pure gold, like transparent glass.

The glory of *God* illuminated it, and *the Lamb* was its light.

The nations of those who are saved will walk in its light, and the monarchs of the earth will bring their glory and honor into it. (Revelation 21:1, 2, 12–24)

When people read this, they understand it only in literal terms. They think that the visible heavens are going to be destroyed along with the earth and that new heavens are going to come into being and come down onto the new earth in the form of a holy city, a Jerusalem with the dimensions given in the description.

[2] Angels understand it in a completely different way, though. They understand in a spiritual way the details that we understand in an earthly way, and they understand what those details really mean. This is the inner or spiritual meaning of the Word. In the deeper or spiritual meaning that angels are engaged in, *a new heaven and a new earth* mean a new church both in heaven and on earth (both will be discussed later [§§2–5]). *The holy city coming down from God out of heaven* means its heavenly teachings. *Its length, breadth, and height, which were equal,* mean everything in those teachings that is good and true, all gathered together. Its *wall* means the truths that protect it. *The measure of the wall,* being *one hundred and forty-four cubits, which is the measure of a human being, that is, of an angel* means all those protective truths gathered together, as well as the nature of those truths. *The twelve gates, which were pearls,* mean introductory truths, as do *the twelve angels on the gates. The foundations of the wall, which were made of precious stones of every kind,* mean the knowledge on which the teachings are based. *The twelve tribes of Israel* mean all elements of the church in general and in particular, as do *the twelve apostles. The gold like clear glass* that the city and streets were made of means good actions done out of love, which cause the teachings and their truths to shine. *The nations of those who are saved* and *the monarchs of the earth who will bring their glory and honor into it* mean everyone in the church who is devoted to what is good and true. *God* and *the Lamb* mean the Lord's divine nature itself and his divine-human nature.

[3] This is what the spiritual meaning of the Word is like; the earthly or literal meaning serves as its foundation. All the same, these

two meanings, the spiritual and the earthly, are bound together by their correspondence. I will not take the time here to show that this kind of spiritual meaning is present throughout because that is not my current task, but the reader may see what is presented in the following passages of *Secrets of Heaven*.[1]

On *earth* in the Word as meaning the church, especially where *earth* means the land of Canaan: §§662, 1066, 1067, 1262, 1413, 1607, 2928, 3355, 4447, 4535, 5577, 8011, 9325, 9643. This is because *earth,* spiritually understood, means the people who live there and their worship: 1262. *The people of the earth* [or *the land*] mean those who are part of the spiritual church: 2928. *The new heaven and the new earth* mean whatever is new in the heavens and on earth in terms of what is good and true, which means in matters of the church in both realms: 1733, 1850, 2117, 2118, 3355, 4535, 10373. On the meaning of *the first heaven and the first earth that had passed away,* see the booklet *The Last Judgment and Babylon Destroyed* from beginning to end, especially §§65–72. [4] On *Jerusalem* meaning the church in regard to its teachings, see *Secrets of Heaven* 402, 3654, 9166. On cities meaning the teachings that are part of a church and a religion, see 402, 2451, 2712, 2943, 3216, 4492, 4493. On *the wall of the city* meaning the protective truth of the teachings, see 6419. On *the gates of the city* meaning truths that lead us to a body of teaching and through that teaching into the church, see 2943, 4477, 4492, 4493. On *the twelve tribes of Israel* as representing and therefore symbolizing everything good and true in the church both in general and in particular, and therefore all aspects of faith and love, see 3858, 3926, 6335, 6640. The meaning of *the twelve apostles of the Lord* is much the same: 2129, 3272, 3354, 3488, 3858, 6397. When it says that the apostles will sit on twelve thrones and will judge the twelve tribes of Israel [Matthew 19:28; Luke 22:30], it means that everyone will be judged according to the true and good principles of the church and therefore by the Lord who is their source: 2129, 6397. *Twelve* means everything taken together: 577, 2089, 2129, 2130, 3272, 3858, 3913. [5] The same holds true for *one hundred and forty-four* because this is twelve times twelve: 7973. It holds true also for *twelve thousand:* 7973. All the numbers in the Word have definable meanings: 482, 487, 647, 648, 755, 813, 1963, 1988, 2075, 2252, 3252, 4264, 6175, 9488, 9659, 10217, 10253. Multiples mean much the same as the individual factors that are

---

1. Swedenborg refers here to his multivolume work *Secrets of Heaven*, published in London in 1749–1756.

multiplied to produce them: 5291, 5335, 5708, 7973. *The measure* means what a given thing is like in regard to its truth and goodness: 3104, 9603, 10262. The *foundations of the wall* mean the knowledge of truth on which elements of the teachings are based: 9643. *Square* means complete: 9717, 9861. *Length* means goodness and its extent, and *breadth* means truth and its extent: 1613, 9861. *Precious stones* mean true perceptions that arise from what is good: 114, 9863, 9865. On the precious stones in the Urim and Thummim, both in general and specifically, see 3862, 9864, 9866, 9891, 9905. On the *jasper* of which the wall was made, see 9872. [6] *The street* of the city means the truth of the teachings that arises from what is good: 2336. *Gold* means good actions that come from love: 113, 1551, 1552, 5658, 6914, 6917, 9510, 9874, 9881. *Glory* means divine truth as it exists in heaven and the intelligence and wisdom that result from it: 4809, 5922, 8267, 8427, 9429, 10574. *Nations* mean the people in the church who are committed to what is good, and in an abstract sense the good actions that are taught by the church: 1159, 1258, 1260, 1285, 1416, 1849, 4574, 7830, 9255, 9256. *Monarchs* mean the people in the church who are committed to what is true, and in an abstract sense the truths that are taught by the church: 1672, 2015, 2069, 4575, 5044. The rituals involved in royal coronations have to do with matters of divine truth, but nowadays awareness of this symbolism has vanished: 4581, 4966 (which contain further discussion about divine truth).

2   Before dealing with the New Jerusalem and its teachings, I need to say something about the new heaven and the new earth. In the booklet *The Last Judgment and Babylon Destroyed* you will find an explanation of the meaning of the first heaven and the first earth that passed away. After they had passed away—that is, after the Last Judgment was complete—the Lord created, or formed, a new heaven. This heaven is made up of all the people who, from the time of the Lord's Coming to the time of the judgment, had lived lives of faith and caring, because only they were forms of heaven. This is because the form of heaven that governs all the relationships and communications there is the form of the divine truth, derived from divine goodness, that radiates from the Lord, and we take on this form spiritually by living in harmony with divine truth. On this as the source of heaven's form, see *Heaven and Hell* 200–212, and on all angels as being forms of heaven, see *Heaven and Hell* 51–58, 73–77.

This makes it possible for us to know which people make up the new heaven and therefore also what they are like—namely, that they are of one mind, because when we live a life of faith and caring we love our neighbors as we love ourselves, and love that is mutually felt joins us to them and them to us. This joining is reciprocal and mutual because in the spiritual world love is a joining together. So when everyone is acting on the same principle, then a single mind arises from the many—from countless individuals, in fact, who are gathered in harmony with heaven's form. People become one in this way because there is nothing that separates or divides them; everything connects and unites them.

Since this heaven was formed out of all such individuals from the Lord's time to the present, we can be sure that it is made up of both Christians and non-Christians. The largest portion, though, consists of all the little children from the whole world who have died since the time of the Lord. All of them, you see, have been adopted by the Lord, raised in heaven, and taught by angels. They have been kept safe so that they could be part of the new heaven along with others. We can therefore determine how vast this heaven is. You may see in *Heaven and Hell* 329–345 that all little children who die are raised in heaven and become angels, and from §§318–328 that heaven is formed just as much from non-Christians as from Christians.

On the subject of this new heaven, it is also important to know that it is distinct from the older heavens—the ones, that is, that existed before the Lord's Coming. Nevertheless, the newer are set in relation to the older in such a way that together they make one heaven.

The reason this new heaven is distinct from the older heavens is that the only body of teaching people of the earlier churches had was one of love and caring; they had no knowledge of any body of teaching about faith apart from love. That is also why the earlier heavens form a higher level while the new heaven forms a level underneath them. The heavens are levels, one above the other. On the highest level are the angels called "heavenly," most of whom come from the earliest church. The people there are called "heavenly angels" because of their heavenly love, which is a love for the Lord. On the levels below them are the angels who are called "spiritual," most of whom come from the ancient church. The people there are called "spiritual angels" because of their spiritual love, which is a caring about their neighbor. Below them are the people who are devoted to doing the good that their faith calls for, people who had lived lives of faith. "Living a life of faith" is living by the teachings of one's church, and "living" includes both intending and acting.

Still, all these heavens make one heaven because of an indirect inflow and a direct inflow, both of which come from the Lord.

You may get a clearer picture of all this, though, from what has been presented in my work *Heaven and Hell.* See particularly the chapter there on the two kingdoms into which the heavens are broadly distinguished (§§20–28), the chapter on the three heavens (§§29–40), and the information in the references assembled from *Secrets of Heaven* at the close of §603 on indirect and direct inflow. On the earliest church and the ancient church, see §46 of the booklet *The Last Judgment and Babylon Destroyed.*

5   That is enough at present about the new heaven; now for the new earth. The *new earth* means a new church on earth, since whenever one church comes to an end the Lord raises up a new one. You see, the Lord makes sure that there is always a church on earth, because the church is the means by which the Lord is joined to the human race, and heaven is joined to the world. This is because the church is where the Lord is known and where we find the divine truths by which we are joined to heaven and the Lord. (See the booklet *Last Judgment* 74 on the fact that a new church is being established at the present time.)

"A new earth" means "a new church," as we learn from a spiritual understanding of the Word, because in the spiritual meaning "earth" does not mean the land itself, but the people there and their worship of God. That is the spiritual equivalent of "earth." Then too, when we find a mention of "the earth" [or "the land"] in the Word with no further regional specification, it means the land of Canaan, and the land of Canaan was where the church had been ever since the earliest times. As a result, all the particular places there and thereabout that are mentioned in the Word, including mountains and rivers, have come to represent and symbolize inner realities of the church—what we speak of as its spiritual side. That is why, as just noted, "the land" in the Word refers to the church—because it means the land of Canaan, and the same holds true for "the new earth" here. This is what has led to the common practice in the church of referring to heaven as "the heavenly Canaan."

In the spiritual meaning of the Word, "the land of Canaan" means the church, as has been shown in various passages of *Secrets of Heaven,* including the following: The earliest church (the church before the Flood) and the ancient church (the church after the Flood) were in the land of Canaan: 567, 3686, 4447, 4454, 4516, 4517, 5136, 6516, 9325. All the specific places then came to represent the kinds of things we find in the Lord's kingdom and the church: 1585, 3686, 4447, 5136. That is why Abraham was commanded to go there—because symbolic religious practices would be instituted among his descendants through Jacob and a

Word would be written whose most outward sense would be made up of the representations and symbolisms found in that place: 3686, 4447, 5136, 6516. That is why "the land" and "the land of Canaan" in the Word mean the church: 3038, 3481, 3705, 4447, 4517, 5757, 10568.

I need to explain briefly what "Jerusalem" means in the spiritual **6** meaning of the Word. "Jerusalem" means the essential church, with a focus on its body of teaching. This is because there in the land of Canaan and nowhere else were the Temple and the altar, there and nowhere else were sacrifices offered and consequently was actual worship of God performed. That is why the three annual festivals were held there, and every male in the whole land was obliged to attend. That is why Jerusalem now, spiritually understood, means the church in regard to its worship or to its body of teaching—which amounts to the same thing, because its worship is defined by its body of teaching and performed as that body of teaching prescribes.

The reason it says "the holy city, the New Jerusalem, coming down from God out of heaven" is that in the spiritual meaning of the Word "a city" means a body of teaching, and "a holy city" means a body of teaching based on divine truth. This is because divine truth is what the Word refers to as "holy." It says "the New Jerusalem" for much the same reason that it refers to the earth as new. That is, as just noted [§5], "the earth" means the church and Jerusalem means that church in regard to its body of teaching. It is described as coming down from God out of heaven because all the divine truth that gives rise to a body of teaching comes down out of heaven from God.

It is obvious that "Jerusalem" does not mean a city (even though it looked like a city), because it says that its height was the same as its length and breadth, twelve thousand stadia (verse 16); that the measure of its wall, one hundred and forty-four cubits, was the measure of a human being, that is, of an angel (verse 17); that it was prepared as a bride adorned for her husband (verse 2); and that later "The angel said, 'Come, I will show you the bride, the wife of the Lamb.' And he showed me the holy city Jerusalem" (verses 9, 10). It is the church that is called the Lord's bride and wife in the Word, his "bride" before they have been joined together and his "wife" afterward—see *Secrets of Heaven* 3103, 3105, 3164, 3165, 3207, 7022, 9182.

Turning specifically to the body of teaching that now follows, it too **7** comes from heaven because it comes from the spiritual meaning of the Word, and the spiritual meaning of the Word is the same as the body of teaching that is found in heaven. You see, there is a church in heaven just as there is on earth. That is, the Word is there, there is a body of teaching drawn from the Word, and there are church buildings there with sermons being delivered—all because there are both ecclesiastical and civil institutions there. In brief, the only difference between things in the heavens and things on earth is that everything in heaven is in a more perfect state because all the people there are spiritual, and spiritual realities are far more perfect than earthly ones. On the fact that this is what heaven is like, see my book *Heaven and Hell* throughout, especially the chapters on forms of government in heaven (§§213–220) and divine worship there (§§221–227).

This shows what it means when it says that a holy city, a New Jerusalem, was seen coming down from God out of heaven.

But I need to turn now to the actual teachings for this new church, which are called "heavenly" because they have been revealed to me from heaven. That is, after all, the reason for this book.

Prologue to the Teachings

I have explained in the booklet *The Last Judgment and Babylon Destroyed* §§8 ($\S\S$33–39 and following) that the end of a church comes when there is no faith because there is no caring. Since the churches in the Christian world at present have identified themselves solely by differences in matters of faith (although the fact is that if there is no caring there is no faith), I should like to preface these teachings with some observations about the body of teaching focused on caring as understood by the ancients. By "the churches in the Christian world" I mean those among the Reformed and Evangelicals, but not among Roman Catholics, because the Christian church is not found there. That is, the church exists wherever the Lord is worshiped and the Word is read, and this is not the case among Roman Catholics. They worship themselves in place of the Lord, the Word is kept from the laity, and papal decrees are given equal or even higher status.

The body of teaching focused on caring, which is a body of teaching §9 about how to live our lives, was the primary focus in the ancient churches (on these churches, see *Secrets of Heaven* 1238, 2385). That body of teaching brought all the churches together and in this way made one church out of many. People at that time recognized as members of the church all those who lived a good and caring life. They called them family no matter how much they might differ with respect to the truths that we now call matters of faith. They taught each other in such matters, this being one of their acts of caring, and they felt no resentment if someone did not agree with them. They knew that we accept truth only to the extent that we are intent on doing what is good.

[2] Because this was the nature of the ancient churches, its members were individuals of inner depth; and because they had such depth, they were exceptionally wise. The explanation of this fact is that when we are devoted to doing good things that come from love and caring, our inner self is in heaven, in an angelic community there that is devoted to the same kind of goodness. Among the people of the ancient churches, this led to a raising of the mind into its higher reaches, which gave them wisdom. Wisdom cannot come from anywhere but heaven—that is, through heaven from the Lord; and there is wisdom in heaven because the people there are devoted to what is good. Wisdom is seeing what is true in the

light of what is true, and the light of what is true is the light that is found in heaven.

[3] With the passage of time, though, that ancient wisdom declined. As the human race distanced itself from doing good things out of love for the Lord or out of love for one's neighbor (the love that is called "caring"), people distanced themselves from wisdom as well, because they distanced themselves from heaven. That is why step by step people became external instead of deep, and as they became external they became worldly and self-centered. Once we are like this, we have little interest in what is heavenly, because we are completely preoccupied with the pleasures of our earthly loves. This includes the evils that appeal to us because of these loves. So when we hear about life after death, about heaven and hell—about anything spiritual, that is—these seem foreign to us, and not familiar, as they should.

[4] That is also why the body of teaching focused on caring that was so beloved by the ancients is now completely lost. Does anyone nowadays realize what "caring" really means or what "a neighbor" really is? Yet that body of teaching tells us not only this but countless other things as well. People nowadays do not know a thousandth of all this. Yet the entire Sacred Scripture is nothing but a body of teaching focused on love and caring. That is what the Lord is telling us when he says,

> You are to love the Lord your God with all your heart, with all your soul, and with all your mind. This is the first and great commandment. The second is like it: you are to love your neighbor as yourself. All the Law and the Prophets depend on these two commandments." (Matthew 22:37, 38, 39, 40)

"The Law and the Prophets" are the Word in its entirety and in every detail.

 In the following pages I have appended to the specific teachings collections of references to *Secrets of Heaven,* because the passages referred to provide a fuller explanation of the matters under consideration.

Goodness and Truth

ALL things in the universe that are in accord with the divine design **11** go back to goodness and truth. There are no exceptions to this in heaven or in the world, because everything good, like everything true, comes from the Divine, which is the source of everything.

We can see, then, that nothing is more necessary for us than knowing **12** what goodness is and what truth is and how each focuses on the other, as well as how each becomes joined to the other. It is particularly necessary, though, for people of the church, because just as everything in heaven goes back to what is good and what is true, so does everything in the church. This is because the goodness and truth that are in heaven are also the goodness and truth that are in the church. This is why I am starting off with a chapter on goodness and truth.

The divine design calls for goodness and truth to be joined together **13** and not separated—to be one, then, and not two. They are together as they emanate from the Lord and they are together in heaven, so they need to be joined to each other in the church.

In heaven, the joining of what is good and what is true is called "the heavenly marriage" because everyone there participates in this marriage. That is why heaven is compared to a marriage in the Word and why the Lord is called the Bridegroom and the Husband, while heaven is called the bride and the wife, as is the church. The reason heaven and the church are so called is that the people there are receptive to the divine goodness that is present within truths.

All the intelligence and wisdom that angels have comes from that **14** marriage. None comes from anything good separated from what is true or from anything true separated from what is good. The same goes for [the intelligence and wisdom of] people in the church.

Since the joining together of goodness and truth is like a marriage, we **15** can see that anything good loves what is true and that correspondingly anything true loves what is good. Each longs to be joined to the other. People in the church who do not have this love and this longing are not participating in the heavenly marriage. This means that the church is not yet in them, because the joining together of goodness and truth is what makes the church.

16 Goodness takes many forms. Basically, it can be spiritual or earthly, and these two types of goodness come together in what is genuinely good on the moral level. The same goes for types of truth as for types of goodness, because truths come from what is good and are forms of what is good.

17 The relationship between what is evil and what is false is the inverse of the relationship between what is good and what is true. That is, just as everything in the universe that is in accord with the divine design goes back to what is good and what is true, so everything that violates that design goes back to what is evil and what is false. Further, just as what is good loves being joined to what is true and what is true loves being joined to what is good, likewise what is evil loves being joined to what is false and what is false loves being joined to what is evil.

And just as all intelligence and wisdom are born of a bond between what is good and what is true, so all madness and stupidity are born of a bond between what is evil and what is false. The bond between evil and falsity is called "the hellish marriage."

18 We can see from the fact that evil and falsity are the opposite of goodness and truth that nothing true can be joined to anything evil and nothing good can be joined to any falsity arising from evil. If anything true is put together with something evil it is no longer true; it is false because it has been distorted. If anything good is put together with some falsity arising from evil it is no longer good; it is evil because it has been polluted. A falsity that does not arise from evil, though, can be joined to goodness.

19 No one who is resolutely and habitually devoted to what is evil and what is false can know what is good and what is true, because such people believe that their evil is good and that their falsity is the truth. On the other hand, anyone who is resolutely and habitually devoted to what is good and what is true can know what is evil and what is false. This is because every type of goodness and its accompanying truth is heavenly in essence, and if any of it is not heavenly in essence it still comes from heaven. Every type of evil and its accompanying falsity, though, is hellish in essence, and any of it that is not hellish in essence still comes from hell. Everything heavenly is in the light, while everything hellish is in darkness.

From *Secrets of Heaven*

ABSOLUTELY everything in the universe goes back to either good- **20**
ness and truth or evil and falsity. If it is in keeping with the divine
design, or is becoming so, it goes back to what is good and true, while if
it is in violation of the divine design it goes back to what is evil and false:
3166, 4390, 4409, 5232, 7256, 10122. This holds true for our understanding and our will, since our understanding is the part of us that is receptive
either to what is true or to what is false and our will is the part of us that
is receptive either to what is good or to what is evil: 10122. Nowadays,
not many people know what "truth" really is in essence because so little is
known about what is good. Yet everything true comes from what is good
and everything good happens by means of what is true: 2507, 3603, 4136,
9186, 9995.

There are four kinds of people.

1. There are people who live lives based on falsity; some of them do so
   with evil intent, and some of them do so without evil intent.
2. There are people who live lives based on truth but lack good intent.
3. There are people who live lives based on truth who use that truth to
   focus on and move toward what is good.
4. And there are people who live lives based on truth who have good
   intent.

Let us take these one at a time.

1. *People who live lives based on falsity with evil intent and people who* **21**
live lives based on falsity without evil intent; and also the nature of false
beliefs that accompany evil intent and of false beliefs that do not. There are
many kinds of falsity—as many as there are kinds of evil—and there are
many sources of things that are evil and of the falsities that they engen-
der: 1188, 1212, 4729, 4822, 7574. Falsity that comes from evil, or evil-
based falsity, is one thing; evil that comes from falsity, or falsity-based
evil, which leads in turn to further or secondary falsity, is another: 1679,
2243. From just one false idea, especially if it is taken as a first principle,
further false ideas flow in an unbroken series: 1510, 1511, 4717, 4721. There
are falsities that are the result of cravings arising from our love for ourselves and for the world, and there are falsities that are the result of misleading sensory impressions: 1295, 4729. There are falsities that arise from

what our religion has taught us and there are falsities that arise from our ignorance: 4729, 8318, 9258. There is falsity that contains some good and there is falsity that contains no good: 2863, 9304, 10109, 10302. There are also things that have been falsified: 7318, 7319, 10648. Everything evil has something false accompanying it: 7577, 8094. The falsity accompanying the cravings that arise from love for ourselves is truly evil; it is the worst kind of falsity: 4729.

[2] Evil is heavy and falls into hell of its own accord, but this is not true of falsity unless it comes from evil: 8279, 8298. Good turns into evil and truth into falsity as they fall from heaven into hell because this is like coming into a dense and polluted atmosphere: 3607. The hells are surrounded by evil-based falsities, which look like storm clouds and unclean waters: 8137, 8146, 8210. The things that are said by the people who are in the hells are falsities that come from evil: 1695, 7351, 7352, 7357, 7392, 7699. Left to their own devices, people intent on evil cannot think anything but falsity: 7437. More on evil that comes from falsity (2408, 4818, 7272, 8265, 8279) and falsity that comes from evil (6359, 9304, 10302).

[3] Every falsity is something we can convince ourselves of, and when we have done so it seems to us to be the truth: 5033, 6865, 8521, 8780. We should therefore make sure something is true before convincing ourselves of it: 4741, 7012, 7680, 7950, 8521. We should be particularly careful not to convince ourselves of falsity in matters of religion because this leads to false convictions that remain with us after death: 845, 8780. How damaging false convictions are: 794, 806, 5096, 7686.

[4] What is good cannot flow into truth as long as we are intent on evil: 2434. To the extent that we devote our lives to what is evil and the falsity that goes with it, to that extent what is good and what is true are moved away from us: 3402. The Lord takes the greatest care to prevent truth from being joined to what is evil and prevent the falsity that comes from evil from being joined to what is good: 3110, 3116, 4416, 5217. If these pairs are mixed, the result is profanation: 6348. Truths put an end to falsities and falsities put an end to truths: 5207. Truths cannot be accepted on any deep level as long as skepticism reigns: 3399.

[5] Examples showing how truths can be falsified: 7318. Why evil people are allowed to falsify truths: 7332. Evil people falsify truths by bending and applying them to an evil purpose: 8094, 8149. Truth is said to have been falsified if it has been used to support evil, which happens mainly through deception and superficial appearances: 7344, 8602. The evil are allowed to attack truth but not to attack what is good; they are allowed

to distort truth by various interpretations and applications: 6677. Truth that has been falsified for an evil purpose is in opposition to what is true and good: 8062. Falsified truth used for evil purposes smells terrible in the other life: 7319. More on the falsification of truth: 7318, 7319, 10648.

[6] Some false religious beliefs harmonize with what is good and some do not: 9258. False religious beliefs that do not clash with what is good do not lead to evil except in people who are intent on evil: 8318. False religious beliefs are not held against people who are intent on doing good, but they are held against people who are intent on doing evil: 8051, 8149. Truths that are not genuine and even falsities can be associated with genuine truths for people who are intent on doing good, but not for people who are intent on doing evil: 3470, 3471, 4551, 4552, 7344, 8149, 9298. The way things appear in the literal meaning of the Word sets elements that are true beside elements that are false: 7344. False beliefs are rendered true and softened by what is good because they are used for and deflected toward what is good, and the evil is put aside: 8149. The false religious beliefs of people who are intent on doing good are accepted by the Lord as if they were truths: 4736, 8149. Any act of goodness whose character has been shaped by false religious belief is accepted by the Lord if it was done in ignorance and innocence, and if the aim behind it was good: 7887. The truths we possess are outward guises of what is true and good, guises deeply stained with misleading appearances, but if our lives are focused on doing what is good the Lord adjusts them toward genuine truths: 2053. Falsities containing something good can be found in people who are outside the church and therefore ignorant of the truth and also in people in a church where there are false teachings: 2589–2604, 2861, 2863, 3263, 3778, 4189, 4190, 4197, 6700, 9256. Falsities in which there is nothing good are more harmful for people within the church than they are for people outside the church: 7688. What is true and good is taken away from evil people in the other life and given to the good, in keeping with the Lord's words "To those who have, more will be given, and they will have abundance; but from those who do not have, even what they have will be taken away" [Matthew 25:29]: 7770.

2. *People who live lives based on truth but lack good intent; and also the nature of truths that lack goodness.* Truths that lack goodness are not truths in and of themselves, because they have no life: the whole life of truth comes from what is good: 3603. This means these truths are like a body without a soul: 8530, 9154. People like this mistake their knowledge about truth and goodness for actual truth and goodness themselves, but their

knowledge resides only in their memory and has not been applied to their lives: 5276. Truths are not internalized for us or made our own if we merely know them and acknowledge them for reasons arising from our self-love and love for the world: 3402, 3834. The truths that are internalized, though, are the ones we acknowledge for the sake of truth and goodness themselves: 3849. Truths apart from what is good are not accepted by the Lord (4368) and do not save us (2261). People who are focused on truths apart from what is good are not part of the church: 3963. They cannot be regenerated, either: 10367. The Lord does not flow into truths except by way of what is good: 10367.

On the separation of what is true from what is good: 5008, 5009, 5022, 5028. What truth is like without anything good and what it is like when it comes from something good: 1949, 1950, 1964, 5951. Some comparisons concerning this topic: 5830. Without what is good, truth is harsh: 1949, 1950, 1951, 1964. In the spiritual world it looks hard (6359, 7068) and sharply pointed (2799). Truth without goodness is like the light of winter, in which everything in the earth is dormant and nothing is produced; but truth that comes from goodness is like the light of spring and summer, in which everything blooms and bears fruit: 2231, 3146, 3412, 3413. This kind of winter light turns into deep darkness when light flows in from heaven; and people devoted to those [wintry] truths then become blind and stupid: 3412, 3413.

People who separate truths from goodness are in darkness; they do not know what truth is and are mired in falsities: 9186. They plunge from false convictions into evil practices: 3325, 8094. The errors and false convictions into which they plunge themselves: 4721, 4730, 4776, 4783, 4925, 7779, 8313, 8765, 9224. The Word is closed to them: 3773, 4783, 8780. They do not pay attention to or even see all the things the Lord said about love and caring and therefore about goodness: 1017, 3416. They do not know what goodness is, and therefore they do not know what heavenly love is or what caring is: 2417, 3603, 4136, 9995. In the other life, people who know the truths that belong to religious faith and yet live evil lives misuse truths in order to gain power; what they are like, and what happens to them there: 4802.

Divine truth condemns us to hell, while divine goodness raises us to heaven: 2258. Divine truth is terrifying, but divine goodness is not: 4180. What it is like to be judged from the standpoint of truth as opposed to being judged from the standpoint of goodness: 2335.

23   3. *People who live lives based on truth and use that truth to focus on and move toward what is good; and also the nature of truths that lead to* *what is good.* We intend whatever we love, and whatever we love or intend we think about and justify by various means. Whatever we love or intend we call good, and whatever thoughts and various justifications we have we call true: 4070. That is why truth turns into goodness when it becomes a matter of our love and will, or when we love and will it: 5526, 7835, 10367. And since our love or our will is the core of our existence, no truth comes to life for us as long as we only know about it and think about it—[it comes to life] only when we love and will to do it and we do it as a result of our love and our will: 5595, 9282. That is how truths receive their life—from what is good: 2434, 3111, 3607, 6077. So truths get their life from what is good, and truths have no life apart from what is good: 1589, 1950, 1997, 2572, 3180, 4070, 4096, 4097, 4736, 4757, 4884, 5147, 5928, 9154, 9667, 9841, 10729. Illustrated [by a comparison]: 9154. When truths can be said to have come to life: 1928. When truth is joined to what is good it becomes part of us because it becomes a matter of our life: 3108, 3161. In order for a truth to be joined to some goodness, our will needs to agree with our understanding; not until our will agrees does the joining take place: 3157, 3158, 3161.

[2] As we are being regenerated, truths become a part of us, along with a feeling of pleasure because we love to do them; and later those truths come back to us with that same feeling again, because the truths and the feeling are joined together: 2480, 2487, 3040, 3066, 3074, 3336, 4018, 5893, 7967. Some feeling related to what we love always attaches itself to any truths we learn, depending on the use we make of those truths in our lives. If those truths come to mind, the feelings come with them: or if those feelings recur, then the truths come with them: 3336, 3824, 3849, 4205, 5893, 7967. Goodness does not recognize anything as true unless it is in harmony with the inclinations of its love: 3161. Truths gain entrance to us by means of things that are pleasurable and delightful [to our earthly self]: 3502, 3512. All genuine love of truth comes from and is shaped by goodness: 4373, 8349, 8356. There is a subtle entry and inflow of goodness into truths, and there is a joining together of goodness and truth (4301); and that is how truths come to life (7967).

[3] Because some feeling of love always attaches itself to any truths we learn, depending on the use we make of those truths in our lives, a given type of goodness recognizes the truth that is its own, and a given type of truth recognizes the goodness that is its own: 2429, 3101, 3102, 3161, 3179, 3180, 4358, 5807, 5835, 9637. The result is a joining together of what is true and what is good: 3834, 4096, 4097, 4301, 4345, 4364, 4368, 5365, 7623–7627, 7752–7762, 8530, 9258, 10555. Truths recognize each other as

well and gather together: 9079. This happens because of an inflow from heaven: 9079.

[4] Goodness is the reality underlying life and truth is how life becomes manifest from that goodness. So goodness finds the manifestation of its life in truth, and truth finds the underlying reality of its life in goodness: 3049, 3180, 4574, 5002, 9144. Thus everything good has its own truth and everything true has its own goodness, because goodness apart from truth has no manifestation and truth apart from goodness has no reality: 9637. Further, goodness gets its form and character from truths, and correspondingly truth is the form and character of goodness (3049, 4574, 6916, 9154); and so truth and goodness need to be joined together in order to be anything at all (10555). So goodness is constantly engaged in the longing and effort to join truths to itself: 9206, 9495. Some illustrations of this: 9207. Correspondingly, truths also strive to join themselves to some goodness: 9206. The joining is reciprocal—goodness with truth and truth with goodness: 5365, 8516. Goodness acts and truth reacts, though it does this as an effect of goodness: 3155, 4380, 4757, 5928, 10729. Truths focus on the good they can do as their origin and aim: 4353.

[5] The joining of truth with goodness parallels the successive phases of our lives beginning in infancy. We gather truths first as information, and then as the basis for rational thinking; ultimately we put them to use in deciding how to live our lives: 3203, 3665, 3690. It is also like a child: it is conceived, lives in the womb, is born, matures, and eventually gains wisdom: 3298, 3299, 3308, 3665, 3690. It is also like seeds and soil (3671) and like the relationship of water to bread (4976). Our first feeling of love for truth is not genuine, but as we are perfected it is purified: 3040, 3089. Still, forms of goodness and truth that are not genuine serve to lead us to forms of goodness and truth that are, at which point we abandon the earlier forms: 3665, 3690, 3974, 3982, 3986, 4145.

[6] Further, we are led to what is good by means of truths, and not in their absence: 10124, 10367. If we do not learn or accept truths, goodness cannot flow into us, so we cannot become spiritual: 3387. The joining of goodness and truth progresses as our knowledge grows: 3141. For all of us, our acceptance of truths depends on our rational capacity: 3385, [3387].

[7] The truths of our earthly self are in the form of information: 3293, 3309, 3310. The information and concepts we have are like containers: 6004, 6023, 6052, 6071, 6077. Truths are containers of goodness because they are receptive to it: 1469, 1900, 2063, 2261, 2269, 3318, 3365, 3365.

[8] Goodness flows in through an inner way for us, or through the soul, while what is true flows in from the outside through our hearing

and sight; and they are joined together within us by the Lord: 3030, 3098. Truths are lifted up from the earthly self and sown in what is good in the spiritual self, and this is how truths become spiritual: 3085, 3086. Then they flow back into the earthly self; goodness in the spiritual self flows directly into goodness in the earthly self but flows indirectly into the truth in the earthly self: 3314, 3573, 4563. Some illustrations of this: 3314, 3616, 3576, 3969, 3995. In brief, how amply and well truths are joined to what is good in us depends on how amply and well we focus on what is good in the way we lead our lives: 3834, 3843. The joining takes place in one way for heavenly people and in another way for spiritual people: 10124. More on the joining together of goodness and truth and on how it takes place (3090, 3203, 3308, 4096, 4097, 4345, 4353, 5365, 7623–7627); and also on how what is good on the spiritual level is given form through truths (3470, 3570).

4. *People who live lives based on truth and have good intent; and also the nature of truths that come from what is good.* Truth that leads to what is good and truth that comes from what is good, and how they differ: 2063. Truth is not true in essence except to the extent that it comes from something good (4736, 10619), because it is from goodness that truth gets its underlying reality (3049, 3180, 4574, 5002, 9144) and its life (3111, 2434, 6077). This is also because truth is the form or outward nature of goodness: 3049, 4574, 5951, 9154. The truth we have relates directly to the goodness we have, the amount and quality of both in us are the same: 2429. For anything true to be true, it must get its essence from our leading a life of caring and innocence: 3111, 6013. The truths that come from leading a good life are spiritual truths: 5951.

[2] Truth that comes from goodness is able to unite itself to goodness so thoroughly that the two become one: 4301, 7835, 10252, 10266. Our understanding and will make one mind and one life when our understanding is subordinate to our will, because our understanding is the part of us that is receptive to truth and our will is the part of us that is receptive to goodness; but this oneness does not occur when what we think and say is at variance with what we intend: 3623. Truth that comes from goodness is truth that lives in our will and in our actions: 4337, 4353, 4385, 4390. When truth comes from goodness, an image of that goodness remains present in that truth: 3180.

[3] Throughout the entire heaven and the entire world and in their every detail, there is some form of a marriage (54, 718, 747, 917, 1432, 2173, 2516, 5194); especially between what is true and what is good (1094, 2173, 2508). This is because everything in the universe, in order to be

anything at all, must go back to what is good and what is true; and in order to accomplish anything, must be the result of their being joined together: 2451, 3166, 4390, 4409, 5232, 7256, 10122, 10555. The ancients established [a custom of referring to] truth and goodness as partners in a marriage: 1904. According to the Lord's words, the law of marriage is that two should become one: 10130, 10168, 10169. True marriage love comes down from heaven from the marriage of what is true and what is good and becomes manifest: 2728, 2729.

[4] The more we are focused on goodness and on the truths that result from it, the wiser we are; no matter how much truth we know, however, if we are not focused on leading a good life wisdom will not be ours: 3182, 3190, 4884. When we have the truths that come from leading a good life, we are actually lifted out of this world's light into heaven's light—out of dimness, then, into clarity. On the other hand, as long as we only know about truths but are not practicing any goodness, we remain in this world's light and in dimness: 3190, 3191. We do not even know what goodness is until we are practicing it and learning from it: 3325, 3330, 3336. Truths grow by leaps and bounds when they come from leading a good life: 2846, 2847, 5345. More on this growth: 5355. This growth happens the way trees bear fruit and seeds multiply to make whole gardens: 1873, 2846, 2847. Wisdom grows to the same extent as well, and this goes on forever: 3200, 4220, 4221, 5527, 5859, 6663. Not only that, to the extent that we have gained truths from leading a good life, to that extent we are enlightened, and to that extent we experience enlightenment when we read the Word: 9382, 10548, 10549, 10550, 10691, 10694. Good actions that we do out of love are like fire, and the insights into truth that result are like light from that fire: 3195, 3222, 5400, 8644, 9399, 9548, 9684. In fact, the truths we learn from living a good life actually do shine in heaven: 5219. The truths we learn from leading a good life, which are the basis of wisdom, increase in proportion to the quality and amount of our love for doing good, and conversely falsities that we absorb from leading an evil life are proportional to the quality and amount of our love for doing evil: 4099. When we are given truths through leading a good life, we come into angelic intelligence and wisdom. These lie hidden within us as long as we are living in this world, but they are opened up for us in the other life: 2494. People who have truths from leading a good life become angels after they die: 8747.

[5] Truths that arise from goodness come in something like successive generations: 9079. They are arranged in sequences: 5339, 5343, 5530,

7408, 10303. The arrangement of truths that arise from goodness is like that of the fibers and blood vessels in our bodies and the complex tissues and structures they form to serve the useful functions of life: 3470, 3570, 3579, 9454. Truths that arise from goodness take the form of a kind of city within us, and this is caused by an inflow from heaven: 3584. At the center are the truths that accompany our primary love, while other concepts are distanced from that center to the extent that they fail to harmonize with [the central truths]: 3993, 4551, 4552, 5530, 6028. For evil people, though, falsity is at the center: 4551, 4552. When the truths we have are a result of our leading a good life, they are arranged in heaven's form (4302, 5339, 5343, 5704, 6028, 10303); and this agrees with the pattern in which heavenly communities are arranged (10303). All truths that result from leading a good life are connected to each other by a kind of kinship, like the branches of families descended from the same ancestor: 2863. Everything true also has an aura reaching out from it into heaven according to the nature and extent of the goodness that is its source: 8063. The marriage of what is good and what is true is the church and heaven for us: 2731, 7752, 7753, 9224, 9995, 10122. The pleasure and happiness felt by people whose truths have goodness inside them: 1470.

[6] When our truths are brought together by goodness, they present an image of us: 8370. As individuals, we are nothing more nor less than our goodness and truth, or our evil and falsity: 10298.

[7] To summarize, we come to faith through truths: 4353, 7178, 10367. We come to caring about our neighbor through truths: 4368, 7623, 7624, 8034. We come to love for the Lord through truths: 10143, 10153, 10310, 10578, 10645. We come to conscience through truths: 1077, 2053, 9113. We come to innocence through truths: 3183, 3494, 6013. We come to purification from evils through truths: 2799, 5954, 7044, 7918, 9088, 10229, 10237. We come to regeneration through truths: 1555, 1904, 2046, 2189, 9088, 9959, 10028. We come to intelligence and wisdom through truths: 3182, 3190, 3387, 10064. Truths beautify angels and therefore also beautify us at the deeper levels of our spirit: 553, 3080, 4985, 5199. We gain power against things that are evil and false through truths: 3091, 4015, 10488. Truths are means of bringing [inner things] into the kind of order that is characteristic of heaven: 3316, 3417, 3570, 5339, 5343, 5704, 6028, 10303. We come to the church through truths: 1798, 1799, 3963, 4468, 4672. We come to heaven through truths: 1900, 9832, 9931, 10303. We become human through truths: 3175, 3387, 8370, 10298. All these things come about, though, by means of truths that arise from goodness and not from truths

apart from goodness; and goodness comes from the Lord: 2434, 4070, 4736, 5147. All that is good comes from the Lord: 1614, 2016, 2904, 4151, 9981.

25 *Everything good and true comes from the Lord.* The Lord is goodness itself and truth itself: 2011, 4151, 10336, 10619. In both his divine and his human natures, the Lord is the divine goodness that results from divine love, and this goodness is the source of divine truth: 3704, 3712, 4180, 4577. Divine truth radiates from the Lord's divine goodness much the way light radiates from the sun: 3704, 3712, 4180, 4577. The divine truth that comes from the Lord takes the form of light in the heavens and is the source of all of heaven's light: 3195, 3222, 5400, 8694, 9399, 9548, 9684. Heaven's light, which is divine truth acting as one with divine goodness, enlightens both the sight and the understanding of angels and spirits: 2776, 3138. Heaven is bathed in light and warmth because it is devoted to what is true and good, since divine truth there is light and divine goodness there is warmth: 3643, 9399, 9400; and [see also] *Heaven and Hell* 126–140. The divine truth that comes from the Lord's divine goodness gives the angelic heaven its form and design: 3038, 9408, 9613, 10716, 10717. In heaven, the divine goodness that is one with the divine truth is referred to as divine truth: 10196.

[2] Divine truth coming from the Lord is the only thing that is real: 6880, 7004, 8200. Everything was made and created by means of divine truth: 2803, 2894, 5272, 7678. Divine truth has all power: 8200.

[3] On our own we cannot do one bit of good or think one bit of truth: 874, 875, 876. On its own, our rational ability cannot grasp divine truth: 2196, 2203, 2209. Any truths that do not come from the Lord come from our own selves and are not true even though they seem to be true: 8868.

[4] Everything that is good and true comes from the Lord, and none of it from us: 1614, 2016, 2904, 4151, 9981. Things that are good and true are good and true to the extent that they have the Lord in them: 2904, 3061, 8480. On divine truth that comes directly from the Lord and on divine truth that comes indirectly, through angels, and on how they flow in for us: 7055, 7056, 7058. The Lord flows into what is good in us, and through what is good into what is true: 10153. He flows through what is good into truths of all kinds, but especially into genuine truths: 2531, 2554. The Lord does not flow, though, into truths that are cut off from goodness, and such truths do not bring us into a parallel relationship with the Lord the way goodness does: 1831, 1832, 3514, 3564.

[5] Doing what is good and true for the sake of what is good and true is loving the Lord and loving our neighbor: 10336. When we are devoted

to the deeper aspects of the Word, the church, and worship, we love to do what is good and true for the sake of what is good and true; but if our involvement is only on a superficial level, with no depth, then we love to do what is good and true only for our own sakes or for worldly reasons: 10683. What it is to do what is good and true for the sake of what is good and true: 10683 (which includes examples by way of illustration).

On different forms of goodness and truth. There is infinite variety, and **26** no one thing can be identical to any other thing: 7236, 9002. There is an infinite variety in the heavens as well: 684, 690, 3744, 5598, 7236. The variations in the heavens are variations of goodness, and they are the basis of all differentiations there: 3519, 3744, 3804, 3986, 4005, 4067, 4149, 4263, 7236, 7833, 7836, 9002. These variations are defined by the truths (which are manifold) that shape the goodness of a given individual: 3470, 3519, 3804, 4149, 6917, 7236. That is how all the angelic communities in the heavens and all the individual angels in the communities are differentiated from each other: 690, 3241, 3519, 3804, 3986, 4067, 4149, 4263, 7236, 7833, 7836. They still act as one because of the love they receive from the Lord and because of their devotion to a single purpose: 457, 3986.

In general terms, goodness and truth are differentiated by level into earthly, spiritual, and heavenly varieties: 2069, 3240. Broadly, the three levels of goodness and of accompanying truth match the three heavens: 4154, 10270. There are three levels of goodness and truth in the inner self and three levels in the outer self as well: 4154. There is earthly goodness, civic goodness, and moral goodness: 3768. The earthly kind of goodness into which some of us are born is not good in the other life unless it becomes spiritual goodness: 2463, 2464, 2468, 3408, 3469, 3470, 3508, 3518, 7761. On earthly goodness that is spiritual and earthly goodness that is not spiritual: 4988, 4992, 5032. There is intellectual truth and there is factual truth: 1904, 1911, 2503.

Wisdom comes into being out of goodness by means of truth. How ratio- **27** nality is conceived and born in us: 2093, 2524, 2557, 3030, 5126. This is brought about by means of an inflow of the Lord through heaven into whatever spiritual and worldly knowledge we have, lifting us up as a result: 1895, 1899, 1900, 1901. This lifting up depends on the useful things we do and on our love of them: 3074, 3085, 3086. Our rationality is born by means of truths, so the nature of the truths determines the nature of our rationality: 2093, 2524, 2557. Our rationality is opened and given form by truths that arise from living a good life; it is closed and destroyed by falsities that arise from living an evil life: 3108, 5126. Our being able to argue that this or that is true does not mean we are rational; we are rational if we are able to see and perceive whether something is actually true or not: 1944. We are not born with any truth, because we are not born with any goodness; we need to learn and absorb everything: 3175. Because of the deceptiveness of our senses and the persuasiveness of falsity, which lead to rationalizations and doubts, we are barely able to accept genuine truths and then become wise: 3175. The beginning of our wisdom occurs when we start to turn our backs on rationalizations that deny what is true, and to cast aside our doubts: 3175. When our rational ability is not enlightened it scoffs at inner truths: 2654 (which includes examples). Our truths can properly be called inner truths only when they have been rooted in our lives, and not merely because we know about them, even though some truths that we know about might be said to be of a deeper kind: 10199.

[2] Within goodness there lies a capacity to grow in wisdom; if our lives have been devoted to doing what is good, we attain angelic wisdom after our departure from this world: 5527, 5859, 8321. Within every type of goodness countless other types of goodness lie hidden: 4005. From goodness countless things can be learned: 3612. How truth multiplies as a result of goodness: 5345, 5355, 5912. By means of truths and by means of living according to them, the goodness we have in early childhood becomes the goodness that belongs to wisdom: 3504.

[3] We can be moved by a desire for truth and we can be moved by a desire for goodness: 1904, 1997. What we are like when we are moved by a desire for truth and what we are like when we are moved by a desire for goodness: 2422, 2429. Which people can come to desire truth and which people cannot: 2689. All truths are arranged under some emotion that they have in common: 9094. In earthly-minded people a desire for truth and a desire for goodness are like brother and sister, while in spiritually minded people they are like husband and wife: 3160.

[4] Pure truths are not to be found in us or even in angels—only in the Lord: 3207, 7902. Any truths that we have are only apparently true: 2053, 2519. The first truths we have are things that seem to be true according to our deceptive senses; we gradually shed these as we increase in wisdom: 3131. If we are devoted to what is good, the things we think are true are accepted as real truths by the Lord: 2053, 3207. The substance and nature of things that seem to be truths: 3207, 3357–3362, 3368, 3404, 3405, 3417. Much of the literal meaning of the Word is adapted to suit the way things seem to people: 1838. The same truths can be more true for one individual, less true for another, and false for yet another because they

have been distorted: 2439. By coordinating the impressions of our earthly self with those of our spiritual self, we can see whether the things we hold as true are actually true or not: 3128, 3138. How true our truths are varies depending on our ideas and concepts of them: 3470, 3804, 6917.

[5] When a truth has been joined to goodness it vanishes from our memory because it has become part of our life: 3108. Truths can be joined to goodness only in a state of freedom: 3158. Truths are joined to goodness by means of the crises of the spirit we go through: 3318, 4572, 7122. All goodness makes a constant effort to put truths in their place and to be restored by means of an inversion of its state: 3610. Truths become unpleasant when their connection with goodness is cut off: 8352. It is hard for us to tell the difference between truth and goodness because it is hard for us to tell the difference between thinking and willing: 9995. In the Word, what is good is called the brother of what is true: 4267. From one point of view, whatever is good is called a lord and whatever is true is called a servant: 3409, 4267.

Will and Understanding

28 WE have two abilities that make up our life, one called *will* and the other *understanding*. They are distinguishable, but they are created to be one. When they are one, they are called *the mind;* so they *are* the human mind and it is there that all the life within us is truly to be found.

29 Just as everything in the universe that is in accord with the divine design goes back to what is good and what is true, so everything in us goes back to will and understanding. This is because whatever is good in us resides in our will and whatever is true in us resides in our understanding. These two abilities, or these two living parts of ours, receive and are acted upon by what is good and true: our will receives and is acted upon by everything that is good, and our understanding receives and is acted upon by everything that is true. Goodness and truth can be found nowhere else in us but in these faculties. Further, since they are not to be found anywhere else, neither are love and faith, since love and goodness are mutually dependent, and similarly faith and truth.

30 Now, since everything in the universe goes back to goodness and truth and everything about the church goes back to good things that are done from love and truth that belongs to faith, and since we are human because of will and understanding, the body of teaching [I am presenting] deals with will and understanding as well. Otherwise we could have no clear concept of them, no solid foundation for our thinking.

31 Will and understanding also form the human spirit, since they are where our wisdom and intelligence dwell—in general, where our life dwells. The body, [by contrast,] is simply a thing that follows orders.

32 There is no knowledge more relevant than knowing how our will and understanding make one mind. They make one mind the way goodness and truth form a unity. There is the same kind of marriage between will and understanding as there is between goodness and truth. You may see quite well what that marriage is like from what has already been presented concerning goodness and truth [§§23–24]. That is, just as goodness is the reality underlying something and truth is how that thing becomes manifest from goodness, so our will is the reality underlying our life, and our understanding is how life becomes manifest from our will. This is because the goodness that is characteristic of our will takes form in our understanding and presents itself to view [there].

People who are focused on what is good and true have both will and understanding, while people who are focused on what is evil and false do not have will or understanding. Instead of will they have craving, and instead of understanding they have mere information. Any will that is truly human is receptive to goodness, and any understanding that is truly human is open to truth. This means anything that is evil cannot [properly] be labeled "will," and anything that is false cannot [properly] be labeled "understanding," because these things are opposites, and opposites are mutually destructive. That is why anyone who is focused on something evil and therefore on what is false cannot be called rational, wise, or intelligent. Then too, the deeper levels of our minds are closed when we are evil, and those levels are where our will and understanding principally reside.

We assume that we have will and understanding even when we are evil because we say that we are willing things and understanding them, but our "willing" is nothing but craving and our "understanding" is mere information.

33

From *Secrets of Heaven*

THINGS that are true on a spiritual level cannot be grasped without knowledge of the following *universal principles.*

34

1. In order to be anything at all, each thing in the universe must go back to goodness and truth and their partnership, and therefore to love and faith and their partnership.
2. We humans have will and understanding, the will being the part of us that is receptive to goodness and the understanding being the part that is receptive to truth. Everything in us goes back to these two and their partnership, just as everything [in general] goes back to goodness and truth and their partnership.

3. There is an inner self and an outer self, as distinct from each other as heaven and earth, and yet these two need to become one if we are to be truly human.

4. Heaven's light is the light that surrounds the inner self, and this world's light is the light that surrounds the outer self. Heaven's light is divine truth itself, which is the source of all intelligence.

5. There is a correspondence between what is in the inner self and what is in the outer, which means that what is in each comes out in a different guise in the other—so different that we cannot sort them out unless we know how this correspondence operates.

Unless we are aware of all this and a great deal more, the only concepts of things spiritual and heavenly we can grasp and form are incoherent. This means that the facts and experiences of the outer self, divorced from these universal principles, cannot be useful to our rational functioning for learning and growth.

We can see, then, how necessary information is. There are treatments of these universal principles in many places in *Secrets of Heaven*.

35 We have two abilities, one called will and the other called understanding: 35, 641, 3539, 3623, 10122. It is these two abilities that make us truly human: 10076, 10109, 10110, 10264, 10284. Our nature depends on the nature of these two abilities of ours: 7342, 8885, 9282, 10264, 10284. These two abilities are also what distinguishes us from animals, because our understanding can be lifted up by the Lord and see divine truths, and our will, too, can be lifted up and perceive divine goodness. And so our partnership with the Lord is made possible by these two abilities that make us who we are—which is not the case with animals: 4525, 5302, 5114, 6323, 9231. And since we can form a partnership with the Lord in this way, we cannot die with respect to our deeper levels—the levels that constitute our spirit; rather, we live to eternity: 5302. We are human not because of our shape but because of what is good and what is true, which are matters of our will and understanding: 4051, 5302.

[2] Just as everything in the universe goes back to goodness and truth, so everything in us goes back to our will and our understanding (803, 10122), because our will is the part of us that receives goodness and our understanding is the part of us that receives truth (3332, 3623, 5835, 6065, 6125, 7503, 9300, 9930). Whether you say "truth" or "faith" it amounts to the same thing, because faith and truth are mutually dependent; and whether you say "goodness" or "love" it amounts to the same thing, because love and goodness are mutually dependent; whatever we believe

we call true, and whatever we love we call good: 4997, 7178, 10122, 10367. It therefore follows that our understanding is the part of us that can have faith and our will is the part of us that can have love, and that faith and love are in us when they are in our will and understanding because there and nowhere else is where our life is: 7178, 10122, 10367. And since our understanding can accept faith in the Lord and our will can accept love for the Lord, we are capable of being joined to the Lord by faith and love; and anyone who can be joined to the Lord by faith and love cannot die to all eternity: 4525, 6323, 9231. In the spiritual world, love is a joining together: 1594, 2057, 3939, 4018, 5807, 6195, 6196, 7081–7086, 7501, 10130.

[3] Our will is the true underlying reality of our life because it is the part of us that receives what is good, while our understanding is the consequent manifestation of our life because it is the part of us that receives what is true: 3619, 5002, 9282. So the life of our will is our primary life, and the life of our understanding emerges from it (585, 590, 3619, 7342, 8885, 9282, 10076, 10109, 10110) the way light comes from fire or a flame (6032, 6314). Whatever enters our understanding and our will together becomes part of us, but what enters only our understanding does not: 9009, 9069, 9071, 9182, 9386, 9393, 10076, 10109, 10110. Whatever is accepted by our will becomes part of our life: [3161, 9386, 9393. It follows then that we are human because of our will] and our consequent understanding: 8911, 9069, 9071, 10076, 10109, 10110. We are all loved and valued by others according to how good our will is and only secondarily how good our understanding is. We are loved and valued if both our intentions and our understanding are good; we are rejected and considered worthless if our understanding is good but our intentions are not: 8911, 10076. Even after death we retain the nature of our will and our consequent understanding: 9069, 9386, 10153. Those things that are in our understanding but not in our will then vanish because they are not in our spirit: 9282. Or to put it another way, after death we retain the nature of our love and the faith that comes from that love—the nature of our goodness and the truth that comes from that goodness—and then anything that is a matter of our faith but not of our love (or of truth in us but not of goodness) vanishes because it is not within us and therefore does not belong to us: 553, 2364, 10153. We are capable of grasping intellectually things that we would not do willingly; that is, we can understand things that run counter to our love and we have no will to do: 3539.

[4] Will and understanding together make one mind: 35, 3623, 5835, 10122. These two life abilities need to act as one if we are to be truly human: 3623, 5835, 5969, 9300. How distorted our state is when our understanding and our will are not acting as one: 9075. This is the kind

of state we find among hypocrites, con artists, flatterers, and imposters: 3527, 3573, 4799, 8250. In the other life our will and our understanding are brought back into unison, and we are not allowed to have a divided mind there: 8250.

[5] Every religious teaching [that we have in our minds] is dependent on concepts [we have gained before]; it is possible [for others in the spiritual world] to perceive how we hold that teaching from seeing the nature of the concepts [that go with it in our minds]: 5510. These concepts of ours determine how we understand a given teaching; without some concept that makes it understandable, the teaching is held in our minds in the form of words alone without substance: 3825. The thoughts in the mind reach out widely all around to communities of spirits and angels: 6599, 6600–6605, 6609, 6613. In the other life the concepts of our understanding are laid open so that their nature is vividly clear: 1869, 3310, 5510. What some people's concepts look like: 6201, 8885.

[6] Every act of will to do what is good and every consequent understanding of what is true comes from the Lord, but this is not the case for an understanding of what is true divorced from any act of will to do what is good: 1831, 3514, 5482, 5649, 6027, 8685, 8701, 10153. Our understanding is what is enlightened by the Lord: 6222, 6608, 10659. When we are receptive to enlightenment the Lord makes us able to see and understand what is true: 9382, 10659. The enlightenment of our understanding varies depending on the state of our life: 5221, 7012, 7233. Our understanding is enlightened to the extent that our will accepts truth—that is, to the extent that we will ourselves to act in accord with it: 3619. Our understanding is enlightened if we read the Word out of a love of truth and a love for living a useful life, but not if we read out of a love for our own reputation, respect, or profit: 9382, 10548, 10549, 10550. Enlightenment is effectively a raising of the mind into heaven's light (10330); see also 1526, 6608, which include evidence from personal experience. Light from heaven gives enlightenment to our understanding just the way light from this world does to our eyesight: 1524, 5114, 6608, 9128. The light of heaven is divine truth, which is the source of all intelligence and wisdom: 3195, 3222, 5400, 8644, 9399, 9548, 9684. It is our understanding that is enlightened by this light: 1524, 3138, 3167, 4408, 6608, 8707, 9128, 9399, 10569.

[7] The nature of our understanding depends on the nature of the love-based truths from which it is formed: 10064. Understanding results from truths that arise from living a good life, not from falsities that arise from living an evil life: 10675. Understanding is seeing, on the basis of our experience and information, things that are true, the causes of events,

their connections, and how they follow from each other: 6125. The faculty of understanding is seeing and perceiving that something is true before we convince ourselves of it; it is not the ability to prove anything we choose: 4741, 7012, 7680, 7950, 8521, 8780. When the light that comes from corroboration strikes someone with no preexisting ability to perceive truth, it becomes an earthly light, available even to people who are not wise: 8780. Seeing and perceiving whether something is true before considering it proven is possible for us only when we love truth for its own sake—that is, when we are in spiritual light: 8521. Any dogma, even a false one, can be supported in such a way that it seems to be true: 2385, 2477, 5033, 6865, 7950.

[8] How rationality is conceived and born in us: 2093, 2524, 2557, 3030, 5126. It comes from an inflow of heaven's light from the Lord through our inner self into the spiritual and worldly knowledge in our outer self, lifting us up as a result: 1895, 1899, 1900, 1901, 1902. Our rationality is born by means of truths and not by means of falsities, so the nature of the truths determines the nature of our rationality: 2093, 2524, 2557. Our rationality is opened and given form by truths that arise from living a good life; it is closed and destroyed by falsities that arise from living an evil life: 3108, 5126. If we are full of false thoughts from evil intent we are not rational; our being able to argue that this or that is true does not mean we are rational: 1944.

[9] It is hard for us to know the difference between our understanding and our will because it is hard for us to know the difference between thinking and willing: 9995.

[10] You can learn more and draw more conclusions about will and understanding from what was cited just above on goodness and truth [§§11–27]: just take goodness to refer to will and truth to refer to understanding, since goodness resides in the will and truth resides in the understanding.

The Inner Self and the Outer Self

36 WE are created in such a way that we are in the spiritual world and the earthly world at one and the same time. The spiritual world is where angels are and the earthly world is where we are. And since that is how we are created, we are given an inner nature and an outer nature—an inner nature that allows us to be in the spiritual world, and an outer nature that allows us to be in the earthly world. Our inner nature is what we refer to as the inner self, and our outer nature is what we refer to as the outer self.

37 Each one of us has an inner level and an outer level, but they are not the same for good people as they are for evil ones. For good people, their inner level is in heaven and in its light, while their outer level is in the world and in its light. Further, for good people this latter light is brightened by heaven's light, so their inner and outer levels act in unison like an efficient cause and its effect, or like what is prior and what is subsequent. For evil people, though, their inner level is in this world and its light, and the same holds true for their outer level as well. This means that they cannot see anything in heaven's light, only in this world's light, which they call "the light of nature." That is why heavenly matters are in darkness for them and worldly matters are in the light.

We can see from this that good people have an inner self and an outer self, while [in effect] evil people have no inner self, only an outer one.

38 It is the inner self that is called a spiritual self because it is in heaven's light, and that light is spiritual. It is the outer self that is called an earthly self because it is in the light of this world, and that light is earthly. Anyone whose inner level is in heaven's light and whose outer level is in this world's light is a spiritual individual in both respects, but people whose inner level is not in heaven's light but in this world's light, where their outer level is as well, are earthly individuals in both respects. Spiritual individuals are the ones called "living" in the Word, while earthly individuals are the ones called "dead."

39 When our inner level is in heaven's light and our outer level is in this world's light, we think in ways that are both spiritual and earthly, but our spiritual thinking flows into our earthly thinking, and that is where we perceive it. However, when our inner level is caught up in this world's light along with our outer level, we think materialistically rather than spiritually. That is, we base our thinking on the kinds of things we find in this physical world, all of which are composed of matter.

To think spiritually is to think about actual things as they really are, seeing truths in the light of truth and perceiving what is good because we love it. It is seeing the qualities of things and perceiving their emotional impact apart from their material characteristics. In contrast, thinking materialistically is thinking, seeing, and perceiving things as inseparable from matter and as in matter, and therefore relatively crudely and dimly.

Seen in its own right, a spiritual inner self is an angel of heaven, and while it is living in the body it is also in the company of angels even though it is not aware of being so; and once it is released from the body it joins them. A merely earthly inner self, though, when seen in its own right, is not an angel but a spirit and is also in the company of spirits while it is living in the body. However, it is with spirits who are in hell, and after its release from the body it joins them.

The deeper levels of [the minds of] people who are spiritual are actively raised up toward heaven because that is their primary focus, while the deeper levels of the minds of people who are merely earthly are actively turned toward this world because that is their primary focus. For all of us, our inner levels, which are levels of our higher mind, are turned toward what we love above all, and our outer levels, which are levels of our lower mind, are turned in the same direction as the inner.

People who have only a vague concept of the inner self and the outer self believe that it is the inner self that thinks and intends and the outer that speaks and acts as a result, since thinking and intending are internal activities, and speaking and acting are external. It should be borne in mind, though, that when we think intelligently and intend wisely, we are thinking and intending from a spiritual inner nature, but when we do not think intelligently and intend wisely we are thinking and intending from an earthly inner nature. This means that when our thoughts about the Lord and about matters that involve the Lord are good and when our thoughts about our neighbor and about matters that involve our neighbor are good, and when our intentions toward them are good, we are thinking and intending from our spiritual inner nature. This is because our thinking is based on a belief in what is true and a love for what is good, and is therefore coming from heaven. However, when our thoughts about them are evil and our intentions toward them are evil, then we are thinking and intending

40

41

42

from our earthly inner nature because our thinking is based on a belief in what is false and a love for what is evil, so our thinking is coming from hell.

In short, to the extent that we are focused on loving the Lord and loving our neighbor, our inner nature is spiritual. We are thinking and intending from that nature and are speaking and acting from it as well. To the extent that we are focused on loving ourselves and loving the world, though, our inner nature is earthly. We are thinking and intending from that nature and are speaking and acting from it as well.

43 The Lord has foreseen and arranged matters in such a way that the more we derive our thoughts and intentions from heaven, the more our inner spiritual self opens and takes shape. This is an opening to heaven all the way to the Lord, and a taking shape in accord with the priorities of heaven. In direct contrast, the more we derive our thoughts and intentions not from heaven but from the world, the more our inner spiritual self closes and our outer self opens. This is an opening to the world and a taking shape in accord with the priorities of this world.

44 When our inner spiritual self has been opened to heaven all the way to the Lord, we are in heaven's light and in an enlightenment that comes from the Lord, which means that we come into intelligence and wisdom. We see what is true because it is true and we perceive what is good because it is good.

On the other hand, when our inner spiritual self has been closed we are not aware that our spiritual self exists, let alone aware of what that spiritual self is. We do not believe that there is anything divine, either, or that there is a life after death, so we do not believe anything that has to do with heaven or the church. Since we are solely in the light of this world and its enlightenment, we believe that nature is God, what is false looks true to us, and what is evil is perceived as good.

45 We refer to people as "sense-oriented" when their inner nature is so external that they cannot believe anything unless they can see it with their own eyes and touch it with their own hands. They have the lowest possible level of earthly human nature and are subject to misconceptions about everything having to do with the faith of the church.

46 The inner and outer levels we have been dealing with are the inner and outer levels of our spirit. Our bodies are nothing but a shell in which these inner and outer levels reside. That is, the body does nothing on its own, acting only from the spirit that is within it.

Bear in mind that after it is released from the body our spirit keeps right on thinking and intending and speaking and acting. Its thinking and intending constitute the inner level of our spirit, while its speaking and acting constitute its outer level. In this connection, see *Heaven and Hell* 234–245, 265–275, 432–444, 453–484.

From *Secrets of Heaven*

O N *our inner and outer natures.* While it is recognized in the Christian world that we have an inner level and an outer level or an inner self and an outer self, there is little knowledge of the nature of either: 1889, 1940. The inner self is spiritual and the outer self is earthly: 978, 1015, 4459, 6309, 9701–9708. An inner self that is spiritual is formed into an image of heaven, and an outer self that is earthly is formed into an image of this world—how this happens, and how it is the reason the ancients called the human being a microcosm: 3628, 4523, 4524, 6057, 6314, 9706, 10156, 10472. This means that the spiritual world and the earthly world are joined together in us: 6057, 10472. It means that we have the ability to look upward toward heaven and downward toward earth: 7601, 7604, 7607. When we look up we are in heaven's light and see what it shows us, while when we look down we are in the world's light and see what it shows us: 3167, 10134. In humankind a pathway has been created from the spiritual world into the earthly one: 3702, 4042.

[2] The inner self (which is spiritual) and the outer self (which is earthly) are completely distinct from each other: 1999, 2018, 3691, 4459. The distinction is like that between a cause and its effect and like that between what is prior and what is subsequent; it is not along a continuum: 3691, 4145, 5146, 5711, 6275, 6284, 6299, 6326, 6465, 8603, 10076, 10099, 10181. So the difference is like that between heaven and this world or between something spiritual and something earthly: 6055. Our inner and outer natures are not along a continuum but are separated on distinctly different levels that have well-defined boundaries: 3691, 4145, 5114, 6326, 6465, 8603, 10099. Anyone who does not perceive the distinctions

47

between our inner and outer natures in keeping with their levels and who does not understand what the levels are like cannot comprehend our inner and outer selves: 5146, 6465, 10099, 10181. Things that are on a higher level are more perfect than things that are on a lower level: 3405. There are three levels in us that are in accord with the three heavens: 4154. The outer things in us are relatively remote from the Divine, so they are more obscure and general: 6451. They are also relatively disorganized: 996, 3855. Inner things are more perfect because they are closer to the Divine: 5146, 5147. There are thousands upon thousands of things in our inner self that appear as one general thing in the outer self: 5707. So the more inward our thinking and perception are, the clearer they are: 5920. It follows then that we should concentrate on what lies in the deeper levels: 1175, 4464.

[3] When we are focused on love and caring, the deeper levels of our mind are actually raised up by the Lord. Otherwise they would face downward: 6952, 6954, 10330. When our inner natures are actively raised up by the Lord, the result is an inflow and enlightenment for us out of heaven: 7816, 10330. When we turn our attention to spiritual matters we are raised up: 9922. To the extent that we are raised up from outward concerns toward inward ones we come into the light and therefore into intelligence; or as the ancients used to say, this happens when the mind withdraws from sense impressions: 6183, 6313. Being raised up from outward to inward concerns is like being lifted out of a fog into the light: 4598.

[4] The inflow from the Lord comes through our inner self into our outer self: 1940, 5119. There can be an inflow from our inner self into our outer self, because inflow is spiritual, not physical—that is, there can be a flow from the spiritual self into the earthly self but not from the earthly self into the spiritual self: 3219, 5119, 5259, 5427, 5428, 5477, 6322, 9110. From the inner realm, where it is peaceful, the Lord governs the outer realm, where it is chaotic: 5396a.

[5] The inner self can see everything in the outer self, but not the reverse: 1914, 1953, 5427, 5428, 5477. While we are living in this world, the thinking in our outer self comes from our inner self; our spiritual thinking flows into our earthly thinking and presents itself in earthly forms: 3679. When we are thinking well, those thoughts are coming from our inner or spiritual self into our outer or earthly self: 9704, 9705, 9707. How the outer self thinks and intends depends on its relationship with the inner self: 9702, 9703.

There is inner thinking and there is outer thinking: 2515, 2552, 5127, 5141, 5168, 6007 (which include information about what each type of thinking is like). As long as we are living in this world we do not perceive the thinking and feeling that are going on in our inner self; we perceive only the thinking and feeling that result from this in our outer self: 10236, 10240. In the other life, though, our outer layer is stripped away and we are brought into our true inner nature: 8870. We can then see what inner things are like: 1806, 1807.

[6] Our inner self produces our outer self: 994, 995. The inner self then clothes itself in whatever enables it to get results in the outer self (6275, 6284, 6299) and to live in the outer self (1175, 6275). When the Lord regenerates us, he joins our inner or spiritual self to our outer or earthly self: 1577, 1594, 1904, 1999. The outer or earthly self is then put in its rightful place by means of the inner or spiritual self and becomes subservient. 9708.

[7] The outer self needs to be subservient and subject to the inner self: 5077, 5125, 5128, 5786, 5947, 10272. The outer self was designed and created to serve the inner self: 5947. The inner self must be the master and the outer self a servant and in a certain respect even a slave: 10471.

[8] The outer self needs to correspond to the inner in order for the two to be joined together: 5427, 5428. What the outer self is like when it corresponds to the inner self and what it is like when it does not: 3493, 5422, 5423, 5427, 5428, 5477, 5512. There are things in the outer self that correspond to and stand in harmony with the inner, and there are things that do not correspond or stand in harmony: 1563, 1568.

[9] The outer self derives its nature from the inner: 9912, 9921, 9922. How great the beauty of the outer self is when it is joined to the inner self (1590) and how ugly it is when it is not (1598). Love for the Lord and caring about our neighbor join the outer self to the inner: 1594. Unless the inner self is joined to the outer there is no fruitfulness: 3987.

[10] Things that are deep within flow down into more outward levels by stages until finally they flow into the outermost or last, which is where they become manifest together and persist: 634, 6239, 9216. They not only flow in by stages, they also all come together on the last [and lowest] level in accord with the design: 5897, 6451, 8603, 10099. All that lies within is held in a connection from first to last: 9828. This also gives things that are on the outermost level strength and power: 9836. The result is that answers and revelations come through the outermost level: 9905, 10548.

This is also why the outermost level is more holy than the inner levels: 9824. So in the Word, "the First and the Last" means every single thing and therefore all there is: 10044, 10329, 10335.

[11] The inner self is open when we are in accord with the divine design and closed when we are not in accord with the divine design: 8513. Without the inner self, heaven has no way of being joined to the outer self: 9380. Both evils and the falsities that come from them close the inner self and limit us to the outermost level (1587, 10492); especially evils that result from self-love (1594). If we refuse to receive what flows in from the Divine, our deeper levels are closed until we are reduced to the sensory level, which is the last [and lowest]: 6564. In the intelligent and learned of this world who take stances against the truths of heaven and the church on the basis of facts they have learned, the inner level is more completely closed than it is for similarly minded simple people: 10492.

[12] Since the inner self is in heaven's light and the outer is in this world's light, if we are focused on the outer to the exclusion of the inner (that is, if our inner self is closed) we have no appetite for profound truths about heaven and the church: 4464, 4946. In that case, in the other life we cannot bear things of an internal nature: 10694, 10701, 10707. We do not believe anything: 10396, 10400, 10411, 10429. We love ourselves and the world more than anything else: 10407, 10412, 10420. No matter how we may seem outwardly, our deeper levels—the processes of our thinking and feeling—are ugly, foul, and profane: 1182, 7046, 9962. Our ideas and thinking are materialistic and not in the least spiritual: 10582. What we are like when our inner level, which faces heaven, is closed: 4459, 9709, 10284, 10286, 10429, 10472, 10492, 10602, 10683.

[13] As our inner, spiritual self is more and more opened, the kinds of goodness and truth we have multiply; as our inner, spiritual self is more and more closed, the kinds of goodness and truth we have disappear: 4099. The church exists in our inner, spiritual self because that self is in heaven; it does not exist in our outer self apart from the inner: 10698. Therefore if we do not have the church in our internal life, having the trappings of it in our external life does nothing for us: 1795. Outward worship apart from inner worship is no worship at all: 1094, 1175. About people who are focused on the inner aspects of the church, worship, and the Word; people who are focused on outward aspects that contain the inner; and people who are focused on outward aspects that lack the inner: 10683. When the inner aspects are lacking, the outward aspects take on a hardness: 9377, 10429.

[14] Merely earthly people are an embodiment of hell unless they become spiritual by means of regeneration: 10156. Everyone who is absorbed in the outer level apart from anything inner, or anyone whose inner, spiritual self is closed, is in hell: 9128, 10483, 10489.

[15] Our inner selves turn actively toward the things we love: 10702. Absolutely everything must have both an inner level and an outer level if it is to exist at all: 9473.

[16] In the Word, "lofty and high" means inner: 1735, 2148, 4210, 4599. So in the Word, "higher" means more inward and "lower" means more outward: 3084.

What is earthly and what is spiritual. How wrong-headed it is that today's world attributes almost everything to the physical world and almost nothing to the Divine: 3483. Why this is the case (5116) when the fact is that absolutely everything in the physical world not only arose but also continues to exist from the Divine, through the agency of the spiritual world (775, 8211). Things divine, heavenly, and spiritual have their outermost boundaries in the physical world: 4240, 4939. The physical world is the foundation on which they stand: 4240, 5651, 6275, 6284, 6299, 9216. Heavenly, spiritual, and earthly realities follow and progress in proper sequence, and are accompanied by what is divine because they come from the Divine: 880, 4938, 4939, 9992, 10005, 10017, 10068. Heavenly realities act as the head [in the universal human], spiritual realities the torso, and earthly realities the legs and feet: 4938, 4939. One of these flows into the next in the same order just mentioned: 4938, 4939. The goodness of the central or third heaven is called "heavenly," the goodness of the intermediate or second heaven is called "spiritual," and the goodness of the outermost or first heaven is called "spiritual-earthly," which make it possible for us to know what the terms "heavenly," "spiritual," and "earthly" mean: 4279, 4286, 4938, 4939, 9992, 10005, 10017, 10068. See also my book *Heaven and Hell* 20–28, 29–40.

[2] Everything in the physical world comes from the Divine through the spiritual world: 5013. So there is something spiritual within everything earthly, like an efficient cause within an effect (3562, 5711), like the impetus within motion (5173), and like an inner level within an outer level (3562, 5711, 5326); and since a cause is the essential element within an effect, the impetus is the essential element within a motion, and the inner level is the essential element within an outer level, it follows that what is spiritual is actually the essential element within what is earthly, and therefore so is the Divine, which is the source of all things (2987–3002, 9701–9709).

Spiritual realities are manifested in what is earthly, and those manifestations are representations and correspondences: 1632, 2987–3002. Because of this, the whole physical world is a theater that portrays the spiritual world—that is, heaven: 2758, 2999, 3000, 4939, 8848, 9280. All things in the physical world are arranged in a design and sequence according to the purposes they serve: 4104. This [purposiveness] comes from the spiritual world (that is, heaven) because purposes, which are ways of being useful, are dominant there: 454, 696, 1103, 3645, 4054, 7038. We have been created in such a way that we perceive in ourselves divine things that are descending all the way into physical matter in accord with the divine design: 3702.

[3] If we are in accord with the divine design, we invariably have an inner level and an outer level. Our inner level is called "the spiritual level" or "the spiritual self," and our outer level is called "the earthly level" or "the earthly self": 978, 1015, 4459, 6309, 9701–9709. Our spiritual self is in heaven's light and our earthly self is in this world's light: 5965. Our earthly self cannot grasp anything on its own; its comprehension is a result of our spiritual self: 5286. Our earthly level is like a surface in which our deeper qualities see themselves; this is how thinking takes place: 5165. Our spiritual self produces thought in our earthly level and therefore thought in earthly terms, as long as our spiritual concerns come into our awareness down on the sensory level: 3679, 5165, 6284, 6299. The earthly plane is where what is spiritual has its outermost boundaries: 5651, 6275, 6284, 6299, 9216. Our spiritual self does not see anything in our earthly self unless our earthly self corresponds to our spiritual self: 3493, 3620, 3623. Our spiritual or inner self can see what is going on in our earthly or outer self, but not the reverse, because what is spiritual flows into what is earthly, but what is earthly does not flow into what is spiritual: 3219, 4667, 5119, 5259, 5427, 5428, 5477, 6322, 9110. On the basis of its own light, which is called earthly light, our earthly self does not know anything about God or heaven or life after death; and it does not believe anything it hears unless some spiritual illumination, which is light from heaven, flows into that [earthly] light: 8444.

[4] From birth and by nature, our earthly self is opposed to our spiritual self: 3913, 3928. As a result, as long as these selves remain opposed we find it irksome to think about spiritual and heavenly subjects but pleasant to think about earthly and bodily ones: 4096. We feel sick when we are faced with heavenly subjects—even when they are merely mentioned: 5006, 9109 (which include evidence from eyewitness experience). People who are entirely earthly regard anything that is spiritually good and true

as a slave: 5013, 5025. Yet the earthly self should be subject to the spiritual self and should serve it: 3019, 5168. Our spiritual self can be said to be a slave to our earthly self when we use our intellect to garner justification, especially from the Word, for the kind of things that we crave: 3020, 5013, 5025, 5168. What merely earthly people look like in the other life, and what their state and destiny is there: 4630, 4633, 4940–4951, 5032, 5571.

[5] The truths that we have in the earthly self are called "factual" and "conceptual": 3293. In its natural state, our earthly self has a materialistic imagination and has drives like those of animals: 3020. When, however, the vision, action, and life of our earthly self depend on our inner or spiritual self, then we develop genuine thought and imagination: 3493, 5422, 5423, 5427, 5428, 5477, 5512.

[6] Relative to the contents of our spiritual self, the contents of our earthly self are very general (3513, 5707); and are therefore comparatively in the dark: (6686).

[7] Our earthly self has an inner and an outer layer: 3293, 3294, 3793, 5118, 5126, 5497, 5649. There is also a bridge between them: 4570, 9216. It is in and by means of our earthly self that our spiritual self is relieved of its burdens: 9572.

People who do good things solely because of the earthly disposition they were born with and not on the basis of religion are not accepted into heaven: 8772.

The light of heaven that surrounds our spiritual self. The light in the heavens is immense: 1117, 1521, 1533, 1619–1632. The light in the heavens vastly surpasses earth's noonday light: 1117, 1521, 4527, 5400, 8644. I have often seen this light: 1522, 4527, 7174. For angels in the central or third heaven the light is like the light of the sun, while for angels in the second heaven it is like the light of the moon: 1529, 1530. The light in the central heaven is flamelike, while in the second heaven it is gleaming white: 9570.

[2] All the light in the heavens comes from the Lord as the sun there: 1053, 1521, 3195, 3341, 3636, 3643, 4415, 9548, 9684, 10809. The Lord is the sun of the angelic heaven, and that sun is his divine love: 1521, 1529, 1530, 1531, 1837, 4321, 4696, 7078, 7171, 7173. The divine truth that radiates from the Lord in the heavens is seen as light; it is the source of all the light in heaven, which is why that light is a spiritual light: 3195, 3222, 5400, 8644, 9399, 9548, 9684. This is why the Word refers to the Lord as "the light": 3195. Since that light is divine truth, it contains divine wisdom and intelligence: 3195, 3485, 3636, 3643, 3993, 4302, 4413, 4415, 9548, 9684.

How light from the Lord flows into the heavens, illustrated by golden haloes around the sun: 9407. The Lord is the sun for the heavens and all the light there comes from him (see *Heaven and Hell* 116–125); the light from that sun is divine truth and the warmth from that sun is the divine goodness that comes from divine love (*Heaven and Hell* 126–140).

[3] Heaven's light enlightens both the sight and the understanding of angels and spirits: 2776, 3138. The nature of the light they experience depends on their intelligence and wisdom: 1524, 3339. Evidence for this from the Word: 1529, 1530. There are as many different types of light in the heavens as there are angelic communities: 4414. Since goodness and truth come in endless varieties in the heavens, the same goes for wisdom and intelligence: 684, 690, 3241, 3744, 3745, 5598, 7236, 7833, 7836. Heaven's having light and warmth means that it has wisdom and love: 3643, 9399, 9400.

[4] Heaven's light is what enlightens our understanding: 1524, 3138, 3167, 4408, 6608, 8707, 9128, 9399, 10569. When we are lifted out of the level of our physical senses, we come into a gentler light and ultimately into heavenly light: 6312, 6315, 9407. When we come into a greater understanding, we have been lifted into heavenly light: 3190. The great light that I have perceived when I have been withdrawn from worldly ideas: 1526, 6608. Our inner self sees in heaven's light, which is why we can think analytically and rationally: 1532. Heaven's light from the Lord is always present with us; it actively flows into us to the extent that we are focused on what is true for the sake of what is good: 4060, 4214. That light is proportional to the truth we have from leading a good life: 3094. Truths shine in the spiritual world: 5219. Spiritual warmth and spiritual light give us true life: 6032.

[5] This world's light is for the outer self, and heaven's light is for the inner self: 3222, 3223, 3337. Heaven's light flows into earthly light; the wisdom of our earthly self is proportional to our acceptance of heaven's light: 4302, 4408. There is a relationship of correspondence between these two kinds of light: 3225. The things that are visible in heaven's light cannot be seen in the light we have in this world, the light we call "earthly light"; and conversely, the things that are visible in earthly light cannot be seen in heaven's light: 9577. That is why people who are in this world's light alone, the light we call "earthly light," do not perceive things that exist in heaven's light: 3108. For people who have embraced false beliefs because they love evil, heaven's light is darkness: 1783, 3337, 3413, 4060, 6907, 8197.

For evil people this world's light comes to have a warm glow, and the brighter it glows, the darker the things that are in heaven's light become for them: 6907. Angels cannot see this world's light: 1521, 1783, 1880.

[6] In the heavens all the light comes from the Lord and all the shade comes from the ignorance and selfhood of angels and spirits, giving rise to the modifications and variations of light and shade that are colors there: 3341. The variations of light that shone through the Urim and Thummim: 3862.

[7] The light of people who are given to a faith separate from caring is snowy and is like winter light: 3412, 3413. That light turns into mere darkness as heaven's light flows in: 3412. The light of people whose faith is merely expedient and whose lives are given to evil: 4416. What the light is like for people whose intelligence comes from themselves and what it is like for people whose intelligence comes from the Lord: 4419.

[8] There is light in the hells, but it is deceptive: 1528, 3340, 4214, 4418, 4531. The light there is like that of glowing charcoal: 1528, 4418, 4531. People in the hells look human to themselves in their own light, but in heaven's light they look like demons and monsters: 4532, 4533, 4674, 5057, 5058, 6605, 6626. In heaven's light, everything looks like what it truly is: 4674. The reason why the hells are referred to [in the Word] as being in "darkness" and "thick darkness" is that they have false thoughts and evil intent: 3340, 4418, 4531. "Darkness" means falsities, and "thick darkness" means falsities from evil intent: 1839, 1860, 7600, 7711.

The sense-oriented people mentioned in the teachings in §45 above, who are the lowest of the earthly. The sensory level is the outermost limit of our life, attached to and embedded in our bodies: 5077, 5767, 9212, 9216, 9331, 9730. We call people sense-oriented who pass final judgment on everything on the basis of their physical senses and who do not believe in anything unless they can see it with their own eyes and touch it with their own hands, saying that only such a thing actually is something and rejecting everything else: 5094, 7693. People like this think on the outermost level and not more deeply within themselves: 5089, 5094, 6564, 7693. Their deeper levels are closed so that they do not see any bit of truth there: 6564, 6844, 6845. In short, they are in a crude earthly light and therefore perceive nothing in heaven's light: 6201, 6310, 6564, 6598, 6844, 6845, 6612, 6614, 6622, 6624. They are therefore inwardly opposed to everything having to do with heaven and the church: 6201, 6316, 6844, 6845, 6948, 6949. Scholars who are adamantly opposed to the truths of the church are sense-oriented: 6316.

[2] Sense-oriented people are able to dispute with cleverness and with vehement certainty because their thinking is closely enmeshed with their speaking, and because, as they see it, intelligence in its entirety consists of words assembled solely out of facts recalled from the memory: 195, 196, 5700, 10236. The reasons they offer in their disputes, however, are based on deceptive sense impressions, which they use to ensnare ordinary people: 5084, 6948, 6949, 7693.

[3] Sense-oriented people are more shrewd and vicious than others: 7693, 10236. Misers, adulterers, hedonists, and deceivers are especially sense-oriented: 6310. Their deeper levels are befouled and filthy: 6201. They are in touch with hell through those levels: 6310. The people in the hells are sense-oriented, more and more so the deeper in hell they are: 4623, 6311. The aura of hellish spirits is joined to our sensory level from behind us: 6312. The ancients called people who reason on the basis of their senses and therefore against the truths that belong to religious faith "serpents of the tree of knowledge": 195, 196, 197, 6398, 6949, 10313.

[4] Further description of our sensory level and sense-oriented people (10236) and of the extension of our senses (9731).

[5] [Thoughts and desires] based on our senses should be put last, not first. In the wise and intelligent they are put last and are subject to the inner self. In those who are not wise, though, they are put first and are in control. These are the people who are properly called "sense-oriented": 5077, 5125, 5128, 7645. If a sensory perspective is put last and is subject to our inner self, a path to the understanding is opened through it and truths are refined from it by means of a kind of distillation: 5580.

[6] Our sensory functions are most directly exposed to the world; they let in things that enter from the world and filter them: 9726. Through these sensory functions our outer or earthly self is in touch with the world; through rational faculties it is in touch with heaven: 4009. In this way our sensory functions provide things that are useful to our deeper functions: 5077, 5081. Some of our senses support our understanding and others support our will: 5077.

[7] Unless our thinking is lifted out of sensory concerns we have little wisdom: 5089. Wise people think on a level higher than that of the senses: 5089, 5094. When our thinking rises above sensory concerns we come into a clearer light and eventually into a heavenly light: 6183, 6313, 6315, 9407, 9730, 9922. The ancients knew that it was desirable to rise above sensory concerns and be released from them: 6313. In our spirit

we can see things that are in the spiritual world if we can be released from the sensory concerns that arise from our bodies and be lifted into heaven's light by the Lord: 4622. This is because it is not the body that is conscious but the spirit within the body, and to the extent that it is in the body the spirit's consciousness is coarse and cloudy and therefore in darkness. To the extent that it is not in the body, the spirit's consciousness is clear and is in the light: 4622, 6614, 6622.

Facts derived from the senses are the lowest level of our understanding, and sensory gratification is the lowest level of our will: 9996 (which includes discussion). The difference between the sensory functions we have in common with animals and the sensory functions we do not have in common with them: 10236. There are sense-oriented people who are not evil because their deeper levels are not completely closed. On their state in the other life: 6311.

The worldly knowledge and spiritual knowledge that serve for the opening of our inner spiritual self. "Worldly knowledge" refers to the knowledge we have in our outer or earthly self and its memory, but not to the knowledge we have in our inner or spiritual self: 3019, 3020, 3293, 3309, 4967, 9918, 9922. Since worldly knowledge belongs to the outer or earthly self it is relatively menial. This is because the outer or earthly self is made to serve the inner or spiritual self the way the world serves heaven: 5077, 5125, 5128, 5786, 5947, 10272, 10471. The outer self is like the world because the laws of the divine design that prevail in the world are written into it, and the inner self is like heaven because the laws of the divine design that prevail in heaven are written into it: 4523, 4524, 5368, 6013, 6057, 9278, 9279, 9283, 9709, 10156, 10472; [see also] *Heaven and Hell* 51–58.

[2] There are bodies of knowledge of an earthly nature that have to do with our civic condition and our civic life; there are bodies of knowledge that have to do with our moral condition and our moral life; and there are bodies of knowledge that have to do with our spiritual condition and our spiritual life: 5774, 5934. For clarity's sake, though, I refer to knowledge about our spiritual condition and our spiritual life as "spiritual knowledge," which mainly consists of theological teachings: 9945.

[3] It is important for us to become steeped in worldly and spiritual knowledge, because it is through this that we learn to think, then to understand what truth and goodness are, and eventually to be wise— that is, to live by what we have learned: 129, 1450, 1451, 1453, 1548, 1802.

Worldly and spiritual knowledge are basic things on which our life is built and founded—both our civic and our moral life as well as our spiritual life; but they need to be learned with the goal of living a useful life: 1489, 3310. Spiritual knowledge opens a pathway to the inner self and then joins the inner and the outer self together according to our usefulness: 1563, 1616. Our rationality is born by means of worldly and spiritual knowledge (1895, 1900, 3086), yet it is not born through that knowledge itself, but through and according to our desire to put it to use (1895). The inner self is opened and gradually perfected through worldly and spiritual knowledge if we seek good and useful goals, especially goals related to eternal life: 3086. Then spiritual insights from the heavenly and spiritual self encounter the knowledge of worldly and spiritual things that is in the earthly self and adopt what is suitable: 1495. Then from the knowledge about worldly and spiritual things that is in our earthly self the Lord, by means of our inner self, draws out, refines, and raises up what is useful for heavenly life (1895, 1899, 1900, 1901, 1902, 5871, 5874, 5901), but information that is incompatible or conflicting is pushed aside and excluded (5871, 5886, 5889). The sight of our inner self calls forth from the worldly and spiritual knowledge in our outer self only those things that relate to what we love: 9394. Our worldly and spiritual knowledge is arranged in bundles and bound together according to the type of love that drove us to learn it: 5881. Then to the eye of our inner self the information that relates to what we love is at the center and in bright light, while the information that does not relate is off to the sides and in darkness: 6068, 6085. Worldly and spiritual knowledge is gradually sown in our loves and takes up residence there: 6323. If we were born loving the Lord and loving our neighbor we would be born into all knowledge and understanding, but since we are born loving ourselves and the world we are born into total ignorance: 6323. Knowledge, intelligence, and wisdom are the offspring that are born of love for the Lord and love for our neighbor: 1226, 2049, 2116.

[4] Since knowledge of worldly and spiritual things belongs to the outer or earthly self, it is in this world's light, but truths that have become matters of love and faith and therefore have been applied to life are in heaven's light: 5212. Even so, earthly concepts are needed to help us understand the truths that we are applying to life: 5510. There is a spiritual inflow through the inner self into the knowledge of worldly and spiritual things that is in the outer self: 1940, 8005. Knowledge of worldly and spiritual things is a

container and vessel for the truth and goodness that belong to the inner self: 1469, 1496, 3068, 5489, 6004, 6023, 6052, 6071, 6077, 7770, 9922. That is why "vessels" in the Word, spiritually understood, means knowledge of worldly and spiritual things: 3068, 3069, 3079, 9394, 9544, 9723, 9724. Our worldly knowledge is like a mirror in which we can see and perceive in a kind of image things that are true and things that are good in the inner self (5201); all three meet together there on the outermost level (5373, 5874, 5886, 5901, 6004, 6023, 6052, 6071, 6077). Since worldly information is in this world's light, it is tangled and dark compared to things that are in heaven's light, which means that the same holds true for the contents of the outer self in comparison to those of the inner self: 2831. In fact, in the Word "a thicket" (2831) and "clouds" and "darkness" (8443, 10551) mean worldly knowledge.

[5] We need to make our start from the truths of a body of teaching from the Word and acknowledge them first, and then it is allowable to turn to worldly knowledge in order to find support for them and verify them: 6047. So if people have a positive attitude toward the truths that belong to religious faith, it is all right for them to look to worldly knowledge for intellectual support, but it is not all right for people who have a negative attitude to such truths, because a positive attitude as a starting point pulls everything in a positive direction, but a negative attitude as a starting point pulls everything in a negative direction: 2568, 2588, 3913, 4760, 6047. There is an affirmative way of doubting and a negative way of doubting, the former being characteristic of the good and the latter characteristic of the evil: 2568. Engagement with worldly knowledge on the basis of the truths that belong to religious faith accords with proper order; but the reverse, engaging on the basis of worldly knowledge with the truths that belong to religious faith, is contrary to proper order: 10236. Since inflow is spiritual and not physical or earthly it is a flow from the truths that belong to religious faith (because these are spiritual) into worldly knowledge (because this is earthly): 3219, 5119, 5259, 5427, 5428, 5479, 6322, 9109, 9110.

[6] People who doubt in a truly negative way, and say that they will not believe until they are convinced by objective evidence, will never believe: 2094, 2832. People who do this become insane in regard to matters of the church and heaven: 128, 129, 130. They fall prey to false beliefs and evil cravings (232, 233) and in the other life when they think about spiritual matters they become like drunks (1072). More about what they

are like: 196. Some examples illustrating the fact that spiritual matters cannot be grasped if they are approached from the wrong direction: 233, 2094, 2196, 2203, 2209. Many scholars are more insane in spiritual matters than ordinary people because they are resolutely negative and have an abundant supply of facts to support their denial: 4760. An example of a scholar who was incapable of understanding anything about spiritual life: 8629. People who use worldly knowledge to dispute the truths that belong to religious faith do so with vehemence, since their arguments are based on the deceptive impressions of the five senses. These impressions, being hard to dispel, are arresting and persuasive: 5700. People who understand nothing of what is true and who are also given to evil are able to reason about the truths and the good actions taught by faith, and yet they have no enlightenment: 4214. Simply confirming a dogma is not a sign of intelligence, because a dogma that is false is as easy to confirm as one that is true: 1017, 2477, 2490, 4741, 5033, 6865, 7012, 7680, 7950, 8521, 8780. People who reason about the truths of the church by asking whether something exists or not are completely in the dark about truths and have no spiritual light yet: 215, 1385, 3428.

[7] There are types of knowledge that support divine truths and types that do not: 5213. Empty facts have to be eliminated from our minds: 1489, 1492, 1499, 1500. Facts are empty if they intend and support our love for ourselves and the world and lead us away from loving the Lord and our neighbor, because this kind of thing closes the inner self so completely that we can then not accept anything from heaven: 1563, 1600. Worldly knowledge is a means to both wisdom and madness; by it the inner self is either opened or closed and our rational functioning is either developed or destroyed: 4156, 8628, 9922.

[8] Worldly learning means nothing after death except what we have gained through it for our understanding and life: 2480. Nevertheless, all our worldly knowledge remains intact after death, though it is dormant: 2476–2479, 2481–2486.

[9] The same facts that are false for evil people because they are used for evil purposes are true for good people because they are used for good purposes: 6917. The truths that evil people know are not actually true no matter how true they may seem when they say them, because there is something evil within those truths and they are falsified as a result; not even the knowledge they have deserves to be called knowledge, because it has no life within it: 10331.

[10] It is one thing to be wise, another to be intelligent, another to be knowledgeable, and another to act; all the same, for people engaged in a spiritual life, these follow in order and correspond to each other, and they are all present together in the doing and in the deeds: 10331. It is also one thing to know the truth, another to acknowledge it, and still another to believe it: 896.

[11] An example of the kind of craving for information that spirits have: 1973. Angels have an immense desire for knowledge and wisdom because knowledge, intelligence, and wisdom are spiritual food: 3114, 4459, 4792, 4976, 5147, 5293, 5340, 5342, 5410, 5426, 5576, 5582, 5588, 5655, 6277, 8562, 9003.

[12] Among the ancients the most important field of study was knowing correspondences, but nowadays that body of knowledge has been erased: 3021, 3419, 4280, 4844, 4964, 4965, 6004, 7729, 10252. There was a knowledge of correspondences among the people of the Near East and in Egypt: 5702, 6692, 7097, 7779, 9391, 10407. This was the source of their hieroglyphics: 6692, 7097. Through their knowledge of correspondences the ancients gained access to spiritual knowledge of various kinds: 4749, 4844, 4966. The Word was written in pure correspondences, and that is the source of its inner or spiritual meaning. Without a knowledge of correspondences we cannot know that this meaning exists or know what the nature of the Word is: 3131, 3472–3485, 8615, 10687. How superior a knowledge of correspondences is to other forms of knowledge: 4280.

The earthly memory that belongs to the outer self and the spiritual memory that belongs to the inner self. Human beings actually have two faculties of memory, an outer memory and an inner memory, or an earthly memory and a spiritual memory: 2469–2494. We are not aware that we have this inner memory: 2470, 2471. How much better the inner memory is than the outer memory: 2473. The contents of our outer memory are in an earthly light, while the contents of our inner memory are in a spiritual light: 5212. Our inner memory is the basis of our ability to think and speak rationally and with understanding: 9394. Every least detail of everything we have thought and said and done as well as what we have heard and seen is inscribed in our inner memory: 2474, 7398. That memory is our book of life: 2474, 9386, 9841, 10505. Our inner memory stores the [truths] that have become part of our faith and the goodness that has become part of our love: 5212, 8067. Our inner memory also stores things that have taken on the force of habit for us and have become part of our

52

life: 9394, 9723, 9841. Knowledge of worldly and spiritual things is stored in our outer memory: 5212, 9922. That information is extremely dark and tangled compared to the contents of our inner memory: 2831. In this world our ability to speak our various languages depends on our outer memory: 2472, 2476. Angels and spirits speak from their inner memory, so they have a universal language such that no matter what country people come from they can talk with each other: 2472, 2476, 2490, 2493. For information about this language, see *Heaven and Hell* 234–245, and on the astoundingly detailed nature of the inner memory that we retain after death, see *Heaven and Hell* 463.

53 *The fallacies arising from the senses that preoccupy the merely earthly and sense-oriented people mentioned in §45 above.* People who are completely earthly and sense-oriented derive their thinking and reasoning from fallacies arising from the senses: 5084, 5700, 6948, 6949, 7693. The nature of fallacies arising from the senses: 5084, 5094, 6400, 6948. To this I may add the following: There are fallacies arising from the senses that concern earthly matters, others that concern civic matters, others moral matters, and still others spiritual matters, and there are many of each kind; at this point I would like to list a few that concern spiritual matters.

If we base our thinking on fallacies arising from the senses, we cannot understand the idea that after death people still look human, that they enjoy the use of their senses as they did before, and that they can become angels. We think [instead] that

1. The soul is simply something barely alive, something purely ethereal, and we can have no concept of it.
2. It is only the body that feels, sees, and hears.
3. We are just like animals except that we can say what we are thinking.
4. Nature is all there is—it came first and is the source of everything.
5. We learn to think and we develop that ability because the inner things of nature and its order flow into us.
6. Spiritual reality does not exist; or if it does it is just a purer aspect of earthly reality.
7. It would be impossible for us to enjoy any sense of blessedness if we were deprived of the gratifications that come from loving glory, high rank, and profit.
8. Conscience is nothing but a feeling of distress caused by physical weakness or lack of success.
9. The Lord's divine love is a love of glory.

10. There is no such thing as providence; everything depends on our own prudence and intelligence.

11. High rank and wealth are the real blessings granted by God.

Not to mention many more such things.

These are just some of the fallacies arising from the senses that concern spiritual matters. These examples show that what is heavenly cannot be grasped by people who are completely earthly and sense-oriented. And we become completely earthly and sense-oriented when our inner spiritual self is closed and only our earthly self is open.

Love in General

54 WHAT we love constitutes life itself to us: what our love is like determines what our life is like and therefore what we are like as human beings. In particular, it is the love that is dominant or supreme in us that makes us who we are.

That love has many loves that are subordinate to it, loves that derive from it. They take on various guises, but they are all nevertheless present within the dominant love, and together with it make one kingdom. The dominant love acts as the monarch or head of the rest; it governs them and works through them as intermediate goals, in order to focus on and strive for its primary and ultimate goal of all, doing this both directly and indirectly.

The object of our dominant love is what we love more than anything else.

55 Whatever we love more than anything else is constantly present within our thoughts and also within our will. It constitutes the very core of our life. For example, if we love wealth more than anything else, whether in the form of money or of possessions, we are constantly considering how we can acquire it. We feel the deepest joy when we do acquire it and the deepest grief when we lose it—our heart is in it.

If we love ourselves more than anything else, we are mindful of ourselves at every little moment. We think about ourselves, talk about ourselves, and act to benefit ourselves, because our life is a life of pure self.

56 We have as our goal whatever we love more than anything else. This is what we focus on overall and in every detail. It is within our will like the hidden current of a river that draws and carries us along even when we are doing something else, because it is what animates us.

What is loved above all is also something we look for and see in others, and something we use to influence them or to cooperate with them.

57 The way we are is entirely determined by what controls our life. This is what distinguishes us from each other. This is what determines our heaven if we are good and our hell if we are evil. It is our essential will, our self, and our nature. In fact, it is the underlying reality of our life. It cannot be changed after death because it is what we really are.

58 All the pleasure, satisfaction, and happiness we feel comes from and accords with what we love above all. We call whatever we love a pleasure because that is how it feels to us. While we can also call something a pleasure that we think about but do not love, that kind of pleasure is not alive for us.

What we see as good is what is pleasing to our love, and what we see as evil is what is displeasing to our love.

There are two kinds of love that generate all that is good and true, and two kinds of love that generate all that is evil and false. The two kinds of love that are the source of everything good and true are love for the Lord and love for our neighbor; the two kinds of love that are the source of everything evil and false are love for ourselves and love for this world. **59**

The latter two kinds of love are the exact opposites of the former two kinds of love.

The two kinds of love that are the source of everything good and true (which as just stated are love for the Lord and love for our neighbor) make heaven for us, so they reign in heaven as well; and since they make heaven for us they also constitute the church. **60**

The two kinds of love that are the source of everything evil and false (which as just stated are love for ourselves and love for this world) make hell for us and therefore reign in hell as well.

The two kinds of love that are the source of everything good and true (which as just stated are the kinds of love in heaven) open and give form to our inner, spiritual self because that is where they live. However, when the two kinds of love that are the source of everything evil and false are in control, they close and wreck our inner, spiritual self and cause us to be materialistic and sense-oriented according to the extent and nature of their domination. **61**

From *Secrets of Heaven*

LOVE is the underlying reality of our life: 5002. Every person in this world, every spirit, and every angel is exactly the same as her or his love is: 6872, 10177, 10284. What we love is what we hold as our goal: 3796. Whatever we love and have as our goal reigns universally in us—that is, throughout us and in our every detail: 3796, 5130, 5949. Love is spiritual warmth and is what is actually alive in us: 1589, 2146, 3338, 4906, **62**

7081–7086, 9954, 10740. All the things within us, all the elements of our understanding and our will, are arranged in a form that is determined by our dominant love: 3189, 6690. Love is a spiritual joining together: 1594, 2057, 3939, 4018, 5807, 6195, 6196, 7081–7086, 7501, 10130. Therefore all the people in the spiritual world are gathered into communities in accord with their loves: 10130. Our feelings are extensions of our love: 3938. Every pleasure, gratification, satisfaction, and happiness we feel, and every heartfelt joy, relates to what we love, and its nature depends on the nature of our love: 994, 995, 2204. There are as many genera and species of pleasure and gratification as there are emotional responses that arise from what we love: 994, 995, 2204. The more superficial are the pleasures we love, the poorer they are: 996. After death, what our life is like is determined by what our love is like: 2363.

63   There is more information above on love and its essence and nature, in the statements and passages referred to concerning goodness and truth [§§11–27]; in the statements and passages referred to concerning will and understanding [§§28–35]; and in the statements and passages referred to concerning the inner and the outer self [§§36–53]. This is because everything that has to do with [what we] love goes back to either good or evil, and the same holds true for everything that has to do with [what we] will to do, and also because the two kinds of love in heaven open the inner, spiritual self and give form to it while the two kinds of love in hell close it and destroy it. By inference, that information will allow you to see the nature of love both in general and in particular.

64   The kinds of love are also discussed in my book *Heaven and Hell,* where it is explained that the Lord's divine nature is present in heaven as love for him and love for one's neighbor (§§13–19); that all the people who are in the hells are absorbed in evils and consequent falsities because of their love for themselves and the world (§§551–565); that in the other life the pleasures of everyone's love are turned into things that correspond (§§485–490); and that spiritual warmth in its essence is love (§§133–140).

Love for Ourselves and Love for the World

L OVE for ourselves is intending benefit only to ourselves and not to others unless it is in our own interests—having no goodwill toward the church or our country or toward any group of people or any fellow citizen. It is also being good to the church, our country, and other people only for the sake of our own reputation, advancement, or praise, so that unless we see some such reward in the good we may do for them we say at heart, "What's the use? Why should I? What's in it for me?" and forget about it. This shows that when we live a life of self-love we are not loving the church, our country, our community, our fellow citizens, or anything worthwhile—only ourselves. **65**

If we give no consideration to our neighbor in what we are thinking and doing and therefore no consideration to the public good, let alone the Lord, then we live a life of self-love; we think only of ourselves and our immediate circle. This means that everything we do is done for the sake of ourselves and our own; if we do anything to benefit the public and our neighbor, it is only for the sake of appearances. **66**

In referring to "ourselves and our immediate circle," I mean that when we love ourselves we also love those we see as our own, in particular our children and grandchildren, and in general everyone with whom we identify, whom we call "ours." Loving them is loving ourselves. This is because we see them as virtually part of us and see ourselves in them. Also included in those we call "ours" is everyone who praises, honors, and reveres us. **67**

If we despise our neighbors or regard people as our enemies for merely disagreeing with us or not showing us reverence or respect, our life is a life of self-love. If for similar slights we hate our neighbors and persecute them, then we are even more deeply entrenched in self-love. And if we burn with vengeance against them and crave their destruction, our self-love is stronger still; people with this attitude eventually love being cruel. **68**

We can tell what self-love is like by contrasting it with heavenly love. Heavenly love is loving service for its own sake, loving for their own sakes the good things we do for church, country, community, and fellow **69**

57

citizen. When we love these things for the sake of ourselves instead, we love them only as servants who wait on us. Therefore when we live in self-love we want the church, our country, our community, and our fellow citizens to serve us rather than wanting to serve them. We place ourselves above them, and them beneath us.

70   Not only that, the more we live a life of heavenly love (which is loving to be useful and do good things and having heartfelt delight when we do them), the more we are led by the Lord, since this is the love in which he is and which comes from him. On the other hand, the more we live a life of self-love, the more we are led by ourselves, and the more we are led by ourselves the more we are led by our own intrinsic characteristics; and those characteristics are nothing but evil. This is in fact the evil that we inherit—loving ourselves more than God, and the world more than heaven.

71   Further, to the extent that we give self-love free rein (that is, with the removal of the outward restraints exerted by fear of the law and its penalties, and of loss of reputation, respect, wealth, office, and life), this love by its very nature goes so wild that it wants to rule not only over every country on earth but even over heaven and over the Divine itself. It knows no boundary or limit. Even if this desire is not visible in the world, where the reins and restraints just mentioned keep it in check, it nevertheless lies hidden within all who devote their lives to this love. When such people find that the way forward is blocked, they stay there until the way is not blocked. The result of all this is that when their life is one of self-love they have no idea that such an insane, boundless craving lies hidden within them.

Still, no one can help but see this in powerful figures and heads of state who lack these kinds of reins, restraints, and obstacles, who charge off to conquer as many territories and countries as they can and thirst for unlimited power and glory. It is even more obvious in the people who extend their dominion into heaven and claim all of the Lord's divine power for themselves—and ceaselessly crave for more.

72   There are two kinds of governing. One arises out of love for our neighbor and the other out of love for ourselves. Fundamentally, these two ways of governing are exact opposites. If we govern out of love for our neighbor, we wish good things for everyone. We love nothing more than being helpful and therefore serving others (serving others is doing good and useful things for them because we have goodwill toward them). This is what we love and what delights our hearts. The more we are promoted to higher office the happier we are; but this is not because of the office but because of the greater and higher service we can perform. This is the kind of governing that exists in heaven.

In contrast, if we govern out of love for ourselves, then we wish good things for no one but ourselves and our immediate circle. Any service we perform is to gain respect and glory for ourselves because that is the only outcome we consider useful; as far as we are concerned, the only reason for serving others is to be served and respected and obeyed. We strive for high office not because of the good things we can do but in order to bask in eminence and glory to our hearts' delight.

The kind of love we had for governing stays with us after our life in this world; but it is those who have governed out of a love for their neighbor who are entrusted with governing in the heavens. In that case, it is not in fact we ourselves who are in control but the good and useful things we do, and when good and useful actions are in control, the Lord is governing. But if in this world we have governed out of love for ourselves, then after our life in this world we are in hell and are lowly slaves. **73**

So these points can help us recognize the characteristics of people who devote their lives to self-love, but this recognition does not depend on how they appear outwardly, whether they come across as proud or submissive. The characteristics mentioned above are in the inner self, and for most people their inner self is hidden away and their outer self is trained to pretend to love the public good and their neighbors—the very opposite of what is inside. This too is for selfish reasons. They know that everyone is deeply moved by examples of a love for the public good and for one's neighbor and that they themselves will be loved and valued to the extent that they exhibit this love. (The reason everyone is moved by such things is that heaven flows into that kind of love.) **74**

The evils characteristic of people devoted to self-love are, broadly speaking, contempt for others, envy, ill will toward those who do not agree with them, a consequent hostility, and various kinds of hatred, vengefulness, guile, trickery, ruthlessness, and cruelty; and wherever we find these evils we also find a contempt for the Divine and for the truths and the good practices from the Divine that are taught by the church. If such people do pay respect to these things, it is with the mouth only and not with the heart. **75**

Further, since self-love is the source of these evils it is also the source of corresponding falsities, since evils give rise to falsities.

76 As for love for the world, this is wanting to use any available means to divert others' resources to ourselves, setting our hearts on wealth, and letting the world distract and seduce us away from the spiritual love that is love for our neighbor, and therefore away from heaven.

If we are obsessed with diverting others' assets to ourselves by various means, especially if we use guile and trickery to do so, with no regard for our neighbor's well-being, we have devoted our lives to love for the world. When this is the love we live in, we crave what others have, and to the extent that we do not fear the law or losing our reputation, purely for the sake of our own gain we will deprive them even to the point of taking everything they have.

77 All the same, love for the world is not so completely opposed to heavenly love as love for ourselves is, because the evils hidden within it are not as horrendous.

Love for the world takes many forms. Wealth can be loved as a means of gaining high office; a prominent position or high office can be loved for the wealth it brings; wealth can be loved because it affords us various kinds of pleasure; wealth can even be loved purely for its own sake, which is called miserliness; and so on. The goal for which we seek the wealth is called its use, and the goal or use is what determines what the love is like, since the nature of the love depends on the goal that it seeks. The other factors serve that goal as means.

78 In a word, love for ourselves and love for the world are exact opposites of love for the Lord and love for our neighbor. Therefore love for ourselves and love for the world are hellish loves. They actually rule in hell, and for us as well they constitute hell. In contrast, love for the Lord and love for our neighbor are heavenly loves. They actually rule in heaven, and for us as well they constitute heaven.

79 We can see from what has now been said that all our evils are contained in and come from this pair of loves. The evils listed in §75 are basic categories; other evils not listed there are subcategories that derive and flow from them.

This shows that since we are born with these two loves we are born with evils of all kinds.

80 If we are to know what evil is we need to know where it comes from; and unless we know what evil is we do not know what goodness is and therefore cannot know what we ourselves really are. That is the reason for dealing here with these two sources of evil.

From *Secrets of Heaven*

L *OVE for ourselves and love for the world.* Just as love for the Lord and   **81**
love for our neighbor, or caring, make heaven, so love for ourselves
and love for the world, where they are dominant, make hell; so the two
pairs of loves are opposites: 2041, 3610, 4225, 4776, 6210, 7366, 7369,
7489, 7490, 8232, 8678, 10455, 10741, 10742, 10743, 10745. Love for ourselves and love for the world are the source of all evils: 1307, 1308, 1321,
1594, 1691, 3413, 7255, 7376, 7488, 7489, 8318, 9335, 9348, 10038, 10742.
Love for ourselves and love for the world are the source of contempt for
others, enmity, hatred, vengefulness, cruelty, trickery, and therefore every
evil and all maliciousness: 6667, 7372, 7373, 7374, 9348, 10038, 10742. To
the extent that we give these loves free rein they run wild, and self-love
even races all the way to the throne of God: 7375, 8678. Love for ourselves
and love for the world are destructive of our communities and of heavenly order: 2045, 2057. It is because of these loves that the human race
had to institute governments and people had to subject themselves to a
ruling authority in order to be safe: 7364, 10160, 10814. Wherever these
loves rule, acts of goodness that are inspired by love and acts of goodness
that are inspired by faith are rejected, or stifled, or corrupted: 2041, 7491,
7492, 7643, 8487, 10455, 10743. In these loves there is no life, but instead
there is spiritual death: 7494, 10731, 10741. Descriptions of what these
loves are like: 1505, 2219, 2363, 2364, 2444, 4221, 4227, 4947, 4949, 5721,
7366–7377, 8678. All craving and obsession come from loving ourselves
and the world: 2041, 8910.

[2] Love for ourselves and love for the world should serve as means,
and not at all as goals: 7377, 7819, 7820. When we are being reformed
these loves are inverted so that they serve as means and not as goals, and
the result is that they become like the feet rather than the head: 8995,
9210. People who devote their lives to self-love and love for the world
have in effect no inner level, only an outer level without an inner one,
because their inner level is closed to heaven but their outer level is open
to the world: 10396, 10400, 10409, 10412, 10422, 10429. People who live
in self-love and love for the world do not know what caring is, what
conscience is, or what the life of heaven is: 7490. To the extent that we
devote our lives to self-love and love for the world we do not accept either

the love of doing what is good or the truth that builds faith, although these are constantly flowing into us from the Lord: 7491.

[3] For people who devote their lives to self-love and love for the world there are outer restraints, but no inner restraints, so when the outer restraints are removed they plunge into every kind of wickedness: 10744, 10745, 10746. In the spiritual world we all turn toward what we love. If we have devoted our lives to loving the Lord and loving our neighbor, we turn toward the Lord; but if we have devoted our lives to loving ourselves and loving the world, we turn our backs on the Lord: 10130, 10189, 10420, 10742. The nature of worship that has self-love within it: 1304, 1306, 1307, 1308, 1321, 1322. The Lord uses evil people to govern the world, leading them by their own loves, which go back to love for themselves and love for the world: 6481, 6495. Evil people can serve functions and do good and useful things just as much as good people can, because they are intent on prestige and wealth as their rewards, so they act outwardly the same way good people do: 6481, 6495.

[4] All the people in the hells have lives that are devoted to evil practices and consequent false beliefs because of their love for themselves and love for the world: *Heaven and Hell* 551–565.

82   *Our own intrinsic characteristics, as mentioned above in the teachings in §70, are love for ourselves and love for the world.* Our intrinsic characteristics are evil through and through: 210, 215, 731, 874, 875, 876, 987, 1047, 2307, 2308, 3518, 3701, 3812, 8480, 8550, 10283, 10284, 10286, 10731. The part of us that belongs to ourselves is our will: 4328. What is intrinsic to us is our loving ourselves more than God, loving the world more than heaven, and regarding our neighbor as nothing in comparison to the self, so it is love for ourselves and love for the world: 694, 731, 4317, 5660. From this intrinsic selfhood of ours gushes not only everything evil but everything false as well, and this falsity is the kind that comes from evil intent: 1047, 10283, 10284, 10286. This selfhood is hell for us: 694, 8480. So no one led by his or her own selfhood can be saved: 10731. Anything good that we do from this selfhood of ours is not good but is essentially evil because it is done for selfish and worldly reasons: 8480.

This selfhood needs to be put aside so that the Lord can be present: 1023, 1044. It is effectively put aside when we are being reformed: 9334, 9335, 9336, 9452, 9453, 9454, 9938. This is done by the Lord alone: 9445. We are given a heavenly selfhood through rebirth: 1937, 1947, 2882, 2883, 2891. Although this heavenly selfhood seems to us to belong to ourselves,

it is not ours but is something within us that belongs to the Lord: 8497.
When we have this kind of selfhood we have true freedom, because freedom is being led by the Lord and by his kind of selfhood: 892, 905, 2872,
2886, 2890, 2891, 2892, 4096, 9586, 9587, 9589, 9590, 9591. All our freedom is experienced in our sense of self, and what our freedom is like
depends on what our selfhood is like: 2880. The nature of a heavenly
selfhood: 164, 5660, 8480. How a heavenly selfhood is planted in us: 1712,
1937, 1947.

What we inherit (discussed above in the teachings in §§70 and 79) is   **83**
loving ourselves and loving the world. All people without exception are
born with evils of every kind, so much so that our intrinsic characteristics are utterly evil: 210, 215, 731, 874, 875, 876, 987, 1047, 2307, 2308,
3701, 3812, 8480, 8550, 10283, 10284, 10286, 10731. Therefore we need to
be born again—that is, regenerated—in order to receive new life from
the Lord: 3701.

[2] The evils we inherit from our parents and ancestors reach back in
a long sequence, increasing and building up. They do not, however, come
from the first human because of his eating from the tree of knowledge
[Genesis 3:1–24], as is commonly believed: 313, 494, 2910, 3469, 3701,
4317, 8550. This means that the evils we inherit nowadays are more malig-
nant than those of the past: 2122. Even babies who die in infancy and are
brought up in heaven are nothing but evil because of their heredity: 2307,
2308, 4563. Children's heredity makes them different from one another
in nature and inclination: 2300. Our inner evils come from our fathers
and our outer ones from our mothers: 4317.

[3] Left to ourselves, we add new evils to the ones we inherit; our new
evils are therefore called "active": 8551. In the other life none are punished
for the evils they have inherited; they are punished only for the evils they
actively and repeatedly commit: 966, 2308. The more vicious hells are
kept apart by themselves to prevent them from activating the inherited
evils that are in us and in spirits: 1667, 8806.

[4] Our inherited evils are evils that arise from self-love and love for
the world—loving ourselves more than God, loving the world more than
heaven, and considering our neighbors to be of no importance what-
soever: 694, 4317, 5660. And since these evils are opposed to the good
loves espoused by heaven and opposed to the divine design, we cannot
avoid being born into utter ignorance: 1050, 1902, 1992, 3175. Some of
us are born with a nature that has an earthly kind of goodness, but this

is still not true goodness, because it readily lends itself to being used in all kinds of evil and false ways, and this kind of goodness is not allowed into heaven unless it becomes spiritual goodness: 2463, 2464, 2468, 3304, 3408, 3469, 3470, 3508, 3518, 7761.

Love for Our Neighbor, or Caring

FIRST of all, I need to define *neighbor,* because this is the one we are ▮84▮ to love and the one toward whom caring is to be extended. Unless we know what *neighbor* means, we may extend caring in basically the same manner indiscriminately—just as much to evil people as to good ones. But in that case our caring can become the opposite of caring, because although the good people will use what they have been given to do good to their neighbor, the evil people will use it to do harm.

Most people nowadays think that everyone is equally their neighbor ▮85▮ and that we should be generous to anyone who is in need. It should be part of Christian prudence, though, to check carefully what someone's life is really like and to extend caring accordingly. People who constitute the inner church do this with discernment and therefore intelligently; but people who constitute the outer church act indiscriminately because they are unable to make distinctions like this.

People in the church should be very aware of the different catego- ▮86▮ ries of the neighbor. The category to which particular neighbors belong depends on which type of goodness they have devoted their lives to. And since every type of goodness comes from the Lord, in the highest sense and to the utmost degree the Lord himself is our neighbor, and is the source [of what makes others our neighbors]. It therefore follows that people are neighbors to us to the extent that they have the Lord in themselves; and since no two people are receptive to the Lord (that is, the goodness that comes from him) in the same way, no two people are our neighbor in the same way. With respect to the particular good they do, all the people in the heavens and all good people on earth are different. It never happens that exactly the same goodness is found in any two individuals. The goodness needs to vary so that each kind of goodness can persist independently.

However, none of us can know all these distinctions and all the consequent distinct kinds of neighbor that arise in accordance with the different ways the Lord is received—that is, the way the goodness from him is received. Not even angels can know this except in a general way, by genus and species. Therefore the Lord requires no more of people in the church than that we live by what we know.

87 Since the sort of goodness in every individual is different, it follows that the nature of each person's goodness determines both the level at which and the way in which that individual is "a neighbor." We can see that this is the case from the Lord's parable about a man who fell among thieves, whom both a priest and a Levite passed by, leaving him half dead, while a Samaritan, after he had bound up his wounds and poured in oil and wine, lifted him onto his own beast and brought him to an inn and made arrangements for his care. The Samaritan is called "a neighbor" because his actions were those of a caring person (Luke 10:29–37). We can tell from this that the people who are "a neighbor" are the ones whose lives are devoted to doing good. In fact, the oil and the wine that the Samaritan poured into the wounds mean goodness and the truth that it shows us.

88 We can see from what has been said thus far that in the broadest sense goodness itself is one's neighbor, since people are neighbors according to the nature of the good that they do, which they get from the Lord. Further, since goodness is one's neighbor, love too is one's neighbor, because everything good that we do is inspired by love. This means that any individual is a neighbor according to the nature of her or his love, which comes from the Lord.

89 The fact that love is what makes someone a neighbor and that we fulfill the role of a neighbor depending on the nature of our love becomes clear in the case of people whose lives are devoted to loving themselves. Such people recognize as neighbors those who love *them* the most—that is, those who are most closely connected to them. These they embrace, these they kiss, these they benefit, and these they call family. In fact, because [people devoted to self-love] are evil, they consider the types of people just mentioned to be their neighbors more than others are; only if others show them love do they consider them too to be their neighbors. They accept someone else as their neighbor, then, to the extent that they receive love from that person and depending on the kind and amount of love they receive. People like this start with themselves to determine who their neighbor is because the determining and deciding factor is whatever one loves.

People who do not love themselves above all, though (and this is true of all who are in the Lord's kingdom), start in determining who their neighbor is with the One whom we should love above all—that is, with the Lord—and they consider an individual to be their neighbor depending on the love that individual has for and from the Lord.

This makes it quite clear where we of the church should start in deciding who our neighbor is and shows that people are our neighbors depending on the goodness they have from the Lord—that is, goodness itself is where we should start.

In fact the Lord tells us in Matthew that this is true. He said to the ones who had done good things that they had given him something to eat, given him something to drink, taken him in, clothed him, visited him, and come to him in prison, and then said that as much as they had done this to one of the least of his people, they had done it to him (Matthew 25:34–40). These six good deeds, understood spiritually, comprise all the kinds of neighbor. `90`

This also shows that when we love doing what is good we are loving the Lord, because the Lord is the source of what is good, the one who is devoted to what is good, and the one who is goodness itself.

However, it is not just people as individuals who are one's neighbor but people in the plural. That is, it is any smaller or larger community, our country, the church, the Lord's kingdom, and above all the Lord himself. These are "our neighbor" to whom we should do good out of love. `91`

These are also ascending levels of neighbor. A community of many is a neighbor on a higher level than one individual. On a level still higher is our country, on a level still higher is the church, and on a level still higher is the Lord's kingdom; but on the highest level, our neighbor is the Lord. These ascending levels are like the rungs of a ladder with the Lord at the top.

A community is a neighbor to a greater extent than an individual is because it is made up of many individuals. We are to practice caring about it just the way we do with respect to individuals, namely, according to the goodness that we find in it. This means that the exercise of caring directed toward a community of honest people is totally different from caring directed toward a community of dishonest people. We love a community when we are concerned for its welfare because of our love of what is good. `92`

Our country is our neighbor to a greater extent than our community is because it is a kind of parent. It is where we were born; it nourishes us and protects us from harm. `93`

We should do good to our country out of love according to its needs, which focus particularly on its being sustained and on the civil life and the spiritual life of the people who live in it.

If we love our country and do what is good for it with goodwill, then in the other life we love the Lord's kingdom because there the Lord's kingdom is our country. Further, anyone who loves the Lord's kingdom loves the Lord because the Lord is everything to all of his kingdom.

94 The church is our neighbor to a greater extent than our country is because if we care for the church we are caring for the souls and the eternal life of the people of our country. This means that if we care for the church out of love we are loving our neighbor on a higher level because we are longing and striving for others to reach heaven and have happy lives forever.

95 The Lord's kingdom is our neighbor on a still higher level because the Lord's kingdom is made up of all whose lives are devoted to doing good, both people on earth and people in the heavens. This means that the Lord's kingdom is goodness of all kinds gathered together. When we love this, we love every individual who is devoted to doing good.

96 These are the levels of neighbor, the steps by which love ascends in people who are devoted to loving their neighbor. These levels are in a definite sequence in which the primary or higher is preferable to the secondary or lower; and since the Lord is on the highest level and is to be our central focus on every level as the ultimate goal of our actions, he is to be loved above all people and above all things.

This now makes it possible for us to tell how love for the Lord becomes joined to love for our neighbor.

97 It is often said that we are neighbors to ourselves, meaning that we need to look after ourselves first. However, teachings on caring tell us how we should understand this.

We all need to make sure that we have the necessities of life, such as the food, clothing, housing, and more that are necessary for whatever civic life we are involved in. We need to provide these not only for ourselves but also for our dependents, and not only for the present time but also for the future, since unless we acquire the necessities of life for ourselves we are not in any condition to extend caring to others; we ourselves are instead in need of everything.

98 The following example may show how we are to be neighbors to ourselves. We all need to provide our bodies with their food and clothing. This needs to come first, but the object is to have a sound mind in a sound body. Further, we all need to provide food for our minds, meaning things that build our intelligence and wisdom, but the object is that our minds will be able to be of service to our fellow citizens, our community, our country, the church, and therefore the Lord. If we do this we are providing for our well-being to eternity. We can see from this that what should come first is the purpose for which we do something, because everything depends on that.

It is also like building a house. First we need to lay the foundation, but the purpose of the foundation is the house, and the purpose of the house is living in it. If we think being neighbor to ourselves is actually the most important thing, this is like regarding not the house or living in it but the foundation as our final goal. But in reality, from start to finish, living in the house is the true goal, and the house and its foundation are only means to this end.

It is our goal that can tell us in what way we are being neighbors to ourselves and looking after ourselves first. If our goal is to become richer than others solely for the sake of wealth or for pleasure or eminence or anything like that, our goal is evil—we are loving ourselves, not our neighbor. If, however, our goal is to acquire wealth in order to be able to be of service to our fellow citizens, our community, our country, and the church, this is like seeking office for the same reasons, and we are loving our neighbor. **99**

The actual goal of our actions makes us the people we are, because our goal is what we love. For everyone, our goal from start to finish is whatever we love above all else.

All this has been about who our neighbor is. Now I need to discuss what loving our neighbor is, or *caring*.

Many people believe that love for their neighbor is giving to the poor, providing means to the needy, and doing good to just anyone. In fact, true caring is acting prudently and with the intent that some good will come of it. If we provide resources to evildoers who are poor or needy, we are doing harm to our neighbors through the resources we provide, because those resources will empower the evildoers to do more evil and supply them with greater means of harming others. The situation is the opposite when we provide resources to good people. **100**

Caring, though, applies to much more than just helping the poor and needy. Caring is doing what is right in everything we do, doing our duty in every position of responsibility. **101**

A judge who does what is fair for the sake of fairness is practicing caring. Judges who punish the guilty and acquit the innocent are practicing caring because in doing so they are showing concern for their fellow citizens and concern for their country.

Priests who teach people truth and lead them to do good are practicing caring, if they do so for the sake of truth and goodness. If they do these things for the sake of themselves or for worldly purposes, though, they are not practicing caring, because they are loving themselves rather than their neighbor.

102   It is the same for others whether they hold some office or not—children toward their parents, for example, and parents toward their children, servants toward their employers and employers toward their servants, subjects toward their monarch and monarchs toward their subjects. If they do their duty for the sake of duty and do what is fair for the sake of fairness, they are practicing caring.

103   The reason all these things are related to love for our neighbor or caring is that everyone is our neighbor, as just noted, but to differing extents. A community, whether small or large, is more of a neighbor than an individual is, the country is still more of a neighbor, the Lord's kingdom still more, and the Lord is the neighbor above all. In the most universally applicable sense the goodness that comes from the Lord is our neighbor, and this means that what is honest and fair is our neighbor as well. So people who do anything good because it is good and who do what is honest and fair because it is honest and fair are loving their neighbor and practicing caring. This is because their actions are motivated by a love of what is good, honest, and fair and therefore by a love for people in whom there is goodness, honesty, and fairness.

104   Caring, then, is an inner desire that makes us want to do what is good, not because we are hoping for a reward but because doing it is the joy of our life.

When we are doing good as the result of an inner desire to do so, caring is present in every detail of what we are thinking and saying, what we are intending and doing. Whether we are angels or people [still on earth], if we hold goodness to be our neighbor, it can be said that in respect to our deeper natures we have become caring itself. That shows how far caring is able to go.

105   If people set loving themselves and the world as their goal there is no way they can live a life of caring. They do not even know what caring is. Further, they completely fail to grasp the fact that intending and doing good for their neighbor without a goal of being rewarded for it is a heaven inside them—that inherent in this desire there is as great a happiness as heaven's angels have: more than words can convey. This is because selfish and worldly people believe that if they were deprived of the joy they take in their display of prestige and wealth they would no longer have any joy at all, when in fact that would be the beginning of an infinitely transcendent heavenly joy.

From *Secrets of Heaven*

H EAVEN is divided into two kingdoms, one of which is called the heavenly kingdom, the other the spiritual kingdom. The love that characterizes the heavenly kingdom is love for the Lord and is called "heavenly love," while the love that characterizes the spiritual kingdom is love for one's neighbor or caring, and is called "spiritual love": 3325, 3653, 7257, 9002, 9835, 9961. On the division of heaven into these two kingdoms, see *Heaven and Hell* 20–28; and on the Lord's divine presence in the heavens taking the form of love for him and caring about one's neighbor, see §§13–19 of the same work.

106

[2] People cannot know what is good and what is true unless they know what love for the Lord and love for one's neighbor are, since all goodness comes from love and all truth comes from goodness: 7255, 7366. Caring is a result of knowing things that are true, being willing to do what they teach, and being moved by them for their own sakes—that is, because they are true: 3876, 3877. Caring consists of an inner desire to do what truth teaches and not an outer desire apart from an inner desire: 2439, 2442, 3776, 4899, 4956, 8033. So caring consists of doing useful things because they are useful things to do: 7038, 8253. Caring is a spiritual way of life for us: 7081. The whole Word is a body of teaching focused on love and caring: 6632, 7262. No one these days knows what caring is: 2417, 3398, 4776, 6632. Nevertheless the light of our reason could tell us that love and caring are what make us human (3957, 6273) and that what is good and what is true are in harmony, each belonging to the other, so the same goes for love and faith (7627).

[3] In the highest sense, the Lord is our neighbor, because he is to be loved above all else. So everything that comes from him and has him

within it is our neighbor—in other words, everything good and true: 2425, 3419, 6706, 6819, 6823, 8124. The type of neighbor someone is can be identified by the nature of the good that he or she does, and therefore by the Lord's presence in him or her: 6707, 6708, 6709, 6710. Every individual and every community, also our country and the church, and in the most universal sense the Lord's kingdom, are our neighbor; and loving our neighbors is doing them good out of a love of what is good, according to the nature of their state; so our "neighbor" is the well-being of others, for which we are to be concerned: 6818–6824, 8123. Our "neighbor" includes civic goodness, too, which is whatever is fair; and moral goodness, which is what is good for our life together in community and is called honesty: 2915, 4730, 8120, 8121, 8122. Loving our neighbors is not loving the personality they project in public but loving what motivates them from within, therefore the goodness and truth they have: 5028, 10336. If we base our love on their public personality and not on what motivates them from within, we will have as much love for evil people as for good people (3820) and we will support both the evil and the good, even though supporting evil people is harming good people, which is not loving our neighbor (3820, 6703, 8120). A judge who punishes the evil in order to correct them and to protect the good from them is loving his neighbor: 3820, 8120, 8121.

[4] Loving one's neighbor is doing what is good, fair, and right in every task and in every function: 8120, 8121, 8122. So caring about our neighbor extends to every least thing that we think, intend, and do: 8124. Doing what is good and what is true is loving our neighbor: 10310, 10336. People who do this are loving the Lord, who is our neighbor in the highest sense: 9210. The life of caring is a life in accord with the Lord's commandments; therefore to live by divine truths is to love the Lord: 10143, 10153, 10310, 10578, 10645.

[5] Genuine caring is not something in which we engage in order to get something in return (2371, 2380, 2400, 3887, 6388–6393), because it comes from an inner desire to do what is good and therefore from a living joy in doing it (2371, 2380, 3887, 6388–6393). If we separate faith from caring, then in the other life we want credit for our faith and for any outwardly good deeds that we have done: 2371. People who lead evil lives because they love themselves and the world above all do not know what it is to do good without seeking a reward, so they do not know what it is to extend caring to someone without claiming credit: 8037.

[6] The teachings of the ancient church were teachings about how to live our lives, that is, teachings focused on caring: 2385, 2417, 3419, 3420,

4844, 6628. These teachings were the source of their intelligence and wisdom: 2417, 6629, 7259–7262. The intelligence and wisdom of people who have led caring lives in this world increase immensely in the other life: 1941, 5859. The Lord flows with divine truth into caring because he flows into our very life: 2363. We are like gardens when caring and faith are joined to each other within us and like deserts when they are not: 7626. The less we care, the less wise we are [6630]; if we are not engaged in caring we are ignorant of divine truths, no matter how wise we may think we are (2417, 2435). An angelic life consists of doing good deeds of caring, which are acts of service: 454. Spiritual angels, the angels whose lives are devoted to caring, are embodiments of caring: 553, 3804, 4735.

[7] All spiritual truths focus on caring as their fundamental principle and their aim: 4353. The teachings of the church are pointless unless they have caring as their goal: 2049, 2116.

[8] The Lord's presence with us and with angels depends on our state of love and caring: 904, 981. Caring is the image of God: 1013. Although we do not realize it, love for the Lord, and therefore the Lord himself, lies deep within caring: 2227, 5066, 5067. When we live caring lives we are welcomed as citizens anywhere in this world and in heaven: 1121. We must do no harm to any good thing that arises out of caring: 2359.

[9] If we have not devoted our lives to caring we are incapable of acknowledging and worshiping the Lord except hypocritically: 2132, 4424, 10177. Forms of hatred and forms of caring cannot coexist: 1060.

I need to append some information about the teachings concerning love for the Lord and concerning caring that were held by the ancient people among whom there was a church. The purpose is to make known the nature of a body of teaching that used to exist but is not in existence today. This is drawn from *Secrets of Heaven* 7257–7263.

Good that is done out of love for the Lord is called "heavenly good," and good that is done out of love for one's neighbor or caring is called "spiritual good." The angels who live in the inmost or third heaven are devoted to doing good because they love the Lord, so they are called "heavenly angels"; while the angels who live in the intermediate or second heaven are devoted to doing good because they love their neighbor and are therefore called "spiritual angels."

[2] The teachings concerning how to do good in a heavenly way, which is good that is done out of love for the Lord, are the most extensive and at the same time the deepest of all teachings. They are the teachings that are followed by the angels of the inmost or third heaven, which are so extensive and deep that if we heard them from the angels' own mouths

we would understand scarcely a thousandth part of them. These teachings also contain things that simply cannot be expressed. While it is the inner meaning of the Word that contains teachings concerning spiritual love, it is the Word's inmost meaning that contains these heavenly teachings.

[3] The teachings concerning how to do good in a spiritual way, which is good that is done out of love for one's neighbor, are also extensive and deep, but much less so than the teachings concerning how to do good in a heavenly way, which is good that is done out of love for the Lord. How extensive the teachings are that concern loving our neighbor or caring is established by the fact that they touch every least thing we think and intend and therefore everything we do and say, and also from the fact that caring is not the same thing in one person as in another and that one neighbor is not the same as another.

[4] Because the teachings concerning caring were so extensive, the ancient people (for whom that was the main thing taught by their church) distinguished caring about one's neighbor into many categories. These they then went on to subdivide, assigning designations to the individual types and teaching how caring was to be practiced toward people of one particular type and toward people of another particular type. In this way they imposed an order on their teachings about caring and on the practice of caring so that it was clearly understandable.

[5] They had many designations for the people to whom caring was extended. Some they called "the blind"; some "the deaf"; some "the lame"; some "the poor," as well as "the wretched" and "the afflicted"; some "orphans"; and some "widows." In general, though, they spoke of "the hungry" to whom they would give food, "the thirsty" to whom they would give drink, "the strangers" whom they would take in, "the naked" whom they would clothe, "the sick" whom they would attend, and those "bound and in prison" whom they would visit.

The particular kinds of people intended by each category have been laid out in *Secrets of Heaven* as follows: "the blind" in §§2383, 6990; "the deaf" in §4302; "the poor" in §§2129, 4459, 9209, 9253, 10227; "the wretched" in §2129; "the afflicted" in §§6663, 6851, 9196; "orphans" in §§4844, 9198, 9199, 9200; "widows" in §§4844, 9198, 9200; "the hungry" in §§4958, 10227; "the thirsty" in §§4958, 8568; "the strangers" in §§4444, 7908, 8007, 8013, 9196, 9200; "the naked" in §§1073, 5433, 9960; "the sick" in §§4958, 6221, 8364, 9031; and those "bound in prison" in §§5037, 5038, 5086, 5096.

Everything we can be taught about caring is summed up in the services extended to the hungry, the thirsty, the strangers, the naked, the sick, and those bound in prison, of whom the Lord spoke in Matthew 25:34, 35, 36, and following; see §§4954–4959.

[6] These designations were given from heaven to the ancient people who were part of the church; they used them to refer to the spiritual condition of others. That church's teachings, focused on caring, told them not only what other people were like but also which particular kind of caring was appropriate for each.

That is why we find these same designations in the Word and why when spiritually understood they mean people of these kinds.

The Word truly understood teaches nothing else except loving the Lord and caring about our neighbor, as the Lord himself taught:

> You are to love the Lord your God with all your heart, with all your soul, and with all your mind. This is the first and great commandment. The second is like it: you are to love your neighbor as yourself. All the Law and the Prophets depend on these two commandments. (Matthew 22:37, 38, 39, 40)

"The Law and the Prophets" are the whole Word: 2606, 3382, 6752, 7463.

[7] These designations are found in the Word so that the Word, which in its own right is spiritual, might be earthly in its outermost form. As a result, people whose devotion was external would show caring toward people who were in that condition physically; but those whose devotion was internal would show caring toward people who were in that condition spiritually. Therefore the simple would understand and do what the Word teaches in a simple way and the wise would do so in a wise way; and through their outward caring the simple might be introduced into its inner forms.

Faith

108 NO one knows what faith is in its essence who does not know what caring is, because where there is no caring there is no faith. This is because caring is just as inseparable from faith as goodness is from truth. What we love or really care about is what we regard as good, and what we believe is what we regard as true. We can therefore see that the oneness of caring and faith is like the oneness of what is good and what is true. The nature of that union was made clear in the earlier material on goodness and truth [§§11–27].

109 The oneness of caring and faith is also like the oneness of our will and our understanding. These are, after all, the two faculties in us that are receptive to goodness and truth, our will being the faculty receptive to goodness and our understanding being the faculty receptive to truth. These two faculties are also receptive to caring and faith, because caring has to do with goodness and faith has to do with truth. Everyone knows that caring and faith are with us and in us, and since they are with us and in us, the only place they can be is in our will and in our understanding. Our whole life resides there and comes forth from there. Yes, we do have a faculty of memory as well, but that is only a waiting room where things gather that are going to enter our understanding and our will. We can see, then, that the oneness of caring and faith is like the oneness of our will and our understanding. The nature of this oneness can be seen from the information already presented on our will and our understanding [§§28–35].

110 Our caring is joined to our faith when we choose to do what we know and perceive to be true. Our caring is a function of what we choose to do, and our faith is a function of what we know and perceive to be true. Faith first enters us and becomes part of us when we choose to do what we know and perceive to be true, and when we come to love that truth. Until that happens, faith remains outside us.

111 Faith is not faith for us unless it becomes spiritual, and it does not become spiritual unless it arises out of our love. This happens when we love to live a life of truth and goodness—that is, to live by what we are commanded in the Word.

Faith is a passion for truth that comes from wanting to do what truth **112**
teaches because it is the truth; and wanting to do what truth teaches
because it is the truth is the very definition of human spirituality. That is,
it transcends our earthly nature, which involves our wanting to do what
truth teaches not because it is the truth but for the sake of praise or fame
or profit for ourselves. Truth detached from such concerns is spiritual
because it comes from the Divine. Whatever comes from the Divine is
spiritual, and this is joined to us through love because love is a spiritual
joining together.

We can know and think and understand a great deal, but when we **113**
are left to the privacy of our own thoughts we discard anything that is
not in harmony with our love. We discard such things after our physical
lives as well, when we are in the spirit, since the only things that are left
to us once we are in the spirit are the things that have entered into our
love. After death all the rest strikes us as foreign matter that we throw out
of our house because it is not part of our love. And I say "in the spirit"
because we live as spirits after death.

We can form some image of the relationship between good actions **114**
that come from caring and the truth that belongs to religious faith if we
think in terms of the warmth and light of the sun. When the light that
radiates from the sun is joined to warmth, as is the case in spring and
summer, then everything on earth sprouts and blossoms. When there is
no warmth in the light, though, as is the case in winter, then everything
on earth becomes dormant and dies. The truth that belongs to religious
faith is spiritual light, and love is spiritual warmth.

This makes it possible for us to form some image of what people of
the church are like when faith is joined to caring in them. They are just
like a garden paradise. Their image, though, when faith is not joined to
caring in them is like that of a desert or a land buried in snow.

The assurance or trust which people say faith provides, and which they **115**
call a "truly saving faith," is not a spiritual assurance or trust but an earthly
one when it is based on faith alone. Spiritual assurance or trust derives
its essence and life from good actions done out of love and not from the
truth that belongs to religious faith apart from those good actions. The
assurance provided by a faith separated from good actions is dead; therefore real assurance is not possible for us when we are leading evil lives. An
assurance that we are saved because of the Lord's merit with the Father no
matter how we have lived is a long way from the truth as well.

All who have spiritual faith, though, have an assurance of being saved by the Lord, because they believe that the Lord came into the world to give eternal life to those who both believe and live by the principles that he taught. They know that he is the one who regenerates such people and prepares them for heaven, doing so all by himself without their help, out of pure mercy.

116   Believing what the Word or the church teaches and not living by it may look like faith, and some may even conjecture that they are saved by it; but the truth is that no one is saved by faith alone. Faith alone is a conviction one deliberately induces in oneself; therefore I need now to describe the nature of such self-induced convictions.

117   A self-induced conviction is when we believe and love the Word and the teachings of the church not for the sake of their truth or in order to live by them but for the sake of profit and respect and to be thought learned. As a result, when this is the kind of faith we have we are not focusing on the Lord or heaven but on ourselves and this world. People who aspire to worldly greatness and crave an abundance of material things express stronger conviction that what the church teaches is the truth than people who have no such aspirations or cravings. This is because for the ambitious the church's teachings are only a means to their own ends, and the more they love those ends, the more they love—and trust—the means.

In reality, though, what determines the strength of their conviction at a given moment is how intensely their love for themselves and for the world is burning and how much that fire is affecting their conversation, preaching, and actions. During moments on fire they are completely convinced that what they are saying is true. When they are not feeling the fire of those loves, however, they believe very little—some have no belief at all. This shows that a self-induced conviction is a faith of the mouth and not of the heart, so it is really no faith at all.

118   People whose faith is self-induced do not know from any inner enlightenment whether what they are teaching is true or false, and as long as the crowd believes them, they do not care. In fact, they have no interest whatever in knowing the truth for its own sake. As a result, if they cannot obtain status or profit they abandon their faith (or at least if they can do so without putting their reputation in jeopardy), because self-induced conviction does not live deep within us. It remains on the outside, only in our memory, so we can call on it when we are teaching. This means that this type of faith vanishes after death, and so do the truths that go with it, because the only kind of faith that remains then is the kind that lives within us—that is, that has taken root in our doing of good and has therefore become part of our life.

The following passage in Matthew is about people whose faith is self-induced: **119**

> On that day many will say to me, "Lord, Lord, haven't we prophesied in your name, cast out demons in your name, and done many great things in your name?" But then I will declare to them, "I do not know you, you workers of iniquity." (Matthew 7:22, 23)

Then it says in Luke:

> Then you begin to say, "We ate and drank in your presence, and you taught in our streets." But he will say, "I tell you, I do not know where you are from. Depart from me, all you workers of iniquity." (Luke 13:26, 27)

They are also described as the five foolish young women in Matthew who did not have oil for their lamps:

> Later the other young women came along and said, "Lord, Lord, open up for us." But he will answer and say, "I tell you truly, I do not know you." (Matthew 25:11, 12)

The oil [that should have been] in their lamps means the good actions from love [that should be] in our faith.

From *Secrets of Heaven*

IF people do not know that everything in the universe goes back to **120** *goodness* and *truth* and that these two must be joined together if they are to accomplish anything, they also do not know that everything in the church must go back to *faith* and *love* and that these must be joined together if there is to be any church among humankind: 7752–7762, 9186,

9224. Everything in the universe that is in accord with the divine design goes back to goodness and truth and to their being joined together: 2451, 3166, 4390, 4409, 5232, 7256, 10122, 10555. Truths are related to faith, and good actions are related to love: 4352, 4997, 7178, 10367. This is why I have discussed goodness and truth [§§11–27] as part of this body of teaching. So, knowing the nature of goodness and truth, both when they are joined together and when they are not, you can determine the relationship between faith and love from what has previously been presented, simply by substituting "love" for "goodness," and "faith" for "truth," and drawing the resulting conclusions.

[2] If people do not know that everything in us must—if we are to be truly human—go back to the *will* and the *understanding* and the joining together of these two, they can have no clear knowledge of the fact that everything in the church must go back to *faith* and *love* and the joining together of those two if there is to be any church within us: 2231, 7752, 7753, 7754, 9224, 9995, 10122. We have two basic faculties, one called understanding and the other called will: 641, 803, 3539, 3623. Our understanding is designed as a home for truths—and therefore the components of our faith—while our will is designed as a home for desires to do good—and therefore the components of our love: 9300, 9930, 10064. This is why I have also discussed will and understanding [§§28–35] in this body of teaching, since from what has been presented there you can also draw conclusions about faith and love, knowing what their nature is when they are joined together and what their nature is when they are not, by thinking about the love that lives in our will and the faith that lives in our understanding.

[3] People cannot know what *spiritual faith* and *spiritual love* are unless they know that within each of us there is an internal level and an external level—an *inner self* and an *outer self*, therefore—and that everything heavenly is on the level of our inner self and everything earthly is on the level of our outer self; therefore the relationship between the two selves is like the relationship between the spiritual world and the earthly world: 4292, 4570, 5013, 6055. We have an inner self and an outer self; the inner self is our spiritual self and the outer self is our earthly self: 978, 1015, 4459, 6309, 9701–9709. True faith is spiritual; therefore our faith is true faith if it resides in our inner self. The same holds true for love: 1594, 3987, 8078. Further, the more we love the truths that belong to religious faith, the more spiritual those truths become: 1594, 3987. This is why I have discussed the inner self and the outer self above [§§36–53], because

from what has been presented there you can draw conclusions about faith and love, what they are like when they are spiritual and what they are like when they are not, and therefore what kinds of faith and love create a church and what kinds do not.

Faith separated from love or caring is like the light of winter, in which everything in the earth is dormant and no flower, fruit, or harvest is produced; but faith together with love or caring is like the light of spring and summer, in which everything blooms and bears fruit: 2231, 3146, 3412, 3413. The light of winter, which is the light of faith separated from caring, turns into deep darkness when light flows in from heaven; and people devoted to that faith become blind and stupid: 3412, 3413. People who separate faith from caring in the teachings they accept and in the lives they lead are in darkness; they do not know what truth is and are mired in falsities, and these constitute [spiritual] darkness: 9186. They plunge themselves into false convictions and therefore into evil practices: 3325, 8094. The errors and false convictions into which they plunge themselves 4721, 4730, 4776, 4783, 4925, 7779, 8313, 8765, 9224. The Word is closed to them: 3773, 4783, 8780. They do not pay attention to or even see all the many things the Lord said about love and caring and about their fruits, which are good actions: 1017, 3416 (which include examples). They do not know what goodness is, and therefore they do not know what heavenly love is or what caring is: 2417, 3603, 4126, 9995.

[a] Faith separated from caring is no faith at all: 654, 724, 1162, 1176, 2049, 2116, 2343, 2349, 3419, 3849, 3868, 6348, 7039, 7342, 9783. In the other life this kind of faith perishes: 2228, 5820. When people make faith alone the most important principle, the truths they have are corrupted by the falseness of their starting point: 2435. Yet they will not let themselves be convinced otherwise, because it goes against their fundamental belief: 2385. The teachings concerning faith alone are destructive of caring: 6353, 8094. People who separate faith from caring are represented by Cain, Ham, Reuben, the firstborn of the Egyptians, and the Philistines: 3325, 7097, 7317, 8093. People who regard faith alone as ensuring salvation say that it is all right to live an evil life; yet those who devote themselves to leading evil lives actually have no faith, because there is no caring in them: 3865, 7766, 7778, 7790, 7950, 8094. Inwardly, they are consumed with false thoughts caused by their evil, although they do not realize this: 7790, 7950. This means that goodness cannot be joined to them: 8981, 8983. In the other life they are opposed to what is good and opposed to people who are engaged in doing anything good: 7097, 7127, 7317, 7502,

121

7545, 8096, 8313. People who are simple-hearted (and are therefore actually wise) know what it is to lead a good life and therefore know what caring is, but they cannot comprehend what faith would be apart from that: 4741, 4754.

[3] Everything about the church goes back to goodness and truth and therefore goes back to caring and faith: 7752, 7753, 7754. The church does not exist within us until truths have been planted in our lives and in this way have turned into good actions done from a caring heart: 3310. Caring, and not faith separated from caring, is what constitutes the church: 809, 916, 1798, 1799, 1834, 1844. Caring is the heart of the church: 1799, 7755. Therefore there is no church where there is no caring: 4766, 5826. If all people were viewed from a perspective of caring no matter how they differed in the teachings of their faith and in the forms of their worship, the church would be unified: 1285, 1316, 1798, 1799, 1834, 1844, 2385, 2982, 3267, 3451. How great a goodness there would be in the church if caring were seen as first in importance and faith as second: 6269, 6272. Every church is initially devoted to caring, but with the passage of time turns instead toward faith and eventually to faith alone: 1834, 1835, 2231, 4683, 8094. In the last times of a church there is no faith because there is no caring: 1843. Worship of the Lord consists of a life of caring: 8254, 8256. The nature of our devotion depends on the nature of our caring: 2190. People who constitute the outer church nevertheless have an inner dimension if they have devoted themselves to caring: 1100, 1102, 1151, 1153. The body of teaching of the ancient church consisted of teachings about how to live one's life and was focused on caring, not on faith separated from caring: 2385, 2417, 3419, 3420, 4844, 6628, 7259–7262.

[4] As the Lord regenerates us, he sows and implants truth in our goodness and caring: 2063, 2189, 3310. Otherwise the seed, which is the truth that belongs to religious faith, could not take root: 880. The amount of goodness and truth within us then grows in proportion to the nature and extent of the caring we have allowed ourselves to feel: 1016. The new light experienced by those who are being reborn does not come from faith but from the way caring illuminates faith: 854. As we are being regenerated, the truths that belong to religious faith become a part of us, along with a feeling of pleasure because we love to do them; and later those truths come back to us with that same feeling again, because the truths and the feeling are joined together: 2487, 3040, 3066, 3074, 3336, 4018, 5893.

[5] When people have devoted their lives to loving the Lord and caring about their neighbor, throughout all eternity they lose nothing,

because they are joined to the Lord; the outcome is different, though, for people devoted to a faith separated from caring: 7506, 7507. The nature that becomes permanent within us is the nature of our life of caring, not the nature of our faith by itself: 8256. If we have lived a life devoted to caring, all our states of pleasure return to us in the other life and are immensely amplified: 823. Heavenly bliss flows from the Lord into our caring because it flows into our active life, and not into any faith we might have apart from caring: 2363. In heaven we are all evaluated on the basis of our caring; no one is evaluated on the basis of faith separated from caring: 1258, 1394. For all who are in the heavens, what they love is what brings them into association with others: 7085. No one gets into heaven for merely thinking about goodness; we must actually want to do some good: 2401, 3459. If doing what is good is not joined to willing to do what is good and thinking what is good, there is no salvation for us and no joining of our inner self and our outer self: 3987. In the other life the only people who are receptive to the Lord and to faith in him are the ones who have been devoted to caring: 2343.

[6] Goodness ceaselessly longs and strives to join itself to truths; therefore caring ceaselessly longs and strives to join itself to faith: 9206, 9207, 9495. Each type of goodness or caring recognizes the truth that goes with it from among those that belong to religious faith; and each type of truth that belongs to religious faith recognizes the type of goodness or caring that goes with it: 2429, 3101, 3102, 3161, 3179, 3180, 4358, 5807, 5835, 9637. As a result a bond forms between a given truth that belongs to religious faith and a given type of goodness that comes from caring: 3834, 4096, 4097, 4301, 4345, 4353, 4364, 4368, 5365, 7623–7627, 7752–7762, 8530, 9258, 10555 (which include further details). This bond is like a marriage: 1904, 2173, 2508. The law of marriage, as the Lord's Word says, is that two should become one [Genesis 2:24; Matthew 19:5–6; Mark 10:7]: 162, 10168, 10169. Faith and caring therefore should become one: 1904, 2173, 2508. This means that in order to be genuine, faith must have caring as its essence: 2228, 2839, 3180, 9783. As goodness is the reality underlying a thing and truth is how that thing becomes manifest from goodness, so caring is the reality underlying the church, and faith is how [the church] becomes manifest from goodness: 3049, 3180, 4574, 5002, 9144. The truth that belongs to religious faith gets its life from good actions that embody caring, which means that to care is to lead a life in accord with the truth that belongs to religious faith: 2571, 4070, 4096, 4097, 4736, 4757, 4884, 5147, 5928, 9154, 9667, 9841, 10729. Faith can exist only in the context of caring. If a given kind of faith is not devoted to caring, then there is

nothing good in that faith: 2261, 4368. Faith is not alive in us when all we do is know about faith and think about it. Rather, faith comes to life when we will to do, and when we actively do, what it teaches: 9224.

[7] There is no salvation through faith, but there is salvation through a life in accord with the truths that faith teaches, which is a life of caring: 379, 389, 2228, 4663, 4721. People who have been taught by their church to think that faith alone saves, but who nevertheless do what is right because it is right and do what is good because it is good, are saved, because they are in fact devoted to caring: 2442, 3242, 3459, 3463, 7506, 7507. If having thoughts about faith were all that were required for salvation, everyone would be saved: 2228, 10659. Caring creates a heaven within us; faith apart from caring does not: 3513, 3584, 3815, 9832, 10714, 10715, 10721, 10724. In heaven all are evaluated on the basis of their caring, not their faith: 1258, 1394, 2364, 4802. Our faith does not join us to the Lord; what joins us to the Lord is living by the truths that faith teaches: 9380, 10143, 10153, 10310, 10578, 10645, 10648. The "tree of life" [Genesis 2:9, 3:22, 24; Revelation 2:7, 22:2, 14] is the Lord, its "fruits" are good actions that come from caring, and its "leaves" are faith: 3427, 9337. Faith is "the lesser light" and love is "the greater light" [Genesis 1:16]: 30–38.

[8] Angels of the Lord's heavenly kingdom do not know what faith is, so much so that they do not even mention it; but angels of the Lord's spiritual kingdom talk about faith because they reason about matters of truth: 202, 203, 337, 2715, 3246, 4448, 9166, 10786. Angels in the Lord's heavenly kingdom say only "Yes, yes" or "No, no"; but angels from the Lord's spiritual kingdom discuss whether something is so or not when they are talking about spiritual truths, which are matters of faith: 2715, 3246, 4448, 9166, 10786 (these passages deal with the interpretation of the Lord's words "Let your communication be 'Yes, yes; no, no.' Whatever is more than these comes from evil" [Matthew 5:37]). The reason heavenly angels are like this is that they put the truths that belong to religious faith directly into their lives, rather than putting them first into their memories the way spiritual angels do; and as a result heavenly angels have a higher perception of everything that has to do with faith: 202, 597, 607, 784, 1121, 1387, 1398, 1442, 1919, 5113, 5897, 6367, 7680, 7877, 8521, 8780, 9995, 10124.

[9] The trust or assurance that is called "saving faith" in the most valid sense is found only in people whose lives are devoted to doing what is good, people therefore who are devoted to caring: 2982, 4352, 4683,

4689, 7762, 8240, 9239–9245. Few people know what this assurance is: 3868, 4352.

[10] The difference between believing the truth that comes from God and actually believing in God: 9239, 9243. It is one thing to know about some truth, another thing to acknowledge it, and still another thing to have faith in it: 896, 4319, 5664b. Faith has a factual aspect, a rational aspect, and a spiritual aspect: 2504, 8078. The first phase of faith is to acknowledge the Lord: 10083. Everything that flows into us from the Lord is good: 1614, 2016, 2751, 2882, 2883, 2891, 2892, 2904, 6193, 7643, 9128.

[11] A faith that you have talked yourself into is no faith at all: 2343, 2682, 2689, 3417, 3865, 8148.

[12] For various reasons it seems as though faith comes before caring, but this is an illusion: 3324. We can know simply from the light of reason that goodness (and therefore caring) comes first and that truth (and therefore faith) comes second: 6273. Goodness (and therefore caring) is actually primary and is the first element of the church; while truth (and therefore faith) is actually secondary and is the second element of the church, even though it may not seem that way: 3324, 3325, 3330, 3336, 3494, 3589, 3548, 3556, 3570, 3576, 3603, 3701, 3995, 4337, 4601, 4925, 4926, 4928, 4930, 5351, 6256, 6269, 6272, 6273, 8042, 8080, 10110. Among the ancients as well there was disagreement as to whether faith or caring was the first element or firstborn of the church: 367, 2435, 3324.

The Lord's twelve disciples represented all the various forms of faith and caring that together constitute the church, as did the twelve tribes of Israel: 2129, 3354, 3488, 3858, 6397. Peter, James, and John represented faith, caring, and good actions that come from caring, respectively: preface to Genesis 18. Peter represented faith: preface to Genesis 22, §§4738, 6000, 6073, 6344, 10087. John represented good actions that come from caring: preface to Genesis 18. The fact that in the last times of the church there would be no faith in the Lord because there would be no caring is represented by Peter's denying the Lord three times before the rooster crowed for the third time; in a symbolic sense, Peter in that passage means faith: 6000, 6073. Both "the crowing of the rooster" and "twilight" in the Word mean the last times of the church (10134); and "three" or "three times" means what is completed (2788, 4495, 5159, 9198, 10127). Much the same is meant by the Lord's saying to Peter, when Peter saw John following the Lord, "What is that to you, Peter? Follow me, John," because Peter had said of John, "What about him?" (John 21:21, 22): 10087. Since John represented good actions that come from caring, he leaned on the

Lord's chest [John 13:23–25; 21:20]: 3934, 10087. Likewise, what the Lord said to John from the cross meant that good actions from a caring heart are what constitute the church: "When Jesus saw his mother, and the disciple whom he loved standing by her, he said to his mother, 'Woman, behold your son!' And he said to the disciple, 'Behold your mother!' And from that hour the disciple accepted her into his household" (John 19:26, 27). John means good actions that come from a caring heart, and "the woman" and "mother" mean the church; therefore the whole statement means that wherever good actions are being done from a caring heart is where the true church will be found. "Woman" in the Word means the church: 252, 253, 749, 770, 3160, 6014, 7337, 8994. The same holds true for "mother": 289, 2691, 2717, 3703, 4257, 5581, 8897, 10490. All the names of individuals and places in the Word symbolize qualities in the abstract: 768, 1888, 4310, 4442, 10329.

Piety

M ANY people think that a spiritual life, the kind of life that leads us to heaven, consists of *piety*, of *outward holiness*, and of *renunciation of the world*. In fact, though, piety without caring, outward holiness without inner holiness, and renunciation of the world without involvement in the world do not make our life spiritual. What does make our life spiritual is piety that comes from a caring heart, outward holiness that is a manifestation of inner holiness, and renunciation of the world that goes along with involvement in the world.

Piety is thinking and speaking reverently, giving ample time to prayer, having a humble attitude when we pray, attending church regularly and listening attentively to what is preached, observing the sacrament of the Supper several times a year, and performing the other ceremonial acts the church prescribes.

A life of caring, though, consists of having goodwill toward our neighbors and doing good things for them; basing all of our actions on what is right and fair, and what is good and true; and applying the same principles in all our responsibilities. In a word, a life of caring consists of being useful. This kind of life is the primary way to worship God; a life of piety is only secondary. This means that if we separate the one from the other, if we lead a pious life but not a caring life at the same time, we are not in fact worshiping God. We may be thinking *about* God, but this comes from ourselves and not from God, because we are constantly thinking about ourselves and not at all about our neighbor. If we do think about our neighbors, we regard them as worthless if they are not like us. Further, we are thinking of heaven as our reward, so our mind is preoccupied with self-love and taking credit. Being actively useful is something we either neglect or regard with contempt; and that is also how we treat our neighbors. Yet at the same time we believe there is nothing wrong with us.

This shows that a pious life apart from a caring life is not the spiritual life that is needed within our worship of God. Compare Matthew 6:7, 8.

Outward holiness is similar to the pious behavior just described (it consists primarily in seeing all worship of God as a matter of the sanctity we experience when we are in church); but this is not holy for us

87

unless we are holy inwardly. This is because our inner nature determines our outer nature—the latter comes from the former the way our actions come from our spirit. This means that outward holiness apart from inner holiness is earthly and not spiritual, which is why it can be found just as readily in evil people as in good people. Furthermore, people whose worship is nothing but external are for the most part empty; that is, they have no knowledge of what is good or true, even though goodness and truth are holiness itself. Goodness and truth are what we are to know and believe and love because they come from the Divine and there is therefore something divine within them. To be inwardly holy, then, is to love what is good and true because it is good and true and to love what is right and honest because it is right and honest. The more we love these things for their own sakes, the more spiritual we become. Our devotion to God becomes more spiritual, too, because we become more and more eager to know what is good and what is true and to put them into practice. On the other hand, as our love for these things diminishes, we become more earthly, our devotion to God becomes more earthly, and we become less and less interested in knowing and doing these things.

We could compare outward worship apart from inner worship to having living breath without having a living heart, while outward worship prompted by inner worship is like living breath that is joined to a living heart.

126 As for *renunciation of the world,* many believe that renouncing the world and living for the spirit and not for the flesh is a matter of casting aside worldly things (primarily wealth and status), going around in constant devout meditation concerning God, salvation, and eternal life, and spending our lives in prayer and in reading the Word and devotional literature, not to mention self-affliction. This, though, is not at all what renouncing the world means; it means loving God and loving our neighbor. We love God when we live by his commandments, and we love our neighbor when we do things that are useful. If we wish to receive the life of heaven, we must by all means live in this world and be involved in its responsibilities and dealings. A life withdrawn from worldly concerns is a life of thought and faith, and yet is completely separate from a life of love and caring. In that kind of life, having goodwill toward our neighbors and doing good things for them ceases altogether; and when our goodwill and our good actions come to an end, our spiritual life is like a house without a foundation that gradually sags into the ground, cracking and splitting, then leans to one side, and finally collapses.

From the Lord's own words we can see that doing what is good is **127** how we are to worship the Lord:

> Everyone who hears my words and does them I will liken to a wise man who built his house on the rock; but anyone who hears my words and does not do them I will liken to a foolish man who built his house on the sand or on the ground without a foundation. (Matthew 7:24–27; Luke 6:47, 48, 49)

This now makes it possible for us to see that a pious life is effective **128** and is accepted by the Lord only to the extent that a caring life is joined to it. The latter is primary and determines the nature of the former.

Likewise, outward holiness is effective and is accepted by the Lord only to the extent that it comes from inward holiness, because the nature of the latter determines the nature of the former.

And again, renunciation of the world is effective and is accepted by the Lord only to the extent that it takes place in the world, since we renounce the world when we lay aside our self-love and our love for the world and do what is right and honest in every office we hold, every item of business we transact, and everything we do, doing so from within and therefore from a heavenly source. This source is present within our life when we do what is good, honest, and right because doing so accords with divine laws.

From *Secrets of Heaven*

APART from a caring life, a pious life is useless, but with a caring life **129** it makes a difference: 8252 and following. Outward holiness apart from inward holiness is not holy: 2190, 10177. What people in the other life are like who have lived lives of outward holiness, but not for reasons of inward holiness: 951, 952.

[2] There is an inner church and there is an outer church: 1098. There is inner worship and there is outer worship: 1083, 1098, 1100, 1151, 1153

(which include information about the nature of each kind of worship). What lies within our worship is what determines what kind of worship it is: 1175. Outward worship without inner worship is no worship at all: 1094, 7724. There is an inner dimension to our worship if our lives are lives of caring: 1100, 1151, 1153. We are engaged in true worship when we are devoted to love and caring—that is, when we are devoted to doing what is good in our daily lives: 1618, 7724, 10242. The nature of our worship depends on the nature of the good that we do: 2190. Real worship is living by the precepts of the church that are drawn from the Word: 7884, 10143, 10153, 10205, 10645.

[3] Real worship comes to us from the Lord; it does not originate in ourselves: 10203, 10299. The Lord wants worship from us for the sake of our salvation and not for the sake of his own glory: 4593, 8263, 10646. People believe that the Lord wants worship from us for the sake of his own glory. However, people who believe this do not know what divine glory is and that divine glory is the salvation of the human race. We gain this salvation when we take no credit ourselves and when, through humility, we put aside our self-centeredness, because only then can anything divine flow into us: 4347, 4593, 5957, 7550, 8263, 10646. For us, heartfelt humility arises from our recognition of what we are: that we are nothing but evil and that on our own we are powerless; followed by our recognition of what the Lord is: that nothing but what is good comes from him and that he is all powerful: 2327, 3994, 7478. What is divine can flow only into a heart that is humble, because the more truly humble we are, the more distant we are from our self-centeredness and our love for ourselves: 3994, 4347, 5957. This means that the Lord wants us to have humility not for his sake but for ours, so that we can be in a state that is receptive to what is divine: 4347, 5957. Worship is not worship if it lacks humility: 2327, 2423, 8873. The nature of outward humility apart from inward humility: 5420, 9377. The nature of heartfelt, inward humility: 7478. There is no heartfelt humility in the evil: 7640.

[4] People who have no caring and no faith may have outward worship but they have no inward worship: 1200. If we are internally ruled by love for ourselves and love for the world, our outward worship has no inner reality no matter what it may look like from the outside: 1182, 10307, 10308, 10309. Outward worship that is a manifestation of inner self-love—the kind of worship that was characteristic of people of Babylon—is profane: 1304, 1306, 1307, 1308, 1321, 1322, 1326. To pretend to have heavenly

feelings in worship when we are actually devoted to evils that come from our self-love is a hellish thing to do: 10309.

[5] From what has been said and cited above about the inner self and the outer self you can see and determine what outward worship is like when it comes from inner worship and what it is like when it does not [§§36–53].

[6] As for what people are like who renounce the world and what people are like who do not renounce it, and how things turn out for them in the other life, this is discussed at some length in the book *Heaven and Hell*, particularly in two chapters: the one titled "Rich and Poor People in Heaven" (§§357–365), and the one titled "A Heaven-Bound Life" (§§528–535).

Conscience

130 A conscience forms in us on the basis of whatever religious tradition we follow, depending on how deeply we internalize that tradition.

131 For people in the [Christian] church, their conscience is shaped either by truths [they themselves have drawn] from the Word that have become part of their faith or else by things based on the Word that they have been taught by others, depending on the extent to which they have taken these to heart. As we come to know and believe truths and comprehend them in our own way, when we will them and do them, then our conscience comes into being. Taking them to heart is taking them into our will, because our will is what we refer to as our heart.

That is why people who have a conscience say from the heart whatever they say, and do from the heart whatever they do. They also have a mind that is not divided, because what they do is consistent with what they understand and believe to be true and good.

132 People who are more enlightened than others concerning the truths of their faith, and who are more perceptive than others, are equipped to have a better conscience than people who are less enlightened and are less perceptive.

133 A genuinely spiritual life is a matter of having a true conscience, because in it our faith is joined to our caring. In that case, we see following our conscience as following the principles of our spiritual life, and going against our conscience as going against the principles of our spiritual life. As a result, when we act in accord with our conscience we feel calm and peaceful and have an inner sense of well-being, but when we go against our conscience we feel disturbed and pained. This pain is what people refer to as "pangs of conscience."

134 People can have a conscience that is focused on what is good, and they can have a conscience that is focused on what is right. A conscience that is focused on what is good is a conscience that resides in our inner self; a conscience that is focused on what is right is a conscience that resides in our outer self. If we are driven from within to live by the precepts of faith, we have a conscience that is focused on what is good; if we are driven by outward considerations to live by civil and moral laws, we have a conscience that is focused on what is right.

People who have a conscience that is focused on what is good also have a conscience that is focused on what is right. People who have only a conscience that is focused on what is right nevertheless have the capacity to develop a conscience that is focused on what is good, and they do so when they are taught about it.

The type of conscience that is found in people whose lives are devoted to caring about their neighbor is a conscience focused on truth, because it is formed through the *faith* they have in the truth. The type of conscience that is found in people whose lives are devoted to love for the Lord, though, is a conscience focused on goodness, because it is formed through the *love* they have for the truth. The conscience the latter people have is of a higher kind and is called a perception of the truth that arises from goodness. **135**

People who have a conscience focused on truth are part of the Lord's spiritual kingdom; people who have the higher conscience, the one called perception, are part of the Lord's heavenly kingdom.

Some examples may help to show what conscience is. Suppose you have another's goods without the other knowing it and can therefore profit from them with no fear of the law or of loss of position or reputation. If you nevertheless return the goods to the other because the goods are not yours, you are someone who has a conscience; you are doing a good thing because it is good, and doing the right thing because it is right. Or suppose you are offered a government position but you know that someone else who also wants that position would be of greater benefit to your country than you would. If you let the other person have the position for the good of your country, you are someone who has a good conscience. A similar principle would apply in many other situations. **136**

On this basis we can tell what people who have no conscience are like; we can identify them because they are the opposite. For example, if for the sake of profit they make something that is wrong look right or something that is evil seem good (or the reverse), they are people who have no conscience. They do not even know what conscience is, and if someone tells them what it is they do not believe it and some of them have no interest whatever in learning more. **137**

That is what people are like who do everything for worldly and selfish reasons.

If we do not develop a conscience in this world we cannot develop one in the other life and therefore we cannot be saved. This is because in that case we do not have a level into which heaven can flow and through which it can work—that is, a way in which the Lord can act by means of heaven **138** to lead us to himself. This is because our conscience is the level within us into which heaven flows; it serves as the part of us that receives heaven's inflow.

From *Secrets of Heaven*

139 *C*ONSCIENCE. People who have no conscience do not know what a conscience is: 7490, 9121. There are some people who laugh at conscience when they are told that there is such a thing: 7217. Some believe that there is no such thing as conscience; some believe that it is a kind of earthly pain and sadness brought on by a change either in physical health or in worldly circumstances; some believe that it is a form of control put on the lower classes by their religious tradition: 206, 847, 950. Some are unaware that they have a conscience even though they do: 2380.

[2] Good people have a conscience; evil people do not: 831, 965, 7490. If our life is devoted to love for God or to love for our neighbor, we have a conscience: 2380. It is especially the case that we have a conscience if we have been regenerated by the Lord: 977. We do not have a conscience if we are focused only on knowing what is true and not on living by it: 1076, 1077, 1919. We do not have a conscience if we do what is good simply because we are good-natured and not for religious reasons: 6208.

[3] We develop a conscience based on the teachings of our church or of whatever religious tradition we follow: 9112. Our conscience is shaped by the principles we believe to be true that we have been taught by our religion: 1077, 2053, 9113. Conscience is an inner restraint that keeps us focused on thinking, saying, and doing what is good and that holds us back from thinking, saying, and doing what is evil, not for selfish and worldly reasons but for the sake of what is good, true, fair, and right: 1919, 9120. Conscience is an inner voice telling us whether or not to act in some particular way: 1919, 1935. Essentially, conscience is an awareness of what is true and right: 986, 8081. The new will in a spiritual, regenerated individual is

a conscience: 928, 1023, 1043, 1044, 4299, 4328, 4493, 9115, 9596. Our spiritual life comes from our conscience: 9117.

[4] Conscience may be true, or spurious, or false: 1033 (which includes discussion). The genuineness of the truths that shape our conscience is what determines how true our conscience is: 2053, 2063, 9114. In general, there are two levels on which conscience can exist, an inner level and an outer level. A conscience on an inner level is a conscience that is focused on what is spiritually good; its essence is truth. A conscience on an outer level is a conscience that is focused on what is morally and civically good; its essence is honesty and fairness—or more broadly, what is right: 5145, 6207, 10296.

[5] The pain felt in our conscience is a mental anxiety because of what is unfair, dishonest, and in any way evil, something we believe to be contrary to God and to the well-being of our neighbor: 7217. If we feel anxious when our thoughts take an evil turn, that comes from our conscience: 5470. The pain felt in our conscience is anguish because of something evil that we are doing, or else because of a loss of goodness or truth: 7217. Because a spiritual crisis is a battle between what is true and what is false in our deeper levels, and because there is pain and anxiety involved in crises of the spirit, only people who have a conscience are allowed to have spiritual crises. 847.

[6] People who have a conscience speak and act from the heart: 7935, 9114. People who have a conscience do not swear empty oaths: 2842. People who have a conscience enjoy a sense of inner well-being when they are doing something good or performing some act of justice that accords with their conscience: 9118. People who have a conscience in this world have a conscience in the other life as well and are among the happy there: 965. Heaven flows into our conscience: 6207, 6213, 9122. The Lord governs spiritual people through their conscience, which serves them as an inner restraint: 1835, 1862. People who have a conscience have an inward kind of thinking, while people who do not have a conscience have only a superficial kind of thinking: 1919, 1935. People who have a conscience base their thinking on what is spiritual, while people who do not have a conscience base their thinking only on what is earthly: 1914. People who do not have a conscience are only outwardly human: 4459. The Lord governs people who do not have a conscience by means of outward restraints, all of which have to do with their love for themselves and for the world and the accompanying fear of losing reputation, status, position, profit, and possessions, as well as fear of the law and of loss of life: 1077, 1080, 1835.

People who have no conscience and yet allow themselves to be controlled by these external restraints can still function well in high offices in this world and do just as much good as people who do have a conscience; but the restraints under which the former are operating are external and the things they do are good outwardly, whereas the restraints under which the latter are operating are internal and the things they do are good inwardly: 6207.

[7] People who do not have a conscience try to destroy the conscience of people who do: 1820. People who have no conscience in this world have no conscience in the other life either: 965, 9122. This means that for people in hell there is no torment of conscience on account of the evil things they did in this world: 965, 9122.

[8] The identity and nature of people who are hyperconscientious: how hard they are on others, and what they correspond to in the spiritual world: 5386, 5724.

[9] People from the Lord's spiritual kingdom have a conscience, and it takes shape in their intellect: 863, 865, 875, 895, 927, 1043, 1044, 1555, 2256, 4328, 4493, 5113, 8521, 9115, 9915, 9995, 10124. People who are in the Lord's heavenly kingdom have something higher than conscience: 927, 1043, 4493, 5113, 6367, 8521, 9915, 9995, 10124.

140   *Perception.* Perception is seeing what is true and good by means of an inflow from the Lord: 202, 895, 7680, 9128. Perception is found only in people who have a love for the Lord that comes from the Lord and who devote their lives to doing good: 202, 371, 1442, 5228. Perception is found in those in heaven who, while they were living in this world, took the church's teachings from the Word and immediately put them into action in their daily lives instead of first storing them away in their memory. Therefore the deeper levels of their minds were formed to accept inflow from the Divine, with the result that in heaven their understanding is continually coming into greater and greater enlightenment: 104, 495, 503, 521, 536, 1616, 5145. They know countless things and are immensely wise: 2718, 9543. People who have perception do not resort to logical argumentation to identify the truths that belong to religious faith, and if they were to use that sort of argumentation, they would lose their perceptiveness: 586, 1385, 5937. If we believe that we are wise and knowledgeable on our own, we cannot have perception: 1386. Scholars have no idea what this kind of perception is: 1387 (which includes evidence from eyewitness experience).

The people who are in the Lord's heavenly kingdom have perception, but the people who are in the spiritual kingdom do not have perception; instead, they have conscience: 805, 2144, 2145, 8081. The people of the Lord's heavenly kingdom do not base their thinking on faith the way the people of the Lord's spiritual kingdom do, because the people of the heavenly kingdom receive from the Lord the ability to perceive everything belonging to faith: 202, 597, 607, 784, 1121, 1387, 1398, 1442, 1919, 7877, 8780. As a result, all that the heavenly angels say about the truths that belong to religious faith is "Yes, yes," or "No, no," because they perceive and see them; but spiritual angels have to use their reason to determine whether the truths taught by their religious faith are actually true or not: 2715, 3246, 4448, 9166, 10786 (these passages explain the Lord's words "Let your communication be 'Yes, yes; no, no.' Whatever is more than these comes from evil" [Matthew 5:37]). Because heavenly angels have this higher perception that allows them to recognize which truths to believe, they do not even like to say the word "faith": 202, 337. The difference between heavenly angels and spiritual angels: 2088, 2669, 2708, 2715, 3235, 3240, 4788, 8521, 9277, 10295. On the perception of the people of the earliest church, which was a heavenly church: 125, 597, 607, 784, 895, 1121, 5121.

There are deeper and shallower levels of perception: 2145, 2171, 2831, 5920. Sometimes people in this world have a perception of what is upright and equitable; they rarely have a perception of what is spiritually good or true: 2831, 5937, 7977. The light of perception is radically different from the light of conviction; the light of conviction may seem like perception to some people, but in fact it is not: 8521, 8780.

Freedom

141 ALL freedom is a function of love, because what we love we do with a sense of freedom. Therefore all of our freedom is connected with our will, because whatever we love we also will to do; and since our love and our will constitute our life, freedom too constitutes our life. This can show us what freedom is, namely, that it is a reflection of our love and our will and therefore our life. That is why anything we do freely seems to us to have come from ourselves.

142 Doing evil freely seems to be a kind of freedom but it is actually slavery, since this freedom comes from our love for ourselves and our love for this world, and these loves come from hell. This kind of freedom actually turns into slavery after we die, since anyone who had this kind of freedom becomes a lowly slave in hell afterward.

In contrast, freely doing what is good is freedom itself because it comes from a love for the Lord and from a love for our neighbor, and these loves come from heaven. This freedom too stays with us after death and then becomes true freedom because anyone who has this kind of freedom is like one of the family in heaven. This is how the Lord expresses it: "Anyone who commits sin is a slave of sin. A slave does not abide in the house forever, but the Son does abide forever. If the Son makes you free, you will be truly free" (John 8:34, 35, 36).

Since everything good comes from the Lord and everything evil from hell, it follows that it is freedom to be led by the Lord and it is slavery to be led by hell.

143 The purpose of our having the freedom to think what is evil and what is false and even to put them into practice (to the extent that the laws do not prevent it) is that it gives us the ability to be reformed. What is good and what is true need to be planted in our love and our will if they are to become part of our life, and there is no way this can happen unless we have the freedom to contemplate both what is evil and false and what is good and true. This freedom is given to each one of us by the Lord. When we are contemplating something that is good and true, then to the extent that we do not at the same time love what is evil and false the Lord plants that goodness and truth in our love and our will and therefore in our life, and in this way reforms us.

Anything that is planted within us while we are in a state of freedom becomes a permanent part of us; anything, though, that is planted under coercion does not last, because our will is not engaged; the will behind it is that of the person supplying the pressure.

That is also why worship in a state of freedom is pleasing to the Lord but forced worship is not. Worship in freedom is worship that comes from love; forced worship does not come from love.

No matter how similar they look on the surface, freedom to do good **144** and freedom to do evil are as different and as remote from each other as heaven and hell. The freedom to do good comes from heaven and is called "heavenly freedom," while the freedom to do evil comes from hell and is called "hellish freedom." To the extent that we have the one freedom we do not have the other—no one can serve two masters (Matthew 6:24). We can also see from this that people who have hellish freedom see it as slavery and bondage if they are not allowed to will what is evil and think what is false whenever they feel like it, while people who have heavenly freedom loathe to will anything evil and to think anything false, and if they are forced to do so, it torments them.

Since acting from freedom seems to us to come from ourselves, heav- **145** enly freedom can also be called "heavenly selfhood" and hellish freedom can be called "hellish selfhood." Hellish selfhood is the sense of self into which we are born, and it is evil. Heavenly selfhood, though, is the sense of self into which we come as we are reformed, and it is good.

This shows us what *freedom of choice* is—namely, doing what is good **146** by choice or intentionally; this is the freedom we have when we are being led by the Lord. We are led by the Lord when we love what is good and true because it is good and true.

We can tell what kind of freedom we have from the pleasure we **147** feel when we are engaged in thought, speech, action, hearing, or seeing, because all the pleasure we feel is a reflection of what we love.

From *Secrets of Heaven*

148 A LL freedom is a function of love and affection, because what we love
we do with a sense of freedom: 2870, 3158, 8987, 8990, 9585, 9591.
Because freedom is a function of what we love, in each of us it constitutes
our life: 2873. There is a heavenly kind of freedom and a hellish kind of
freedom: 2870, 2873, 9589, 9590. Heavenly freedom comes from a love
of what is good and true (1947, 2870, 2872); and since a love of what is
good and true comes from the Lord, it is freedom itself to be led by the
Lord (892, 905, 2872, 2886, 2890, 2891, 2892, 9096, 9586, 9587–9591). We
are led into heavenly freedom by the Lord through regeneration: 2874,
2875, 2882, 2892. We need freedom in order to be regenerated: 1937,
1947, 2876, 2881, 3145, 3158, 4031, 8700. Otherwise a love of what is good
and true cannot be planted in us and incorporated into us in such a way
that it seems to be our own: 2877, 2879, 2880, 8700. Nothing becomes
part of us that happens by coercion: 2875, 8700. If we could be reformed
by coercion, everyone would be saved: 2881. Coercion in reformation is
injurious: 4031.

[2] Worship is real when it comes from freedom, but not when it is
done under pressure: 1947, 2880, 7349, 10097. Repentance, too, needs to
take place in a free state and is not effective if it is done under pressure:
8392. The kinds of states that exert such pressure: 8392.

[3] So that goodness can be granted to us, we are given the ability to
act on the basis of freedom and rationality; therefore we are free to think
and intend evil as well and also to do it to the extent that the laws do not
forbid it: 10777. We are kept between heaven and hell by the Lord and
are therefore kept in an equilibrium so that we can have freedom for the
sake of our reformation: 5982, 6477, 8209, 8987. Whatever is planted
within us when we are free stays with us, but not what is planted when
we are coerced: 9588, 10777. Therefore freedom is never taken away from
anyone: 2876, 2881. The Lord never forces anything on anyone: 1937,
1947. How the Lord leads us toward goodness by means of our freedom:
he uses our freedom to deflect us from evil and bend us toward goodness,
leading us so gently and subtly that we believe the whole process is coming from ourselves: 9587.

[4] Self-compulsion is a type of freedom, but being compelled by
someone else is not: 1937, 1947. We need to compel ourselves not to do

evil (1937, 1947, 7914) and also compel ourselves to do good, doing so as though we were doing it on our own, but acknowledging that goodness comes from the Lord (2883, 2891, 2892, 7914). Although it does not seem so, our freedom is actually stronger when we are undergoing spiritual crises and winning, for the reason that we are then inwardly compelling ourselves to withstand evils: 1937, 1947, 2881. There is in fact a freedom in every crisis of the spirit, but it is hidden deep within us as a gift from the Lord; because of it we fight and try to conquer and not be conquered— something we could not do without freedom: 1937, 1947, 2881. The Lord grants us this freedom by creating a desire for truth and goodness in our inner self, without our realizing it: 5044.

[5] Hellish freedom consists of being led by our love for ourselves and the world and by our own appetites: 2870, 2873. To the people in hell this is the only freedom: 2871. Heavenly freedom is as remote from hellish freedom as heaven is from hell: 2873, 2874. Seen for what it really is, hellish freedom is slavery (2884, 2890), because it is slavery to be led by hell (9586, 9589, 9590, 9591).

[6] All our freedom is experienced in our sense of self and depends on that sense: 2880. Through being regenerated by the Lord we receive a heavenly selfhood: 1937, 1947, 2882, 2883, 2891. The nature of a heavenly selfhood: 164, 5660, 8480. Although this heavenly selfhood seems to us to belong to ourselves, it is not ours but is something within us that belongs to the Lord: 8497. When we have this kind of selfhood we have true freedom, because freedom is being led by the Lord and by his kind of selfhood: 892, 905, 2872, 2886, 2890, 2891, 2892, 4096, 9586, 9587, 9589, 9590, 9591.

Freedom comes from the equilibrium between heaven and hell; if we did not have this freedom we could not be reformed. This has been shown in *Heaven and Hell*; see the discussion of the equilibrium itself in §§589–596 and of the freedom that arises from it in §§597–603. To provide information here about what freedom is and about the fact that it makes our reformation possible, I would like to quote the following from that source.

149

I have just described the balance between heaven and hell and have shown that the balance is between goodness from heaven and evil from hell, which means that it is a spiritual balance that in essence is a freedom.

The reason this spiritual balance is essentially a freedom is that it exists between what is good and what is evil and between what is true and what is false, and these are spiritual realities. So freedom is the ability to intend either good or evil and to think either truth or falsity, the ability to choose one instead of the other.

The Lord grants this freedom to every individual, and it is never taken away. By virtue of its source it in fact belongs to the Lord and not to us, because it comes from the Lord; yet still it is given to us along with our life as though it were ours. This is so that we can be reformed and saved, for without freedom there can be no reformation or salvation.

Anyone who uses a little rational insight can see that we have a freedom to think thoughts that are good or evil, honest or dishonest, fair or unfair, and that we can say and do things that are good, honest, and fair, although we cannot say and do things that are evil, dishonest, and unfair, because of the moral and civil laws that keep our outward nature in restraint.

We can see from this that this freedom applies to our spirit, which does our thinking and intending, but not to our outer nature, which does our talking and acting, unless our outer nature is following the aforementioned laws.

The reason we cannot be reformed unless we have some freedom is that we are born with evils of all kinds, evils that need to be laid aside if we are to be saved. Yet they cannot be laid aside unless we see them within ourselves, admit that they are there, then no longer will them, and ultimately reject them. Only then are they laid aside. This cannot happen unless we are exposed to both what is good and what is evil, since it is from goodness that we can see evil, though from evil we cannot see goodness. As for the kinds of spiritual goodness we can think about, from early childhood we learn them from the reading of the Word and from sermons. We learn the kinds of moral and civic goodness from our life in the world. This is the primary reason we need to be in a state of freedom.

The second reason we cannot be reformed without freedom is that nothing becomes part of us unless we engage with it with love. True, other things can enter us, but no deeper than into our thought, not into our will; and anything that does not enter all the way into our will is not ours. This is because our thinking is derived from our memory, but our will is derived from our life itself. We never experience a sense of freedom unless our feelings, which are extensions of what we love, are engaged, because whatever we intend or love, we do with a sense of freedom. This is why our freedom and the feelings we have from our love or our will are one and the same. So we also have freedom in order to be able to be moved by what is true and good, or to love them, so that they become like part of us. In a word, anything that does not enter us while we are in a state of freedom does not stay with us because it does not belong to our love or will; and anything that does not belong to our love or will does not belong to our spirit. The reality underlying our spirit is love or will.

So that we can be in a state of freedom for the sake of our reformation, we are joined in spirit to heaven and to hell. With each of us there are spirits from hell and angels from heaven. By means of the spirits from hell we encounter our evil, while by means of the angels from heaven we encounter the good we have from the Lord. As a result, we are in a spiritual equilibrium—that is, a state of freedom. On the fact that angels from heaven and spirits from hell are present with all of us, see the chapter on the union of heaven with the human race (*Heaven and Hell* 291–302).

Taking Credit

150 IF we do what is good for the credit we may get, we are doing good not out of a love for doing good but out of a love for getting a reward, since if we are looking for credit we want something in return. When we do this we are focusing on pleasure and thinking it is to be found in receiving a reward rather than in doing some good. This means that we are not spiritual people but earthly ones.

151 Good that is really good must be done from a love of what is good and therefore for the sake of the good that is accomplished. When we devote our lives to this love we do not want even to hear about getting credit because we love what we are doing and find real pleasure in it. Quite the opposite: it saddens us if people think we have done something out of self-interest. It is very much like helping our friends for the sake of friendship, our sisters and brothers for the sake of family, our spouse and children for their sakes, and our country for its sake, and therefore doing what we are doing out of friendship and love. If we think of it, we even tell them with conviction that we are not being helpful for our own sake but for theirs.

152 If we are doing good for the sake of reward, the good we are doing comes not from the Lord but from ourselves, because we are focusing primarily on ourselves and what is good for us. As for the welfare of our neighbor—meaning what is good for our fellow citizens, our community, our country, and the church—this we are regarding only as a means to an end. Therefore any good act we do to get credit will have hidden in it the supposed goodness that belongs to our love for ourselves and for the world, and this type of "goodness" comes from ourselves and not from the Lord. All acts of goodness that come from ourselves are not really good— in fact, to the extent that selfishness and worldliness are concealed within them, they are evil.

153 Genuine caring and genuine faith are completely devoid of any concern for credit because what makes caring for others pleasurable is the goodness itself and what makes faith pleasurable is the truth itself. So people who are committed to this kind of caring and faith know the nature of goodness without concern for credit, while people who are not committed to caring and faith do not.

The Lord himself tells us in Luke that we are not to do good for the sake of reward: **154**

> If you love those who love you, what credit is that to you? Even sinners do the same. Rather, love your enemies, do good, and lend, hoping for nothing in return; then your reward will be great and you will be children of the Highest. (Luke 6:32, 33, 34, 35)

The Lord also tells us in John that on our own we cannot do anything good in such a way that it is truly good:

> People cannot receive anything unless it has been given to them from heaven. (John 3:27)

And again,

> Jesus said, "I am the vine; you are the branches. As a branch cannot bear fruit on its own unless it abides on the vine, the same goes for you unless you abide in me. Those who abide in me and in whom I abide bear much fruit, because without me you cannot do anything." (John 15:4–5)

Since everything good and true comes from the Lord and nothing from us, and since anything good that comes from us is not really good, it follows that none of us has merit; only the Lord has merit. The merit of the Lord is that he saved the human race by his own power and also saves individuals who do good from him. **155**

That is why the Word refers to people as "righteous" if the Lord's merit and righteousness are attributed to them but as "unrighteous" if their righteousness and merit come from themselves.

The delight itself that is found in doing good with no goal of getting something in return *is* the reward, a reward that lasts to eternity, because heaven and eternal happiness are instilled into that kind of goodness by the Lord. **156**

Thinking and believing that we come into heaven if we do what is good and that we are to do what is good in order to get into heaven is not the same as focusing on a reward as our goal or taking credit for our deeds, since people who do good things that come from the Lord have this thought and belief. However, if we think, believe, and act like this **157** but do not love doing good for its own sake, then we are indeed focusing on reward and seeking credit.

From *Secrets of Heaven*

158 ONLY the Lord has merit and righteousness: 9715, 9979. The merit and righteousness of the Lord are that he saved the human race by his own power: 1813, 2025, 2026, 2027, 9715, 9809, 10019. The goodness of the Lord's merit and righteousness is the goodness that reigns in heaven, and that is the goodness of his divine love, the source of his power to save the human race: 9486, 9979. None of us can become righteous on our own, and none has any right to claim to be righteous: 1813. What people are like who proclaim their own righteousness in the other life: 942, 2027. The Word refers to people as "righteous" if the Lord's merit and righteousness are attributed to them, but as "unrighteous" if their righteousness and merit come from themselves: 5069, 9263. Anyone who has received righteousness from the Lord once will receive it from him continually because righteousness never belongs to us but remains constantly the Lord's: 9263. People who believe what the church teaches about justification by faith alone know very little about regeneration: 5398.

[2] We become wise to the extent that we attribute everything that is good and true to the Lord and not to ourselves: 10227. Since everything that is genuinely good and true comes from the Lord and none of it comes from us, and since anything good that does come from us is not really good, it follows that none of us has merit; only the Lord has merit: 9975, 9981, 9988. The people who enter heaven rid themselves of any sense that they have earned it: 4007. They do not think about getting a reward for the good things they have done: 6478, 9174. The more we think in terms of what we deserve, the less willing we are to admit that everything is from the mercy of the Lord: 6478, 9174. People who think

in terms of the credit they deserve are thinking about being rewarded and receiving something in return, so their desire for credit is actually a desire to be paid back: 5660, 6392, 9975. People like this cannot let heaven into themselves: 1835, 8478, 9977. Heavenly happiness consists in a heartfelt desire to do good without any intention of receiving something in return: 6388, 6478, 9174, 9984. In the other life, to the extent that we do what is good without looking for a reward, bliss from the Lord flows into us in ever greater measure, but that bliss evaporates as soon as we think about getting something in return: 6478, 9174.

[3] We are to do what is good without looking to receive something in return: 6392, 6478. Some biblical passages that illustrate this: 9981. True caring is completely devoid of any desire for credit: 2371, 2400, 3887, 6388–6393. The reason is that true caring comes from love and therefore from a delight in doing what is good: 3816, 3887, 6388, 6478, 9174, 9984. "Reward" in the Word means the delight and bliss we experience in helping others without looking for any reward; people who devote their lives to true caring feel and perceive this delight and bliss: 3816, 3956, 6388.

[4] When we do good for the sake of some reward we are actually loving ourselves and not our neighbor: 8002, 9210. Spiritually understood, "hired servants" in the Word means people who do what is good for the sake of some reward: 8002. These people do what is good only in order to get something in return; in the other life they want others to serve them and are never satisfied: 6393. They despise their neighbors, and are angry at the Lord himself because they have not received their reward but say they deserve it: 9976. In the other life, people who have inwardly separated faith from caring want credit both for their faith and for the good actions that they have done, even though they did them only for show and therefore for the sake of themselves: 2371. More about what people are like in the other life if their actions were intended to earn them merit: 942, 1774, 1877, 2027. They are in the lower earth there and seem to themselves to be sawing wood: 1110, 4943, 8740. This is because one particular meaning of wood, and especially acacia wood, is good that is done for a reward: 2784, 2812, 9472, 9486, 9715, 10178.

[5] In the Lord's kingdom, people who have done good for the sake of reward are servants: 6389, 6390. When people who want credit for their actions are spiritually tested, they fail: 2273, 9978. People who devote their lives to loving themselves and the world have no idea what it is to do good with no thought of getting something in return: 6392.

Repentance and the Forgiveness of Sins

159 IF we want to be saved, we must confess our sins and repent.

160 *Confessing sins* is to recognize things that are evil, see them within ourselves, acknowledge them, accept that we are at fault, and condemn ourselves because of them. When this is done in the presence of God, it is confessing our sins.

161 After we have confessed our sins in this way and have prayed for forgiveness with a humble heart, *repenting* is to stop doing them and to lead a new life that follows the principles of caring and faith.

162 If all we do is make a blanket acknowledgment that we are sinners and declare ourselves guilty of all evils but without examining ourselves—that is, seeing our own particular evils—we are making some kind of confession, but not a confession that leads to repentance. Since we do not know what our evils are, we live the same way afterward as before.

163 If we are leading a life of caring and faith we repent every day. We reflect on the evils in ourselves, acknowledge them, take precautions against them, and pray to the Lord for help. You see, on our own we are constantly falling down, but the Lord is constantly raising us up and leading us toward goodness. This is our state if we devote our lives to doing good. If we spend our lives doing evil, then too we are constantly falling down and the Lord is constantly lifting us up, but the result is only that we are steered away from falling into those most serious evils to which we instinctively tend with all our might.

164 If we are practicing self-examination in order to repent, it is important that we examine our thoughts and the intentions of our will, and note what we would do if we could get away with it—that is, if we had no fear of the law or of losing our reputation, our job, or our wealth. Our evils live in our will; that is the source of all the evil things we do physically. Therefore if we do not search out evils in our thoughts and our will, we will be unable to repent, because afterward we will have the same thoughts and intentions as we had before; and intending evils is the same as doing them. This therefore is what self-examination entails.

165 Saying that we repent but not changing the way we live is no repentance at all. Our sins are not forgiven when we say we repent; they are forgiven when we change our lives. Our sins are of course constantly being forgiven by the Lord, because he is mercy itself. Nevertheless, despite what we may think about how our sins are forgiven, they actually still cling to us and are not put aside from us unless we live by the precepts of true faith. As we live by these precepts our sins are put aside, and as our sins are put aside they are forgiven.

People believe that when our sins are forgiven they are washed away **166** or rinsed off the way dirt is rinsed off with water. However, our sins are not washed away; they are just put aside. That is, we are held back from doing them when we are kept focused by the Lord on doing what is good; and when we are focused on doing good it seems as though our sins are gone and therefore as though they have been washed away. Further, the more we have been reformed, the more capable we are of focusing on doing what is good; how we are reformed will be explained in the treatment of regeneration that follows [§§173–186]. If we think that our sins are forgiven in any other way, we are sadly mistaken.

Some signs that our sins have been forgiven (that is, put aside) are **167** the following: we sense a pleasure in worshiping God for God's sake and in helping our neighbor for our neighbor's sake, which means in doing good for its own sake and in speaking truth for its own sake. We do not want credit for our caring or our faith. We reject and turn our backs on evils like enmity, hatred, vindictiveness, adultery, and even the very thoughts that go along with intentions in such directions.

In contrast, some signs that our sins have not been forgiven (that is, put aside) are the following: we worship God but not for God's sake, we help our neighbor but not for our neighbor's sake, which means that we do not do good for its own sake or speak truth for its own sake but for self-serving and worldly reasons. We want credit for what we do. We do not find evils like enmity, hatred, vindictiveness, and adultery at all distasteful, and entertain these evils in our thoughts with a complete lack of restraint.

When we repent in a state of freedom, it works; when we repent under **168** duress, it does not. The following are states of duress: a state of sickness, a state of mental depression because of misfortune, a state in which death seems imminent, as well as any state of fear that robs us of the use of reason. Sometimes people who are evil and are in a state of duress do things that are good and make promises to repent, but when they find themselves in a state of freedom they return to their old life of evil. It is different for people who are good.

169 After we have examined ourselves, acknowledged our sins, and repented of them, we must for the rest of our lives remain constant in our devotion to doing what is good. If instead we backslide into our former evil life and embrace it again, then we commit profanation because we are then joining evil and goodness together. This makes our latter state worse than our former one, according to the Lord's words:

> When an unclean spirit goes out of someone, it wanders through dry places seeking rest, but finds none. Then it says, "I will go back to my house, the house I left." When the spirit comes and finds the house empty, swept, and decorated for it, then it goes and recruits seven other spirits worse than itself, and they come in and live there, and the latter times of that person become worse than the first. (Matthew 12:43, 44, 45)

For what profanation is, see below [§172].

From *Secrets of Heaven*

170 *SIN and evil.* There are countless kinds of evil and falsity: 1188, 1212, 4818, 4822, 7574. There is evil that results from falsity and there is falsity that results from evil, and these lead to still more falsity and still more evil: 1679, 2243, 4818. The nature and characteristics of evil that results from falsity: 2408, 4818, 7272, 8265, 8279. The nature and characteristics of falsity that results from evil: 6359, 7272, 9304, 10302. Evils that are our own fault and evils that are not our fault: 4171, 4172. Evils that come from our understanding and evils that come from our will: 9009. The distinctions among transgression, wickedness, and sin: 6563, 9156.

[2] All our evils cling to us: 2116. Evils cannot be removed from us; we can only be held back from them and be kept focused on doing what is good: 865, 868, 887, 894, 1581, 4564, 8206, 8393, 9014, 9333, 9446, 9447, 9448, 9451, 10057, 10109. Our being held back from doing evil and kept focused on doing good is something accomplished by the Lord alone:

929, 2406, 8206, 10109. Evils and sins are only put aside, and this happens gradually: 9334, 9335, 9336. It happens through our being regenerated by the Lord: 9445, 9452, 9453, 9454, 9938. Our evils cut us off from the Lord: 5696. We need to abstain from evils in order to accept goodness from the Lord: 10109. Goodness and truth flow in to the extent that we abstain from evils: 2388, 2411, 10675. Being held back from doing evil and being kept focused on doing good is what is meant by forgiveness of sins: 8391, 8393, 9014, 9444–9450. Some signs indicating whether our sins have been forgiven or not: 9449, 9450. The forgiveness of our sins means that we are seen from the perspective of our goodness, not of our evil: 7697.

[3] Evil and sin are a separation and a turning away from the Lord; this is what evil and sin mean in the Word: 4997, 5229, 5474, 5746, 5841, 9346. Evil and sin also are, and mean, a separation and a turning away from goodness and truth: 7589. Evil and sin are, and mean, what is contrary to the divine design: 4839, 5076. Evil is hell and damnation: 3513, 6279, 7155. No one knows what hell is who does not know what evil is: 7181. Evils are heavy, so to speak, and naturally fall into hell, and the same holds true for falsities that result from evil: 8279, 8298. No one knows what evil is who does not know what love for ourselves and love for the world are: 4997, 7178, 8318. All evils come from these loves: 1307, 1308, 1321, 1594, 1691, 3413, 7255, 7376, 7488, 7489, 8318, 9335, 9348, 10038, 10742.

[4] All the people who exist are born with evils of all kinds, even to the point that their intrinsic characteristics are nothing but evil: 210, 215, 731, 874, 875, 876, 987, 1047, 2307, 2308, 3518, 3701, 3812, 8480, 8550, 10283, 10284, 10731. That is why we need to be reborn and regenerated in order to accept a life of goodness: 3701.

[5] We cast ourselves into hell when we do evil willingly, then deliberately, and finally with delight: 6203. When we are consumed with leading an evil life, we are also consumed, whether we realize it or not, with the false beliefs that go with that evil: 7577, 8094. If we believe what is actually the case, namely, that everything evil comes from hell and that everything good comes from the Lord, evil does not become part of us: 6206, 4151, 6324, 6325. In the other life, evil characteristics are put aside in good people and good characteristics are put aside in evil people: 2256. In the other life, all are brought into their inner nature, so evil people are brought into their evil nature: 8870.

In the other life, there is inherent in every evil its own punishment, and in every good its own reward: 696, 967, 1857, 6559, 8214, 8223, 8226,

9049. In the other life we are not punished for evils we inherited, because they are not our fault; but we are punished for evils that we ourselves have put into practice: 966, 2308. What lies within evil is filthy and foul, no matter how unlike that it may look in outward form: 7046.

In the Word, evil is attributed to the Lord, when in fact nothing but good comes from him: 2447, 6071, 6991, 6997, 7533, 7632, 7926, 8227, 8228, 8632, 9306. The same holds true for the anger that is attributed to him there: 5798, 6997, 8284, 8483, 9306, 10431. Why it says things like this in the Word: 6071, 6991, 6997, 7643, 7632, 7679, 7710, 7926, 8282, 9010. What "carrying iniquity" means when it is said of the Lord: 9937, 9965. When good people are being assailed and tested, the Lord turns that evil into a good thing for them: 8631. God's allowing us the freedom to do evil is called "permission": 10778. Evil and falsity are governed by the Lord according to the laws of permission; they are tolerated for the sake of the divine design as a whole: 7877, 8700, 10778. The Lord tolerates evil, but not because he wants it to happen; he does not want it to happen, but it cannot be remedied completely, because his overall goal takes precedence: 7877.

171 *Falsity.* There are many kinds of falsity—as many as there are kinds of evil, in fact—and evils and falsities retain the nature of their sources, which are many: 1188, 1212, 4729, 4822, 7574. Falsity that comes from evil, or evil-based falsity, is one thing; evil that comes from falsity, or falsity-based evil, which leads in turn to further falsity, is another: 1679, 2243. From any false idea that is taken as a first principle further false ideas flow in an unbroken series: 1510, 1511, 4717, 4721. There are falsities that are the result of cravings arising from our love for ourselves and for the world, and there are falsities that are the result of misleading sensory impressions: 1295, 4729. There are falsities that arise from what our religion has taught us and there are falsities that arise from our ignorance: 4729, 8318, 9258. There is falsity that contains some good and there is falsity that contains no good: 2863, 9304, 10109, 10302. There are also things that have been falsified: 7318, 7319, 10648.

The nature of falsity that comes from evil: 6359, 9304, 10302. The nature of evil that comes from falsity: 2408, 4818, 7272, 8265, 8279. The hells are surrounded by falsities that come from evil, which look like storm clouds and unclean waters: 8137, 8146, 8210. Waters like these symbolize falsities: 739, 790, 7307. The things that are said by the people who are in hell are falsities that come from evil: 1695, 7351, 7352, 7357, 7392, 7699. Left to their own devices, people intent on evil cannot think anything but falsity: 7437.

Some false religious beliefs harmonize with what is good and some do not: 9258. False religious beliefs that do not clash with what is good do not lead to evil except in people who are intent on leading an evil life: 8318. False religious beliefs are not held against people who are intent on doing good, but they are held against people who are intent on doing evil: 8051, 8149. Every falsity is something we can convince ourselves of, and when we have done so it seems to us to be the truth: 5033, 6865, 8521, 8780. We should be careful not to convince ourselves of falsity in matters of religion because in this arena we are particularly susceptible to false convictions: 845, 8780. How damaging false convictions are: 794, 806, 5096, 7686. False convictions continually generate arguments to support their own falsity: 1510, 1511, 2477. People who are convinced of falsities are inwardly imprisoned: 5096. In the other life, when those who have powerful false convictions encounter other people they shut down the rationality of those others and virtually suffocate them: 3895, 5128.

Truths that are not genuine and even falsities can be associated with genuine truths, but only falsities within which there is goodness, not falsities within which there is evil: 3470, 3471, 4551, 4552, 7344, 8149, 9298. If falsities have goodness within them, they are accepted by the Lord as if they were truths: 4736, 8149. Any act of goodness whose quality has been shaped by falsity is accepted by the Lord if it was done in ignorance and innocence, and if the aim behind it was good: 7887.

Evil falsifies truth because it bends it toward something evil and applies it to that evil: 8094, 8149. A truth that has been applied to some evil and used to support it is called a falsification: 8062. Falsified truth is opposed to what is true and what is good: 8062. More on falsifications of truth: 7318, 7319, 10648.

Concerning what is profane and profanation (discussed above in §169 of the teachings). Profanation is a mingling within us of both goodness and evil and of both truth and falsity: 6348. The only people who can profane what is good and true, or the sacred things taught by the church and the Word, are people who first acknowledged and believed them— especially if they have lived by them—but later relapsed from their faith, ceased to believe these things, and lived for themselves and the world: 593, 1008, 1010, 1059, 3398, 3399, 3898, 4289, 4601, 8394, 10287. People who have true beliefs as children but lose those beliefs as adults commit a mild form of profanation; people, however, who as adults become inwardly convinced of the truth of what they were taught but later turn and deny it commit a severe form of profanation: 6959, 6963, 6971. We also commit profanation if we have true beliefs but live an evil life, or if we live a pious life but disbelieve what is true: 8882. If after heartfelt repentance we relapse into our former evils, we commit profanation, and our latter state is then worse than our former one: 8394. People in the Christian world who pollute the holy contents of the Word through unclean thoughts and speech are committing profanation: 4050, 5390. There are various general categories of profanation: 10287.

[2] We cannot profane holy teachings if we have not acknowledged them, and still less if we have not even known about them: 1008, 1010, 1059, 9188, 10284. People within the church are able to profane holy teachings, but those outside the church are not: 2051. Non-Christians cannot commit profanation, because they are outside the church and do not have the Word: 1327, 1328, 2051, 9021. Jews cannot profane the deeper holy teachings of the Word and the church, because they do not acknowledge them: 6963. That is why deeper truths have not been disclosed to Jews, since if they had been disclosed and acknowledged, they would have been profaned: 3398, 3489, 6963.

Profanation is what is meant by the Lord's words cited in §169 above:

> When an unclean spirit goes out of someone, it wanders through dry places seeking rest, but finds none. Then it says, "I will go back to my house, the house I left." When the spirit comes and finds the house empty, swept, and decorated for it, then it goes and recruits seven other spirits worse than itself, and they come in and live there, and the latter times of that person are worse than the first. (Matthew 12:43, 44, 45)

The departure of the unclean spirit from the individual means repentance on the part of those who are consumed with evil; its wandering through dry places and not finding rest means that this is what leading a good life feels like for such people; the house that the spirit finds empty and decorated for itself and therefore reenters means that within themselves and their will such people have no goodness; the seven spirits it recruits and with whom it returns mean the evil that becomes joined to their good actions; and their last state being worse than their first means profanation. This is the inner meaning of the words, for the Lord spoke by means of correspondences.

The meaning of the Lord's words to the man he healed at the pool of Bethesda is much the same: "See, you have been made well. Do not sin anymore, or else something worse than before may come upon you" (John 5:14). There is this statement as well: "He has blinded their eyes and hardened their hearts, so that they would not see with their eyes and understand with their hearts and turn, and I would heal them" (John 12:40). Their turning and being healed would involve the profanation that happens when truth and goodness are acknowledged and then rejected. This, as just noted, would have happened if Jews had turned and been healed.

[3] The fate of profaners in the other life is the worst of all, since the good and true things that they have acknowledged stay with them, as does what is evil and false, and because these cling to each other their life is torn apart: 571, 582, 6348. That is why the Lord takes the greatest possible care to prevent our committing profanation: 2426, 10287. That is why we are kept far from acknowledgment and faith unless we can remain devoted to them to the end of our lives: 3398, 3402. That is why it is sometimes better for us to be kept in ignorance and in outward worship: 301, 302, 303, 1327, 1328. If we have acknowledged and accepted any goodness and truth in the meanwhile, the Lord hides it away in our deeper reaches: 6595.

[4] To prevent profanation, deeper truths are not revealed until the church is at its end: 3398, 3399. That is why the Lord came into the world and opened deeper truths at a time when the church was utterly in ruins: 3398. See what has been cited on this subject in the booklet *The Last Judgment and Babylon Destroyed* 73–74.

[5] In the Word, "Babylon" means the profanation of goodness and "Chaldea" means the profanation of truth: 1182, 1283, 1295, 1304, 1306, 1307, 1308, 1321, 1322, 1326. The general categories of profanation correspond to "the degrees of forbidden relations," or detestable types of adultery, listed in the Word: 6348. In the Israelite and Jewish church profanation was represented by "eating blood" [Genesis 9:4], which is why that was so strictly forbidden: 1003.

Regeneration

173 ANYONE who does not begin to live a spiritual life—that is, who is not born anew by means of the Lord—cannot come into heaven. This is what the Lord tells us in John: "Truly, truly I say to you, unless you are born again you cannot see the kingdom of God" (John 3:3).

174 We are born by our parents into an earthly life, but not into a spiritual life. A spiritual life is loving the Lord above all and loving our neighbor as ourselves, and doing so by following the precepts of faith that the Lord has taught us in the Word. In contrast, an earthly life is loving ourselves and the world more than we love our neighbor, and in fact more than we love God himself.

175 We are all born from our parents with the evils of love for ourselves and for the world. Every evil that has become part of someone's nature as a result of habitual indulgence is passed on to his or her progeny. Therefore we receive accumulated evil passed down from our parents, grandparents, and ancestors in a long chain going back into the past. The evil we derive from them has over time become so great that all our intrinsic characteristics are nothing but evil.

This continuous accumulation can be broken and changed only by a life of faith and caring from the Lord.

176 We constantly tend toward and lapse into what we have received by heredity, so we ourselves reinforce this evil in ourselves and also add even more to it.

These evils are absolutely opposed to a spiritual life. They destroy it. So unless we get from the Lord a new life, a spiritual life—unless, then, we are conceived anew, born anew, and raised anew (that is, created anew)—we are damned, because we want nothing and think about nothing but loving ourselves and the world, just as the people in hell do.

177 We cannot be regenerated unless we know the kinds of teachings that lead us to a new life, a spiritual life. What we must be taught in order to gain a new, spiritual life are the truths that we need to believe and the good things we need to do—the truths that need to become part of our faith and the good actions that need to become part of our caring.

There is no way any of us can know these on our own, because all we take in is what strikes our senses. From this input we gain the light that is called earthly, which makes it possible for us to see only what has to do with the world and with ourselves. It shows us nothing that has to do with heaven or with God. This we must learn from revelation.

It is only from revelation, for example, that we learn that the Lord who is God from eternity came into the world to save the human race; that he has all power in heaven and on earth; that everything that has to do with faith and caring, that is, all truth and goodness, comes from him; that there is a heaven and a hell; and that we are going to live forever—in heaven if we have led a life of goodness and in hell if we have led a life of evil.

These and much more are matters of faith that we need to know if we are to be regenerated, since if we know them we can think about them, then intend them, and finally do them, thereby having a new life. **178**

For example, if we do not know that the Lord is the Savior of the human race we cannot have faith in him, love him, and therefore do what is good for his sake. If we do not know that everything good comes from him we cannot think that our salvation comes from him, let alone want it to be that way; so we cannot live from him. If we do not know that there is a hell and a heaven and an eternal life we can have no thought whatever about heavenly life, nor can we devote ourselves to receiving it. It is much the same in regard to the other points just mentioned [§177].

Each of us has an inner self and an outer self. The inner self is called our spiritual self and the outer self is called our earthly self. If we are to be regenerated, each of these needs to be regenerated. **179**

If we have not been regenerated, then our outer or earthly self is in control and our inner self is its servant; while if we have been regenerated our inner or spiritual self is in control and our outer self is its servant. So we can see that the proper order of life in us is inverted from birth—what ought to be in control is serving and what ought to serve is in control. This order has to be reversed if we are to be saved; and the only way this reversal can be realized is through our being regenerated by the Lord.

The following may illustrate what it means to say that the inner self is in control and the outer self is serving, or the reverse. If we make pleasure and money and our own pride our highest good, if we take delight in hatred and vengeance, and if we inwardly collect reasons in support of these attitudes, then our outer self is in control and our inner self is its servant. **180**

If, though, we perceive it as a good thing and a pleasure to have thoughts and intentions that are benevolent, honest, and fair, and to have our words and deeds reflect these same qualities outwardly, then our inner self is in control and our outer self is its servant.

181 First the inner self and then the outer is regenerated by the Lord; and the outer is regenerated by means of the inner. The inner self is regenerated by thinking about what is involved in faith and caring, and the outer is regenerated by a life in accord with this.

That is the meaning of the Lord's words: "Unless you have been born of water and the spirit you cannot enter the kingdom of God" (John 3:5). "Water," spiritually understood, is the truth that belongs to religious faith, and "the spirit" is a life according to that truth.

182 When we have been regenerated, our inner self is in heaven and is an angel among the angels we are going to live with after we die. Then we will truly be able to live the life of heaven, love the Lord, love our neighbor, have an understanding of truth, be skilled in goodness, and feel the bliss that all these bring.

From *Secrets of Heaven*

183 W*HAT regeneration is and why it happens.* Nowadays there is little knowledge about regeneration; why this is the case: 3761, 4136, 5398. We are born with a love for evils of every different kind, and for that reason in terms of our intrinsic characteristics, we are nothing but evil right from our birth: 210, 215, 731, 874, 875, 876, 987, 1047, 2307, 2308, 3518, 3701, 3812, 8480, 8549, 8550, 8552, 10283, 10284, 10286, 10731. On *what we inherit* being nothing but evil, see the references assembled above in §83 of this work. On *our own intrinsic characteristics* being nothing but evil as well, see §82. On our own, to the extent that we rely on our inherited and intrinsic characteristics, we are worse than brute animals: 637, 3175. As a result, left to ourselves we are constantly looking toward hell: 694, 8480. So if we are led by this selfhood of ours, there is no way we can be saved: 10731.

Our earthly life is opposed to our spiritual life: 3913, 3928. Anything good that we do on our own or when we are led by our intrinsic characteristics is not good, since we are doing it for our own sake and for worldly reasons: 8478. This selfhood of ours has to be put aside in order for the Lord and heaven to be present: 1023, 1044. It is actively put aside as we are regenerated by the Lord: 9334, 9335, 9336, 9452, 9453, 9454, 9938. That is why we need to be created anew—that is, regenerated: 8549, 9450, 9938. In the Word, our being "created" symbolizes our being regenerated: 16, 88, 10634.

As we are regenerated we are joined to the Lord: 2004, 9338. We are also brought into the company of angels in heaven: 2474. We do not arrive in heaven until we are in a state that makes it possible for us to be led by the Lord through what is good, which happens when we are regenerated: 8516, 8539, 8722, 9832, 10367.

When we have not been regenerated, the outer or earthly self is in control and the inner is its servant: 3167, 8743. The state of our life is thus upside down from birth and therefore needs at all costs to be inverted so that we can be saved: 6507, 8552, 8553, 9258. The goal of regeneration is that the inner or spiritual self should be in control and that the outer or earthly self should be its servant: 911, 913. This is actually what happens when we have been regenerated: 5128, 5651, 8743. After regeneration it is no longer love for ourselves and the world that are dominant in us but love for the Lord and love for our neighbor, so the Lord is ruling and not we ourselves: 8856, 8857. We can see from this that unless we are regenerated we cannot be saved: 5280, 8548, 8772, 10156.

Regeneration is a foundation for the perfecting of our life to eternity: 9334. When we have been regenerated, we are indeed continually perfected to eternity: 6648, 10048. The nature of people who have been regenerated and of people who have not been regenerated: 977, 986, 10156.

Who is regenerated. We cannot be regenerated until we have been instructed in the truths that belong to religious faith and the good actions that constitute caring: 677, 679, 711, 8635, 8638, 8639, 8640, 10729. If we are focused solely on truth and not on goodness, we cannot be regenerated: 6567, 8725. No one who lacks an attitude of caring can be regenerated: 989. No one who lacks a conscience can be regenerated: 2689, 5470. We are all regenerated in keeping with our ability to accept doing what is good out of love for the Lord and out of caring about our neighbor, because of the truths we believe from the Word, which we are taught by the church: 2967, 2975. More on who can be regenerated and who cannot: 2689. People who live lives of faith and caring but have not been regenerated in this world are regenerated in the other life: 989, 2490.

185   *Our regeneration is carried out by the Lord alone.* The Lord alone regenerates us; absolutely none of it is accomplished by us or by angels: 10067. Our regeneration is an image of the Lord's glorification—just as the Lord made his own human nature divine, the Lord makes the people he regenerates spiritual: 3043, 3138, 3212, 3296, 3490, 4402, 5688, 10057, 10076. As he regenerates us the Lord wants us to surrender our whole selves to him and not just a part of ourselves: 6138.

186   *More on regeneration.* We are regenerated by means of the truths that belong to religious faith and through living by them: 1904, 2046, 9088, 9959, 10028. This is the meaning of the Lord's words "Unless you have been born of water and the spirit you cannot enter the kingdom of God" (John 3:5); "water" means the truth that belongs to religious faith and "the spirit" means a life in accord with that truth: 10240. Water in the Word means the truth that belongs to religious faith: 2702, 3058, 5668, 8568, 10238. Spiritual purification, which is purification from evil and falsity, is effected by means of the truths that belong to religious faith: 2799, 5954, 7044, 7918, 9088, 10229, 10237. When we are being regenerated, truths are sown and rooted in doing good so that they become part of our life: 880, 2189, 2675, 2697. What truths must be like before they can be rooted in doing good: 8725. In the process of regeneration, truth is introduced and joined to doing good, and likewise doing good is introduced and joined to truth: 5365, 8516. How that mutual introduction and joining takes place: 3155, 10067. Truth becomes rooted in doing good when we come to will it, because it then becomes something that we love: 10367.

[2] There are two states we go through when we are being regenerated: the first is when we are being led to do what is good by means of truth, and the second is when we act on the basis of what is good and see what is true from what is good: 7992, 7993, 8505, 8506, 8510, 8512, 8516, 8643, 8648, 8658, 8685, 8690, 8701, 8772, 9227, 9230, 9274, 9509, 10057, 10060, 10076. What our state is like when truth is in first place for us and goodness is second: 3610. We can see from this that when we are being regenerated we look toward goodness from the perspective of truth, but when we have been regenerated, we look toward truth from the perspective of goodness: 6247. So there is a kind of reversal in which our state is turned upside down: 6507.

[3] It is important to know, though, how things really stand: while we are being regenerated, truth is only apparently but not actually in first place and goodness in second place; but when we have been regenerated goodness is actually and observably in first place and truth in second place: 3324, 3325, 3330, 3336, 3494, 3539, 3548, 3556, 3563, 3570, 3576, 3603, 3701, 4243, 4244, 4247, 4337, 4925, 4926, 4928, 4930, 4977, 5351, 6256, 6269, 6273, 8516, 10110. This means that goodness comes both first and last in our regeneration: 9337. Because truth seems to come first and goodness seems to come second when we are being regenerated (or when we are becoming a form of the church, which amounts to the same thing), this appearance led to a difference of opinion among the ancients as to which was the firstborn of the church, the truth that belongs to religious faith or the good actions that come from caring: 367, 2435. The good actions that come from caring are the firstborn of the church in actual fact, while the truth that belongs to religious faith is only apparently so: 3325, 3494, 4925, 4926, 4928, 4930, 8042, 8080. "Firstborn" in the Word means what comes first in the church and has preference and higher rank: 3325. That is why the Lord is called "the firstborn"—because all the good that comes from love and caring and faith exists within him and originates from him: 3325.

[4] Once we are in the later state (looking at truth from the perspective of goodness) we should not turn back to the earlier state (looking at goodness from the perspective of truth), and why that is the case: 2454, 3650–3655, 5895, 5897, 7857, 7923, 8505, 8506, 8510, 8512, 8516, 9274, 10184 (which include discussion of the Lord's words "Those who are in the field then should not go back to get their outer garments" [Matthew 24:18] and "Those who are in the field then should not turn back. Remember Lot's wife" [Luke 17:31–32], showing that this is what those sayings mean).

[5] A description of the way the process of our regeneration unfolds: 1555, 2343, 2490, 2657, 2979, 3057, 3286, 3310, 3316, 3332, 3470, 3701, 4353, 5122, 5126, 5270, 5280, 5342, 6717, 8772, 8773, 9043, 9103, 10021, 10057, 10367. There are countless mysteries concerning regeneration, because regeneration goes on throughout our entire lifetime: 2679, 3179, 3665, 3690, 3701, 4377, 4551, 4552, 5122, 5126, 5398, 6751, 9103, 9258, 9296, 9297, 9334. Hardly any of these mysteries come into our knowledge or perception: 3179, 9336. This is what is meant by these words of the Lord: "The wind blows where it wishes, and you hear the sound of it, but cannot tell where it is coming from or where it is going. So it is with everyone who is born of the spirit" (John 3:8). Information about the process of regeneration of those who are part of the spiritual church: 2675, 2678, 2679, 2682.

Information about the process of regeneration of those who are part of the heavenly church, and the differences between the two: 5113, 10124.

[6] It is much the same for someone who is being regenerated as it is for a baby who first learns to talk, then to think, later to live rightly, until finally everything flows freely, seemingly on its own: 3203, 3701. So someone who is being regenerated is led by the Lord through stages: the first is like infancy, the next is like childhood, and the one after that is like adulthood: 3665, 3690, 4377, 4378, 4379, 6751. When we are being regenerated by the Lord, at first we are in a state of outward innocence, which is a state like infancy for us. Then step by step we are led through to a state of inward innocence, which is a state of wisdom for us: 9334, 9335, 10021, 10210. The nature and characteristics of the innocence of infancy and the nature and characteristics of the innocence of wisdom: 1616, 2305, 2306, 3494, 4563, 4797, 5608, 9301, 10021. A comparison between our regeneration and the conception and formation of an embryo in the womb: 3570, 4931, 9258. Because of this parallel, references to conception and birth in the Word mean spiritual conception and birth—that is, stages in our regeneration: 613, 1145, 1255, 2020, 2584, 3860, 3868, 4070, 4668, 6239, 10204. Our regeneration is illustrated by the process of germination in the plant kingdom: 5115, 5116. In the spiritual world the stage of our regeneration is represented as a rainbow: 1042, 1043, 1053.

[7] Both the inner or spiritual self and the outer or earthly self need to be regenerated, and the one is regenerated by means of the other: 3868, 3870, 3872, 3876, 3877, 3882. The inner self is regenerated before the outer because the inner is in heaven's light and the outer is in this world's light: 3321, 3325, 3469, 3493, 4353, 8748, 9325. The outer or earthly self is regenerated by means of the inner or spiritual self: 3286, 3288, 3321. We are not regenerated until our outer or earthly self has been regenerated: 8742–8747, 9043, 9046, 9061, 9325, 9334. If our earthly self is not being regenerated, our spiritual self is closed off (6299) and is in effect blind to the truths and the good actions that are related to faith and love (3493, 3969, 4353, 4588). When the earthly self has been regenerated the whole person has been regenerated: 7442, 7443. This is the meaning of the washing of the disciples' feet and by these words of the Lord: "Those who have bathed need only to have their feet washed to be completely clean" (John 13:10): 10243. Washing in the Word means spiritual washing, which is purification from evils and falsities (3147, 10237, 10241), and feet mean the attributes of our earthly self (2162, 3761, 3986, 4280, 4938–4952), so "washing our feet" means purifying our earthly self (3147, 10241).

[8] How the earthly self is regenerated: 3502, 3508, 3509, 3518, 3573, 3576, 3579, 3616, 3762, 3786, 5373, 5647, 5650, 5651, 5660. The nature of the earthly self when it has been regenerated and its nature when it has not been regenerated: 8744, 8745. The less our earthly self fights with our spiritual self, the more regenerated we are: 3286. When we have been regenerated, our earthly self perceives the spiritual things that are flowing in: 5651.

[9] Our sensory level, which is the lowest level of our earthly self, is not regenerated nowadays, but instead we are raised above it: 7442. When we are being regenerated we are actually lifted up from the sensory level into the light of heaven: 6183, 6454. The nature and characteristics of sense-oriented people may be seen in the references assembled in §50 above.

[10] We are regenerated by means of an inflow into whatever knowledge we have about goodness and truth: 4096, 4097, 1364. When we are being regenerated we are led by means of intermediate forms of goodness and truth into genuine forms of them, after which the intermediate forms are left behind and the genuine ones take their place: 3665, 3690, 3686, 3974, 4063, 4067, 4145. This then brings our truths and our desires to do good into a completely different arrangement: 4250, 4251, 9931, 10303. They are arranged according to our goals (4104); therefore they are arranged according to the use to which we wish to put our spiritual life (9297). When we are being regenerated we undergo many different states, but are steadily being led deeper into heaven and therefore closer to the Lord: 6645. Those who have been regenerated are patterned after heaven: 8512. Their inner reaches are opened into heaven: 8512, 8513. Through regeneration we come into angelic intelligence, but this lies hidden in our deeper levels as long as we are living in this world. It is opened up in the other life, however, and then we have the same kind of wisdom as angels have: 2494, 8747. The state of enlightenment that is given to those who are being regenerated: 2699, 2701, 2704. Through regeneration we are given a new faculty of understanding: 2657. How goodness becomes more fruitful and truth multiplies in people who are being regenerated: 984. When goodness takes charge in those who have been regenerated, the truths that come forth around it form little stars, so to speak, and each of these generates more starlike truths around itself, without end: 5912. In a person who has been regenerated, the truths that come from goodness are arranged in a pattern so that the genuine truths connected with that goodness are in the center; these are like parents to

the next group of truths; and still other truths are placed farther away according to the degree of kinship or family ties, extending all the way to the outermost areas, where it is dark: 3128, 4551, 4552, 5134, 5270. In people who have been regenerated, truths that come from goodness are arranged in the form of heaven: 3316, 3470, 3584, 4302, 5704, 5709, 6028, 6690, 9931, 10303. In the book *Heaven and Hell,* see also the chapters "Heaven's Form, Which Determines How People Associate and Communicate There" (§§200–212) and "The Wisdom of Heaven's Angels" (§§265–275).

[11] In people who have been regenerated there is a correspondence between the spiritual and the earthly contents of their minds: 2850. In people who have been regenerated the whole hierarchy of their lives has been completely inverted: 3332, 5159, 8995. In their spirits, those who have been regenerated are completely new people: 3212. Those who have been through regeneration may seem outwardly like those who have not, but they are not like them inwardly: 5159. Regeneration is the only way we can gain spiritual goodness—which is intending and doing good because we are moved by a love for goodness: 4538. Whatever emotion instilled a given truth in us before has the power to evoke that truth again: 5893. The more our truths are disconnected from their origin in our self-focused life, the more they can be joined to goodness and receive spiritual life: 3607, 3610. Our truths have life to the extent that the evils stemming from our love for ourselves and for the world are put aside: 3610.

[12] When we are being regenerated, the first desire we feel for truth is not pure, but over time that desire is gradually purified: 3089, 8413. When we are being regenerated, the evil and false things in us are put aside slowly, not quickly: 9334, 9335. The evil and false things that have become part of us still continue to exist and are only put aside by our regeneration: 865, 868, 887, 929, 1581, 2406, 4564, 8206, 8393, 9014, 9333–9336, 9445, 9447, 9448, 9451–9454, 9938, 10057. There is no way we can be so completely regenerated that we are declared perfect: 894, 5122, 6648. Evil spirits do not dare attack someone who has been regenerated: 1695. People in the church who believe in justification know very little about regeneration: 5398.

[13] We need freedom in order to be regenerated: 1937, 1947, 2876, 2881, 3145, 3146, 3158, 4031, 8700. Through regeneration we are brought into heavenly freedom: 2874, 2875, 2882, 2892. No joining of goodness and truth takes place under coercion, so no regeneration does either: 2875,

2881, 4031, 8700. For more on our freedom in regard to regeneration, see the teachings given in the chapter on freedom above [§§141–149].

[14] When we are being regenerated, we must of necessity undergo spiritual crises (3696, 8403) because such crises happen for the sake of joining goodness and truth together in us and also joining our inner and outer selves together (4248, 4572, 5773).

Crises of the Spirit

187 ONLY people who are being regenerated experience spiritual crises, because spiritual crises are times of mental anguish for people whose lives are devoted to goodness and truth. These crises are brought about by evil spirits. When they stir up the evils in us, an anxiety wells up inside that is a symptom of our spiritual crisis. We are not aware, however, of where the anxiety is coming from because we do not realize that a spiritual crisis is its source.

188 There are evil spirits and good spirits with each of us. The evil spirits are in our evil tendencies and the good spirits are in our good tendencies. When the evil spirits come closer they stir up our evil tendencies, and the good spirits respond by stirring up our good ones. This leads to a collision and a battle that causes us the inner anxiety that is a crisis of the spirit.

We can see from this that spiritual crises are caused by hell and do not come from heaven. This is also what is taught by the faith of the church, which is that God does not test anyone.

189 There are also times of inner anxiety for people whose lives are not devoted to goodness and truth. Theirs are earthly anxieties, though, not spiritual ones. The distinction is that earthly anxieties focus on worldly concerns, while spiritual anxieties focus on heavenly ones.

190 What is at stake in crises of the spirit is either the dominance of goodness over evil or the dominance of evil over goodness. The evil that wants to take control is in our earthly or outer self, and the goodness is in our spiritual or inner self. If evil wins, the earthly self controls us; if goodness wins, the spiritual self controls us.

191 These battles are waged by means of truths of our religious faith that are drawn from the Word. It is from these resources that we must fight against what is evil and false; if we fight from any other resource we do not win because the Lord is not in it.

Since the battle is waged by means of the truths that belong to religious faith, we are not allowed to engage in these battles until we have some knowledge of goodness and truth and have gained some spiritual life from them. For this reason, these battles do not start in us until we have reached adulthood.

If we give up the fight, our state after the spiritual crisis becomes **192** worse than it was before, because the evil in us has then gained power over the goodness in us and falsity has overpowered truth.

Since faith is rare these days because there is an absence of caring **193** and the church is at its end, few people nowadays are allowed to undergo spiritual crises. That is why it is scarcely known what they are or what good they do.

Crises of the spirit help goodness in us gain control over evil and **194** truth gain control over falsity. They help reinforce truths and join them to goodness and at the same time shatter evils and the falsities that arise from them. They also serve to open our inner, spiritual self and bring our earthly self under its control, break up our love for ourselves and for the world, and tame the cravings that arise from them.

Once this has been done, we come into enlightenment and gain a perception of what is true and what is good, and of what is false and what is evil. This gives us intelligence and wisdom, which then keep growing day by day.

During our spiritual crises the Lord alone is fighting for us. If we do **195** not believe that the Lord alone is fighting for us and winning for us, then we are experiencing only an outer crisis that does not do us much good.

From *Secrets of Heaven*

BEFORE presenting an overview of what is written about spiritual cri- **196** ses in *Secrets of Heaven*, I need to offer something about them by way of a preface so that readers may have a clearer understanding of where these crises come from.

We call a crisis "spiritual" when the truths that belong to religious faith are under attack within us, truths that we believe at heart and love to live by. This is especially so when the attack threatens the good things we do from love, the goodness in which we find our spiritual life.

These attacks are waged by various means—by an inflow, into our thoughts and also into our will, that blocks what is true and good, and by constantly bringing up and calling to mind evil things we have done and false thoughts we have harbored, so that we are flooded by such things. At the same time, too, in the deeper levels of our mind there is an apparent break so that our communication with heaven is cut off. This stops us from thinking on the basis of our faith or forming intentions that relate to what we love. All this is done by the evil spirits who are with us; and as it is being done, it seems to us that we are suffering inner anxieties and pangs of conscience, because what is being done shakes and tortures our spiritual life. All the while, we believe that this is coming not from evil spirits but from ourselves, deep within. The reason we do not believe that this comes from evil spirits is that we do not realize that there are spirits with us—evil ones in our evil tendencies and good ones in our good tendencies—and that they are in our thoughts and feelings.

These crises are most severe when they are accompanied by pains experienced in our bodies, and are even worse if the pains persist and become more severe and we beg for divine mercy but there is still no deliverance. This leads to despair, which is the end of the process.

Here I need first to cite some statements from *Secrets of Heaven* about the spirits who are with us, since they are the cause of these crises.

There are spirits and angels with each of us: 697, 5846–5866. They are in our thoughts and feelings: 2888, 5846, 5848. If the spirits and angels were taken away, we could not remain alive: 2887, 5849, 5854, 5993, 6321. The reason for this is that it is through spirits and angels that we have communication and connection with the spiritual world, and without that we would have no life: 697, 2796, 2886, 2887, 4047, 4048, 5846–5866, 5976–5993. The spirits with us change depending on the feelings we are having, which stem from what we love: 5851. Spirits from hell are in the loves that are intrinsic to us: 5852, 5979–5993. Spirits have access to everything in our memory: 5853, 5857, 5859, 5860, 6192, 6193, 6198, 6199. Angels are in the goals from which and for which we think, intend, and act in one way and not in another: 1317, 1645, 5854. We are not visible to spirits, just as spirits are not visible to us: 5862. So spirits cannot see, through us, anything that is in our subsolar world: 1880. Even though spirits and angels are with us in our thoughts and feelings we are still free to think, intend, and act as we wish: 5982, 6477, 8209, 8307, 10777. In addition, there is material in *Heaven and Hell* in the chapter "The Union of Heaven with the Human Race" (§§291–302).

The origin and characteristics of crises of the spirit. Spiritual crises arise **197** from the evil spirits who are with us; these spirits put barriers between us and the goodness we love and the truths we believe, and also stir up evil things that we have done and false things that we have thought: 741, 751, 761, 3927, 4307, 4572, 5036, 6657, 8960. At such times evil spirits use extreme cunning and malice: 6666. When we are undergoing a spiritual crisis we are close to hell: 8131. There are two forces at work in spiritual crises, a force from the Lord from within and a force from hell from without, and we are in between: 8168.

[2] In spiritual crises, what is under assault is the thing we love the most: 847, 4274. Evil spirits exclusively attack the things we believe and love and therefore our spiritual life itself, so that our eternal life is at stake: 1820. A comparison between the state we are in during a spiritual crisis and the state we are in when being attacked by thieves: 5246. When we are in spiritual crises, angels from the Lord hold us to a path of truth and goodness, while evil spirits hold us to a path of falsity and evil, which causes a conflict and a battle: 4249.

[3] A crisis of the spirit is a battle between the inner or spiritual self and the outer or earthly self: 2183, 4256. So it is a battle between the pleasures of the inner and the outer selves, which at this point are opposite to each other: 3928, 8351. This happens because the two kinds of pleasure clash with one another: 3928. So what is at stake is the control of one self over the other: 3928, 8961.

[4] No one can undergo a spiritual crisis who does not acknowledge the existence of truth and goodness and desire them, since if these are lacking no battle occurs. That is, there is nothing spiritual to counteract what is earthly and therefore there is no battle for control: 3928, 4299. Only those who have gained some spiritual life undergo spiritual crises: 8963. Crises of the spirit affect people who have a conscience—people, then, who have gained a spiritual kind of love. Such crises are more severe, though, for people who have perception—people who have gained a heavenly kind of love: 1668, 8963. Dead people—that is, people who have no faith in or love for God and no love for their neighbor—are not allowed to undergo spiritual crises, because they would give up the fight: 270, 4274, 4299, 8964, 8968. So nowadays not many people undergo spiritual crises: 8965. People do, however, have anxieties caused by various worldly situations—whether those situations have happened, or are happening, or are going to happen—situations that generally include mental affliction or physical illness. These are not, though, the same as the

anxieties caused by spiritual crises: 762, 8164. Spiritual crises may or may not happen during times of physical suffering: 8164. The state we come into during a crisis of the spirit is impure and filthy, because we are inundated with evils and falsities and also doubts about what is good and true (5246) and because in these crises there are resentments, mental anguish, and many feelings that are not good (1917, 6829). There is also an element of darkness and doubt about the outcome (1820, 6829) and also about divine providence and whether we are being heard, because in crises of the spirit, prayers are not heard the way they are outside of such crises (8179), and because when we are in spiritual crises we experience ourselves as being in a state of damnation (6097). This is because we have a clear sense of what is happening in our outer self and therefore of the things that the evil spirits are injecting and evoking (and these shape the way we are thinking about our state). On the other hand, we do not sense what is happening in our inner self, which means we do not sense what is flowing in through angels from the Lord. The result is that we are incapable of judging our own state: 10236, 10240.

[5] Crises of the spirit continue until we reach despair, at which point the process comes to an end: 1787, 2694, 5279, 5280, 6144, 7147, 7155, 7166, 8165, 8567. Why this is so: 2694. Throughout the course of a spiritual crisis there are certain feelings of despair, but at the end they become all-encompassing: 8567. In despair we say some bitter things, but the Lord pays no attention to them: 8165. Once a spiritual crisis is over we at first fluctuate between truth and falsity (848, 857), but then the truth shines forth and we feel peaceful and lighthearted (3696, 4572, 6829, 8367, 8370).

[6] When we are being regenerated we experience crises of the spirit not just once but many times, because we have many evils and falsities that need to be put aside: 8403. If people gain some spiritual life in this world but do not undergo spiritual crises here, they go through them in the other life: 7122. How and where spiritual crises happen in the other life: 537, 538, 539, 699, 1106–1113, 2694, 4728, 4940–4951, 6119, 6928, 7090, 7122, 7186, 7317, 7474, 7502, 7541, 7542, 7545, 7768, 7990, 9331, 9763. The state of enlightenment of people who are emerging from crises of the spirit and being raised into heaven, and what happens to them there: 2699, 2701, 2704.

The nature of a spiritual crisis caused by lack of truth, and the longing for truth that results from it: 2682, 8352. How little children are tested in the other life, a process by which they learn to resist evils: 2294. How spiritual crisis, persecution, and devastation differ from each other: 7474.

How and when crises of the spirit take place. Spiritual battles are waged **198** primarily by means of truths that belong to religious faith: 8962. Therefore truth is the first requirement for the battle: 1685. The crises of the spirit that people of the spiritual church undergo concern the truths that belong to their religious faith, so their battles are waged by means of truths; the crises of the spirit that people of the heavenly church undergo concern the good that they love to do, so their battles are waged by means of goodness: 1668, 8962. For the most part, the people of the spiritual church do not have genuine truths to use in the battle, but instead things they believe to be true because they were taught them by their church; to be effective, though, these teachings need to be capable of being joined to what is good: 6765.

When we are being regenerated we have to experience crises of the spirit. Apart from such crises regeneration is impossible (5036, 8403), and that is why spiritual crises are necessary (7090). As we are being regenerated, we come into spiritual crises when evil tries to gain control over goodness and our earthly self tries to gain control over our spiritual self: 6657, 8961. We also come into spiritual crises at the point when goodness needs to take the lead: 4248, 4249, 4256, 8962, 8963. When we are being regenerated we are brought first into a tranquil state, then into spiritual crises, then back to the tranquil state of peace that has become our goal: 3696.

The benefit of crises of the spirit. An overview of what crises of the spirit **199** accomplish: 1692, 1717, 1740, 6144, 8958–8969. Through spiritual crises our spiritual or inner self gains control over our earthly or outer self; so goodness gains control over evil and truth over falsity, since goodness resides in our spiritual self. In fact, we have no goodness anywhere but in our spiritual self; evil resides in our earthly self: 8961. Since a spiritual crisis is a battle between these two, what is at stake is control—namely, whether or not the spiritual self will gain control over the earthly, whether or not goodness within us will gain control over evil, and therefore whether the Lord or hell will have control over us: 1923, 3928. It is through crises of the spirit that our outer or earthly self accepts truths that align with the desire for truth that has developed in our inner or spiritual self: 3321, 3928. Our inner, spiritual self is opened up by spiritual crises and joined to our outer self, so that both parts of us can be lifted up and can turn to the Lord: 10685. The reason our inner, spiritual self is both opened by spiritual crises and joined by them to our outer self is that the Lord acts from within and flows from there into our outer self, where he puts evils aside and conquers them, and during this process renders our outer self subject and subordinate to our inner self: 10685.

[2] Crises of the spirit happen so that goodness and truth can be joined together in us and so that the falsities that cling to goodness and truth can be dispelled (4572); so through spiritual crises, goodness is joined to truths (2272). Vessels in our minds that are receptive to truths are softened by spiritual crises and take on a state that is also receptive to goodness: 3318. Through spiritual crises, truths and goodness of various kinds take root and are strengthened in us; therefore our faith and caring increase: 8351, 8924, 8966, 8967. Meanwhile, evil and falsity in us are moved aside so that there is room for goodness and truth: 7122. Through spiritual crises, our love for ourselves and our love for the world—the sources of everything that is evil and false—are broken up (5356) and we are taught humility (8966, 8967). Through spiritual crises, what is evil and false in us is tamed, separated, and put aside, but is not destroyed: 868. Through spiritual crises, bodily concerns and cravings are tamed: 857, 858. Through spiritual crises we learn what goodness and truth are, in part from the contrast between them and their opposites, evil and falsity: 5356. We also learn that everything we have is nothing but evil and that anything good we have comes from the Lord and his mercy: 2334.

Through spiritual crises in which we are victorious, evil spirits are deprived of their power to do anything further against us: 1695, 1717. The hells do not dare rise up against people who have undergone spiritual crises and have been victorious: 2183, 8273.

After crises of the spirit in which we are victorious, there is a joy that arises from the joining together of goodness and truth, though we are not aware that this is the source of our joy: 4572, 6829. We then gain an enlightenment regarding the truth that leads to faith and a perception of the goodness that comes from love: 8367, 8370. From crises of the spirit we also gain intelligence and wisdom: 8966, 8967. Truths increase immensely after spiritual crises: 6663. Goodness takes the lead or occupies first place, while truth comes second: 5773. With respect to our inner, spiritual self we are brought into angelic communities, and therefore into heaven: 6611.

Before we undergo crises of the spirit, the truths we have, as well as the good things in us, are set in order for us by the Lord so that we can resist the evil and falsity that are with us from hell and will be stirred up: 8131. In spiritual crises, the Lord provides a good outcome where the hellish spirits intend nothing but evil: 6574. After spiritual crises, the Lord sets our truths, as well as the good things in us, in a new order and arranges them in a heavenly form: 8370. On the arrangement of the deeper parts of the spiritual self into a heavenly form, see the chapter in *Heaven and Hell* titled "Heaven's Form, Which Determines How People Associate and Communicate There" (§§200–212).

People who give up the fight in spiritual crises come into damnation because the evil and falsity win and the earthly self triumphs over the spiritual and takes control; and our latter state becomes worse than our former one: 8165, 8169, 8961.

In crises of the spirit the Lord fights for us. The Lord alone fights for us in spiritual crises; we do nothing on our own: 1692, 8172, 8175, 8176, 8273. Of ourselves there is no way whatever that we could fight against evil and falsity, because this would be fighting against all the hells, which no one but the Lord alone can control and conquer: 1692. The hells fight against us and the Lord fights for us: 8159. Resources we use in the fight are truths and goodness, and therefore our knowledge about and love for truth and goodness. However, it is not we who are fighting, it is the Lord who is doing so by these means: 1661. When we are in crises of the spirit, we think that the Lord is absent because our prayers are not heard then the way they are when we are not in such crises, but in fact the Lord is even more present at such times: 840. When we are in spiritual crises we need to fight as though we were on our own, not drop our hands and wait for direct intervention, yet we should still believe that the Lord is the one doing the work: 1712, 8179, 8969. There is no other way we can receive a heavenly selfhood: 1937, 1947, 2882, 2883, 2891. The nature of this selfhood—it is not ours but is something within us that belongs to the Lord: 1937, 1947, 2882, 2883, 2891, 8497.

[2] A crisis of the spirit does not accomplish anything or bring about any good if even after it is over we do not believe that it was the Lord who fought and conquered for us: 8969. People who want credit for their deeds cannot fight against evils, because they fight by their own efforts and do not let the Lord fight for them: 9978. It is hard for us to be saved if we believe that we ourselves have earned heaven by going through spiritual crises: 2273.

The Lord does not test us but sets us free and leads us to goodness: 2768. Spiritual crises seem to come from the Divine, but in actuality they do not: 4299. What is meant by "Lead us not into temptation" [Matthew 6:13; Luke 11:4] in the Lord's Prayer: 1875 (which includes evidence from eyewitness experience). Contrary to the way we usually think permission works, the Lord does not condone the spiritual crises he permits us to undergo: 2768.

There is freedom in all crises of the spirit even though it does not seem so. But this freedom is deep within us from the Lord; it allows us to fight and try to win and not be overcome, which we could not do without freedom: 1937, 1947, 2881. The Lord creates this freedom through a love for truth and goodness that he has imparted to our inner self without our knowing it (5044), because all freedom is a function of love and affection and depends on what that love is like (2870, 3158, 8987, 8990, 9585, 9591).

201 *The Lord's spiritual crises.* Beyond all others, the Lord suffered the fiercest, most severe spiritual crises; they are barely touched on in the literal sense of the Word but are described extensively in its inner meaning: 1663, 1668, 1787, 2776, 2786, 2795, 2816, 9528. The Lord fought out of his divine love for the whole human race: 1690, 1691, 1812, 1813, 1820. The Lord's love was a love for the salvation of the human race: 1820. The Lord fought from his own power: 1692, 1813, 9937. Through spiritual crises and victories from his own power, the Lord alone became righteousness and merit: 1813, 2025, 2026, 2027, 9715, 9809, 10178. Through crises of the spirit, the Lord united his divine nature, which was within him from conception, to his human nature, and made this latter divine, just as he makes us spiritual through our crises of the spirit: 1725, 1729, 1733, 1737, 3318, 3381, 3382, 4286. The Lord's spiritual crises included despair at the end: 1787. Through the spiritual crises he allowed himself to undergo, the Lord gained control over the hells and brought everything there and in the heavens into proper order; and at the same time he glorified his human nature: 1737, 4287, 9528, 9715, 9937. The Lord alone fought against all the hells: 8273. This is why he allowed himself to undergo spiritual crises: 2816, 4295.

The Lord's divine nature could not have undergone spiritual crises, because the hells cannot attack anything divine. That is why the Lord took on a human nature from his mother, a nature that can undergo spiritual crises: 1414, 1444, 1573, 5041, 5157, 7193, 9315. Through his spiritual crises and victories he drove out everything he had inherited from his mother and divested himself of the human nature he had received from her, even to the point that he was no longer her son: 2159, 2574, 2649, 3036, 10830. Jehovah, who was in him from conception, nevertheless seemed to be absent during his spiritual crises: 1815. This was his state of being humbled: 1785, 1999, 2159, 6866. His last spiritual crisis and final victory was in Gethsemane and on the cross, through which he completely overcame the hells and made his human nature divine: 2776, 2813, 2814, 10655, 10659, 10828.

Not eating bread and not drinking water for forty days [Exodus 34:28; Deuteronomy 9:9] means an entire state of spiritual crisis: 10686. Forty years, forty months, or forty days means a full state of spiritual crisis from beginning to end, and this state is meant by the forty-day duration of the Flood [Genesis 7:4, 17], by Moses' sojourn on Mount Sinai for forty days [Exodus 24:18; 34:28], by the Israelites' sojourn in the wilderness for forty years, and by the forty-day-long crisis the Lord experienced in the wilderness [Matthew 4:2; Mark 1:13; Luke 4:2]: 730, 862, 2272, 2273, 8098.

Baptism

202 BAPTISM was instituted as a sign that an individual belongs to the church and as a reminder that she or he needs to be regenerated. The washing of baptism is actually the spiritual washing that is regeneration.

203 All our regeneration is carried out by the Lord, by means of truths that belong to religious faith and by a life in accord with those truths. This means that baptism is a witness that an individual belongs to the church and is capable of being regenerated, because it is in the church that the Lord, who regenerates us, is acknowledged; and it is there that we find the Word, which contains the truths of religious faith that are required for our regeneration.

204 The Lord teaches us this in John: "Unless you have been born of water and the spirit you cannot enter the kingdom of God" (John 3:5). "Water," spiritually understood, is truth for our faith that is drawn from the Word, "the spirit" is a life in accord with that truth, and "being born" is being regenerated as a result of both.

205 Since everyone who is being regenerated also undergoes crises of the spirit, which are spiritual battles against evil and falsity, the waters of baptism also mean spiritual crises.

206 Since baptism serves as a sign and a reminder of all this, we can be baptized as infants or, if not then, as adults.

207 People who have been baptized should be aware that baptism itself does not give them either faith or salvation but it does bear witness that they will receive faith and be saved if they are regenerated.

208 We can therefore conclude what is meant by the Lord's words in Mark: "Those who believe and are baptized will be saved; but those who do not believe will be condemned" (Mark 16:16). The one who believes is the one who acknowledges the Lord and accepts divine truths from him through the Word; and the one who is baptized is the one whom the Lord regenerates by these means.

From *Secrets of Heaven*

BAPTISM means regeneration by the Lord by means of truths for our faith that are drawn from the Word: 4255, 5120, 9088, 10239, 10386, 10387, 10388, 10392. Baptism serves as a sign that an individual belongs to the church, where the Lord, who is the source of regeneration, is acknowledged; and where the Word is found, which is the source of the truths for our faith that are the means of our regeneration: 10386, 10387, 10388. Baptism does not give us either faith or salvation, but it bears witness to what we will receive if we are regenerated: 10391.

[2] The washing rituals in the ancient churches and in the Israelite church represented and therefore meant processes of purification from evil and falsity: 3147, 9088, 10237, 10239. The ritual washing of clothes meant purification of the understanding from falsities: 5954. The ritual washing of feet meant purification of the earthly self: 3147, 10241. An explanation of the meaning of the Lord's washing the disciples' feet [John 13:1–11]: 10243.

[3] Waters mean truths that belong to our religious faith: 28, 2702, 3058, 5668, 8568, 10238. Springs and wells of living water mean truths for our faith that come to us from the Lord; therefore they also mean the Word: 3424. Bread and water mean all the goodness that comes from love and all the truths that lead to faith: 4976, 9323. The spirit means a life in accord with truth or with faith: 5222, 9281, 9818. What spirit and flesh are: spirit means life that comes from the Lord and flesh means life that comes from ourselves: 10283. We can therefore see what these words of the Lord mean: "Unless you have been born of water and the spirit you cannot enter the kingdom of God" [John 3.5], namely, that unless we have been regenerated through truths that belong to our religious faith and a life in accord with them, we cannot be saved: 10240. All regeneration is effected by means of truths that belong to religious faith and by a life in accord with them: 1904, 2046, 9088, 9959, 10028.

[4] The complete washing that took place by immersion in the waters of the Jordan meant regeneration itself, just as baptism does: 9088, 10239. The meaning of the waters of the Jordan, and what the Jordan River means: 1585, 4255.

[5] A flood and an inundation of waters mean spiritual crises: 660, 705, 739, 756, 790, 5725, 6853. Baptism also symbolizes spiritual crises: 5120, 10389. How baptism was represented in heaven: 2299.

The Holy Supper

THE Holy Supper was instituted by the Lord so that through it the church would be joined to heaven and to himself. Therefore it is the holiest form of worship. **210**

However, people who do not know anything about the inner or spiritual meaning of the Word do not grasp how the Holy Supper accomplishes this joining together, because their thoughts do not go beyond the Word's outward meaning, which is its literal meaning. It is from the Word's inner or spiritual meaning that we know what is meant by the body and the blood, the bread and the wine, and eating. **211**

In the spiritual meaning, the Lord's body or flesh, like the bread, is the goodness of love, and the Lord's blood, like the wine, is the goodness of faith, while eating is our making these kinds of goodness our own and becoming joined to the Lord by them. This is how the angels who are with us when we are taking the Holy Supper understand it, because they perceive everything spiritually. Therefore holy love and holy faith flow into us from the angels—that is, through heaven from the Lord—at that time, and this brings about the partnership. **212**

We can see from this that when we take the bread, which is the body, we are joined to the Lord through the goodness of love for him that comes from him; and that when we take the wine, which is the blood, we are joined to the Lord through the goodness of faith in him that comes from him. **213**

It is important to know, however, that this being joined to the Lord through the sacrament of the Supper occurs only for people who are devoted to the goodness of love for the Lord and faith in the Lord that come from the Lord. For such people this joining together takes place through the Holy Supper; for others there is no joining together, but the Lord is nonetheless present with them.

Furthermore, the Holy Supper includes and encompasses all the worship of God instituted in the Israelite church. In fact, the burnt offerings and sacrifices that were central to the worship of that church were collectively referred to as "bread." The Holy Supper, then, also serves as the culmination of all those practices. **214**

From *Secrets of Heaven*

SINCE we cannot know what lies within the Holy Supper if we do not know the symbolism of its individual components (because these correspond to things that are spiritual), I need to present the meaning of "body" and "flesh," of "bread," of "wine," and of "eating" and "drinking," and also some material showing that the sacrifices that were central to the worship of the Israelite church were collectively referred to as "bread."

215   *Supper.* Midday meals and suppers symbolized the closeness love brings to us: 3596, 3832, 4745, 5161, 7996. The Passover supper symbolized the closeness love brings to those in heaven: 7836, 7997, 8001. The feast of unleavened bread or Passover symbolized our being freed by the Lord from damnation (7093, 7867, 9286–9292, 10655); in its inmost meaning it symbolized our calling to mind the glorification of the Lord's human nature, since his glorification made our liberation possible (10655).

216   *Body and flesh.* The Lord's flesh means the divine goodness of his divine love, which is a property of his divine-human nature: 3813, 7850, 9127, 10283. His body means the same thing: 2343, 3735, 6135. Flesh in general means our will and therefore our intrinsic characteristics, which in and of themselves are evil but which mean something good when they have been brought to life by the Lord: 148, 149, 780, 999, 3813, 8409, 10283. So flesh in the Word means the entire human race and every human being: 574, 1050, 10283.

The reason that here and in what follows I mention the *symbolism* of things is that this is their *correspondence;* the correspondence of things shapes their symbolism: 2179, 2896, 2987, 2989, 3002, 3225. The Word was written in pure correspondences, and that is the source of its inner or spiritual meaning. Without a knowledge of correspondences we cannot know what that meaning is—we can scarcely know that it exists: 3131, 3472–3485, 8615, 10687. It is through the Word, therefore, that heaven and the people of the church are joined together: 10687. You may find more on this subject in the book *Heaven and Hell* 303–310, where it deals with heaven's union with the people of the church through the Word.

217   *Blood.* The Lord's blood means the divine truth that emanates from the divine goodness of his divine love: 4735, 6978, 7317, 7326, 7846, 7850, 7877, 9127, 9393, 10026, 10033, 10152, 10210. The blood sprinkled all around on the altar and at its base meant the oneness of divine truth and divine goodness in the Lord: 10047. "The blood of grapes" [Genesis 49:11; Deuteronomy 32:14] means the truth that feeds our faith and originates in our caring actions: 6378. Grapes and clusters of grapes mean spiritual goodness, that is, goodness that comes from caring actions: 5117. The shedding of blood means doing violence to divine truth: 374, 1005, 4735, 5476, 9127. The meaning of the blood and water that came out of the Lord's side: 9127. The meaning of the Lord's redeeming the human race by his blood: 10152.

Bread. When the context concerns the Lord, "bread" means the divine goodness of his divine love, and also a reciprocal love for him in the people who "eat the bread": 2165, 2177, 3478, 3735, 3813, 4211, 4217, 4735, 4976, 9323, 9545. "Bread" in a general sense includes and means food of all kinds: 2165, 6118. "Food" means everything that nourishes our spiritual life: 4976, 5147, 5915, 6277, 8418. So "bread" means heavenly and spiritual food of all kinds (276, 680, 2165, 2177, 3478, 6118, 8410), and therefore, as the Lord says in Matthew 4:4, it means every word that proceeds from the mouth of God (681). In a general sense bread means good actions that come from love: 2165, 2177, 10686. Wheat, from which bread is made, has the same meaning: 3941, 7605. When the Word mentions bread and water, they mean good actions that come from love and truths that belong to our religious faith: 9323. In the ancient churches breaking bread represented mutual love: 5405. Spiritual food consists of knowledge, intelligence, and wisdom, and therefore of goodness and truth, because the former come from the latter (3114, 4459, 4792, 5147, 5293, 5340, 5342, 5410, 5426, 5576, 5582, 5588, 5655, 8562, 9003), and because knowledge, intelligence, and wisdom nourish the mind (4459, 5293, 5576, 6277, 8418). When someone in the Word is sustained by food, it means spiritual nourishment and the inflow of goodness and truth from the Lord: 4976, 5915, 6277.

[2] The bread on the table in the tabernacle meant the divine goodness of the Lord's divine love: 3478, 9545. The grain offerings in sacrifices, which took the form of unleavened cakes and wafers, meant worship from the goodness of love: 4581, 10079, 10137. The specific meanings of the grain offerings of various kinds: 7978, 9992, 9993, 9994, 10079.

[3] When the ancients spoke of bread in a general sense, they meant food of all kinds. See Genesis 43:16, 31; Exodus 18:12; Judges 13:15, 16; 1 Samuel 14:28, 29; 20:24, 27; 2 Samuel 9:7, 10; 1 Kings 4:22, 23; 2 Kings 25:29.

219   *Wine.* When the context concerns the Lord, "wine" means divine truth emanating from his divine goodness, as does "blood": 1071, 1798, 6377. Wine in a general sense means good actions that come from caring: 6377. "New wine" means truth in the earthly self that grows out of goodness: 3580. Wine was called "the blood of grapes": 6378. A vineyard means the church in respect to the truth it has: 3220, 9139. The drink offering in sacrificial rituals, which was wine, meant spiritual goodness, which is holy truth: 10137. The Lord alone is holy, so everything that is holy comes from him: 9229, 9680, 10359, 10360. The divine truth that emanates from the Lord is what is called "holy" in the Word: 6788, 8302, 9229, 9820, 10361.

220   *Eating and drinking.* "Eating" means making caring and love our own and being joined to the Lord by them: 2187, 2343, 3168, 3513, 5643. It therefore also means being associated with others: 8001. "Eating" is said of making goodness our own and its becoming a part of us, and "drinking" is said of making truth our own and its becoming a part of us: 3168, 3513, 3832, 9412. The meaning of "eating and drinking in the Lord's kingdom" [Luke 22:30]: 3832. That is why in the Word "being hungry and thirsty" means having a love and a longing for goodness and truth: 4958, 10227.

Because they live in a spiritual world, angels understand all the elements just discussed solely in an internal or spiritual way: 10521. Therefore something holy flows from heaven into people of the church when they take the sacrament of the Supper reverently (6789), and this joins them to the Lord (3464, 3735, 5915, 10519, 10521, 10522).

221   *Sacrifices.* Burnt offerings and sacrifices symbolized all worship that arises out of loving what is good and believing what is true: 923, 6905, 8680, 8936, 10042. Burnt offerings and sacrifices symbolized the divine heavenly qualities that are the inner characteristics of the church and give rise to its worship (2180, 2805, 2807, 2830, 3519); various different qualities were reflected in the different rituals (2805, 6905, 8936). So there were many kinds of sacrifices, which involved different processes and different animals: 2830, 9959, 9990. The general meaning of the differences can be determined by unfolding the inner meaning of the details: 10042. The specific meanings of the animals that were sacrificed: 10042. There are secrets of heaven contained in the sacrificial rituals and processes: 10057. In general, they contain secrets about the glorification of the Lord's human nature; and in an analogous sense they contain secrets about our own regeneration and purification from evil and falsity, so the sacrifices were for various kinds of sin, guilt, and purification: 9990, 10022, 10042, 10053, 10057. The meaning of laying hands on the animals that were about to be sacrificed: 10023. The meaning of placing the lower parts of the slaughtered animals on top of their higher parts in burnt offerings: 10051. The meaning of the grain offerings, which were then also burned: 10079. The meaning of the drink offering: 4581, 10137. The meaning of salt, which was also used in sacrifices: 10300. The meaning of the altar and all its features: 921, 2777, 2784, 2811, 2812, 4489, 4541, 8935, 8940, 9388, 9389, 9714, 9720, 9963, 9964, 10028, 10123, 10151, 10242, 10245, 10344. The meaning of the fire on the altar: 934, 6314, 6832. The meaning of eating consecrated food: 2187, 8682. Proof from the Word that sacrifices were not actually commanded, and that caring and faith were what was commanded, so sacrifices were only tolerated: 922, 2180. Why they were tolerated: 2180, 2818.

[2] The burnt offerings and sacrifices (which were performed using lambs, she-goats, sheep, kids, he-goats, calves, and oxen) were collectively referred to as "bread," as can be seen in the following passages:

The priest will burn them on the altar as *the bread of an offering made by fire to Jehovah*. (Leviticus 3:11, 16)

The sons of Aaron will be holy to their God and will not profane the name of their God, because they are offering offerings to Jehovah made by fire, *the bread of their God*. You will consecrate him, because he is offering *the bread of your God*. No man among Aaron's descendants who has any defect may approach to offer *the bread of his God*. (Leviticus 21:6, 8, 17, 21)

Command the children of Israel and say to them, "My offering, *my bread*, made by fire as a restful aroma, you must be careful to offer to me at their appointed time." (Numbers 28:2)

Those who have touched something unclean are not to eat the holy offerings, but are to wash their bodies with water. Afterward they may eat the holy offerings, because *these are their bread*. (Leviticus 22:6, 7)

You offer *defiled bread* on my altar. (Malachi 1:7)

This is the reason for what was said in §214 above:

The Holy Supper includes and encompasses all the worship of God instituted in the Israelite church. In fact, the burnt offerings and sacrifices that were central to the worship of that church were collectively referred to as "bread." The Holy Supper, then, also serves as the culmination of all those practices.

[3] All of this makes it possible for us to see what is meant by the bread in John:

> Jesus said to them, "Truly, truly I say to you, Moses did not give you *bread from heaven,* but my Father gives you *the true bread from heaven. The bread of God is* the one who comes down from heaven and gives life to the world." They said to him, "Lord, always give us *this bread.*" Jesus said to them, "*I am the bread of life.* Those who come to me will not hunger, and those who believe in me will never thirst. Those who believe in me have eternal life. *I am the bread of life. This is the bread* that comes down from heaven so that anyone who eats of it will not die. *I am the living bread* that came down from heaven. Anyone who eats *this bread* will live forever." (John 6:31–35, 47–51)

We can see from these passages that "bread" is everything good that emanates from the Lord, since the Lord himself is present in the goodness that comes from him. So we can see that the bread and the wine in the Holy Supper mean all worship of the Lord that arises out of the goodness of love and of faith.

222 Here I would like to add something from *Secrets of Heaven* 9127.

> People who know nothing about the Word's inner or spiritual meaning cannot help thinking that "flesh" and "blood" in the Word actually mean flesh and blood. The inner or spiritual meaning, however, is not about the life of the body but about the life of our soul— that is, our spiritual life, which we are going to live to eternity. In the literal meaning of the Word this life is described in terms of physical life, in terms of flesh and blood; and since our spiritual life is maintained by good things that we do out of love and the truth that belongs to our religious faith, in the inner meaning of the Word "flesh" means these good things done out of love, and "blood" means this truth of our faith. That is what "flesh" and "blood" are taken to mean in heaven. This is also what "bread" and "wine" mean, since in heaven "bread" has exactly the same meaning as "flesh," and "wine" has exactly the same meaning as "blood."

> Now, people who are not spiritual do not grasp this, so it is acceptable for them to continue in the beliefs they have, as long as they believe there is something holy in the Holy Supper and in the Word because

these come from the Lord. Even though they do not know where this "something holy" is, if they are gifted with some inner perception let them ponder whether "flesh" means flesh and "blood" means blood in the following passages. From the Book of Revelation:

> I saw an angel standing in the sun; and he cried with a loud voice, saying to all the birds that fly in the midst of heaven, "Gather together for the supper of the great God, so that you may eat the flesh of monarchs and the flesh of commanders, the flesh of the mighty, the flesh of horses and of those who ride on them, and the flesh of all people, free and slaves, both small and great." (Revelation 19:17, 18)

What would anyone make of this who does not know the inner meaning of flesh and the inner meaning of monarchs, commanders, the mighty, horses, those who ride on them, the free, and slaves? And in Ezekiel:

> Thus says the Lord Jehovih, "Say to every bird of heaven and to every beast of the field, 'Gather and come. Gather yourselves from all around for my sacrifice, which I am sacrificing for you, a great sacrifice on the mountains of Israel, so that you may eat flesh and drink blood. You will eat the flesh of the mighty and drink the blood of the rulers of the earth. You will eat fat until you are full and drink blood until you are drunk, from my sacrifice, which I will sacrifice for you. At my table you will eat your fill of horses and chariots and the mighty and every man of war. This is how I will establish my glory among the nations.'" (Ezekiel 39:17, 18, 19, 20, 21)

This is about calling everyone to the Lord's kingdom, and is specifically about the establishment of the church among non-Christians; "eating flesh and drinking blood" means their taking into themselves divine goodness and divine truth—therefore something holy that emanates from the Lord's divine-human nature. When it speaks about "eating the flesh of the mighty," "drinking the blood of rulers," and "drinking blood until we are drunk," can anyone fail to see that "flesh" here does not mean flesh and that "blood" does not mean blood? Who cannot see that "eating our fill of horses and chariots and the mighty and every man of war" is not to be taken literally? As for the spiritual meaning of "the birds of heaven and the beasts of the field," see *Heaven and Hell* 110 and footnote c there.

Now consider what the Lord said in John about his own flesh and blood:

> The bread that I will give is my flesh. Truly, truly I say to you, unless you eat the flesh of the Son of Humanity and drink his blood, you will not have life within you. Those who eat my flesh and drink my blood have eternal life; I will raise them up on the last day. My flesh is true food and my blood is true drink. Those who eat my flesh and drink my blood live in me and I in them. This is the bread that came down from heaven. (John 6:51–58)

The fact that the Lord's flesh means divine goodness and that his blood means divine truth, both of which come from him, can be seen from consideration that these are what nourish our spiritual life. This is why it says that "my flesh is true food and my blood is true drink"; and because we are joined to the Lord by means of divine goodness and truth, it also says, "Those who eat my flesh and drink my blood have eternal life" and "live in me and I in them"; and earlier in the chapter we are told, "Do not work for the food that perishes, but for the food that endures to eternal life" (John 6:27). The Lord himself tells us in John 15:2–12 that "abiding in the Lord" is abiding in a love for him.

Resurrection

WE are created in such a way that as far as our inner being is concerned we cannot die. This is because we can believe in God and can also love God; so we can be joined to God by faith and love, and to be joined to God is to live forever. **223**

Everyone who is born has this "inner being." Our outer being is our inner being's means of carrying out the intentions of its faith and love. **224**

The inner being is what we call "the spirit," and the outer being is what we call "the body." The outer being, called the body, is adapted to functioning in an earthly world. It is cast off when we die. But the inner being, called the spirit, is adapted to functioning in a spiritual world. It does not die. If we have been a good person in this world, our inner being is then a good spirit and an angel; if we have been an evil person in this world, our inner being is then an evil spirit.

After the death of the body, our spirit has a human form that is visible in the spiritual world, just as it had a human form that was visible in this world. Our spirit enjoys the abilities to see, hear, speak, and have sensations, just as it did in this world, and is endowed with every faculty of thinking, willing, and doing, just as it was in this world. In a word, we are human beings in absolutely every respect, except that we are not clothed with the dense body we wore in this world. That we leave behind when we die, and we never put it back on. **225**

This continuation of our life is what is meant by "the resurrection." The reason people believe that they will not be resurrected until the Last Judgment, when the whole visible world is allegedly going to perish, is that they have not understood the Word. It is also because sense-oriented people locate life in the body and believe that unless their bodies are revived it will be all over for them. **226**

Our life after death is the life of our love and our faith, so the kind of love and faith we have when we live in this world determines the kind of life that will be ours to eternity. It is a life of hell for people who have loved themselves and the world above all, but it is a life of heaven for people who have loved God above all and their neighbor as themselves. The latter are the ones who have faith; the former do not. **227**

The life of heaven is what is called "eternal life." The life of hell is what is called "spiritual death."

228   The Word tells us that we live after death. It says, for example, that God is not the God of the dead but of the living (Matthew 22:32); that Lazarus was carried up into heaven after his death, but the rich man was cast down into hell (Luke 16:22, 23, and following); that Abraham, Isaac, and Jacob are in heaven (Matthew 8:11; 22:31, 32; Luke 20:37, 38); and that Jesus said to the thief, "Today you will be with me in paradise" (Luke 23:43).

229   THERE is no need to cite anything from *Secrets of Heaven* here, since there is a full presentation of information about our resurrection and life after death in *Heaven and Hell*. See, then, the following chapters in that book.

On the Last Judgment (mentioned in §226 above), and the fact that it is not going to involve the destruction of the world, see the booklet *The Last Judgment and Babylon Destroyed*, from beginning to end.

Heaven and Hell

THERE are two elements that constitute our spiritual life: love and **230** faith. Love constitutes the life of our will and faith constitutes the life of our understanding. A love of what is good and a consequent faith in what is true make up the life of heaven, and a love of what is evil and a consequent faith in what is false make up the life of hell.

Love for the Lord and love for one's neighbor constitute heaven. **231** Faith, too, constitutes heaven, but only to the extent that we lead our lives according to it. Further, since both love and the faith that goes with it come from the Lord, we can see that the Lord himself constitutes heaven.

For each of us, heaven is within us to the extent that we accept love **232** and faith from the Lord; and if we accept love and faith from the Lord while we are living in this world, we enter heaven after death.

The people who accept heaven from the Lord are the ones who have **233** heaven within themselves, because heaven is within us. This is what the Lord teaches us:

> They will not say, "See, the kingdom of God is here!" or "See, it is there!" Behold, the kingdom of God is within you. (Luke 17:21)

The heaven that is within us is in our inner self. It is present in our **234** willing and thinking from love and faith. As a result it is also present in our outer self, in which we act and speak from love and faith. Heaven is not, however, present in our outer self apart from our inner self; after all, every hypocrite can do and say good things without willing and thinking good things.

When we arrive in the other life, which happens immediately after **235** death, others can see whether heaven is within us, though this is not visible while we are living in this world. You see, what shows in this world is our outer self, not our inner self, while in the other life our inner self appears because then we are living as spirits.

Eternal happiness, which is also called heavenly joy, is given to people **236** who live and walk in a love for the Lord that comes from the Lord and a faith in him that comes from him. This love and faith have heavenly joy within them. If we have heaven within ourselves we come into heavenly joy after death; until then it lies hidden in our inner self.

There is in heaven a sharing of everything that is good. The peace, intelligence, wisdom, and happiness of all are shared with every individual there, though the individuals' capacity for it is determined by the amount of love and faith they have accepted from the Lord. This shows how much peace, intelligence, wisdom, and happiness there is in heaven.

237 Just as love for the Lord and love for our neighbor constitute a life of heaven for us, so love for ourselves and love for the world, when they are in control, constitute a life of hell for us, because these latter loves are the opposites of the former. So people whose love for themselves and love for the world are in control are incapable of accepting anything from heaven. What they accept comes from hell. Whatever we love and whatever we believe comes either from heaven or from hell.

238 People in whom love for themselves and love for the world are in control do not realize what heaven and heavenly happiness are. They cannot believe that happiness can be found in any kind of love other than self-love and love for the world. Yet the fact is that we feel the happiness of heaven to the extent that we put these loves aside as our goals. After these loves have been put aside, the happiness that follows is so great that it is beyond human comprehension.

239 Our life cannot be changed after death. It retains the nature it had, because the nature of our spirit depends entirely on what our love is like, and a hellish love cannot be transformed into a heavenly one, because they are opposites. This is the meaning of what Abraham said to the rich man in hell: "Between you and us there is a great gulf, so that those who want to cross over to you cannot, and neither can those from there cross over to us" (Luke 16:26). This shows that people who enter hell stay there to eternity and people who enter heaven stay there to eternity.

240 SINCE heaven and hell have been the subject of a whole book, and relevant material from *Secrets of Heaven* has been cited there, there is no need to add more here.

The Church

WHAT constitutes heaven for us also constitutes the church; just as **241** love and faith constitute heaven, so too love and faith constitute the church. So we can see what the church is from what has already been said about heaven [§§230–240].

The term "church" is applied to the regions where the Lord is acknowl- **242** edged and the Word exists, since the essentials of the church are a love for the Lord that comes from the Lord and a faith in the Lord that comes from the Lord, and the Word teaches us how we need to live in order to receive this love and faith from the Lord.

For a church to exist there also needs to be a body of teaching based **243** on the Word, since without one the Word is not understood. Such teachings alone, however, do not constitute a church for us—that requires living in accordance with such teachings. It therefore follows that faith by itself does not constitute the church, but a church requires living according to faith, which means caring.

A genuine body of teaching is one focused on caring and faith together and not one focused on faith by itself. Clearly, a body of teaching focused on caring and faith together is about how to live, while a body of teaching focused on faith that does not include teachings focused on caring is not.

People outside the church who acknowledge one God and in accor- **244** dance with their religion devote their lives in some way to caring about their neighbor have something in common with people in the church, because no one who believes in God and lives a good life is damned. This shows that although the Lord's church takes a particular form where the Lord is acknowledged and the Word is found, it actually exists everywhere in the whole world.

Everyone in whom the church exists is saved and everyone in whom **245** the church does not exist is damned.

From *Secrets of Heaven*

246 THE church takes a particular form where the Word exists and the Lord is known by means of it, and therefore where divine truths have been revealed: 3857, 10761. Still, though, this does not mean that people are part of the church by merely being born where the Word exists and the Lord is known; people are part of the church only if they are being regenerated by the Lord by means of truths from the Word—that is, they are living caring lives: 6637, 10143, 10153, 10578, 10645, 10829. People who are of the church—that is, people who have the church within themselves—are drawn to the truth for its own sake; that is, they love what is true because it is true. They also search the Word to find out whether the teachings of the church in which they were born are true: 5432, 6047. Otherwise everyone's religion could be declared true merely because someone else said so or because it was the religion of the person's native soil: 6047.

[2] The Lord's church includes all people in the world who are living a good life according to their own religion: 3263, 6637, 10765. All the people who live good lives and acknowledge one God, no matter where they are, are accepted by the Lord and come into heaven. This is because everyone who is devoted to doing good recognizes the Lord, since goodness comes from the Lord and the Lord is present in it: 2589–2604, 2861, 2863, 3263, 4190, 4197, 6700, 9256. In the Lord's view, the whole church throughout the globe is like one human being: 7396, 9276. He sees heaven the same way, since the church is heaven, or the Lord's kingdom, on earth: 2853, 2996, 2998, 3624–3649, 3636–3643, 3741–3745, 4625. However, the church where the Lord is known and the Word exists is like the heart and like the lungs in us relative to the rest of our body, which lives from them as the wellsprings of its life: 637, 931, 2054, 2853. This is why the human race could not be saved if there were no church where the Word exists and the Lord is known by means of it: 468, 637, 931, 4545, 10452. The church is the foundation of heaven: 4060.

[3] There is an inner church and an outer church: 1242, 6587, 9375, 9680, 10762. The inner aspect of the church is love for the Lord and caring about one's neighbor; therefore people who are drawn to what is good and true because they love the Lord and care about their neighbor constitute the inner church, while people who practice outward worship as a matter of

obedience and faith constitute the outer church: 1083, 1098, 4288, 6380, 6587, 7840, 8762. Knowing what is true and good and acting on that basis is the outer form of the church; willing and loving what is true and good and acting on that basis is the inner form of the church: 4899, 6775. The inner church is present within the worship of people who are part of the outer church, but only dimly present: 6775. The inner church and the outer church together make one church: 409, 10762. Each individual has an inner self and an outer self, the inner in the image of heaven and the outer in the image of this world. So for anyone to be a church, the outer self must act in unity with the inner self: 3628, 4523, 4524, 6013, 6057, 9706, 10472. The church resides in the inner self and at the same time in the outer self, but not in the outer self apart from the inner self: 1795, 6581, 10691. The condition of our inner church depends on the nature and quality of the truths we have, and on the extent to which they have been rooted in goodness by the way we live: 10460.

[4] The church, like heaven, is within us as individuals, so the church in general is made up of people who have the church within themselves: 3884. For a church to exist there needs to be a body of teaching focused on how to live, that is, on caring: 3445, 10763, 10764. Caring constitutes the church, not faith apart from caring (916); so what is needed is not a body of teaching focused on faith apart from caring but one focused on faith joined to caring, together with a life in accordance with that teaching (809, 1798, 1799, 1834, 1844, 4468, 4672, 4683, 4766, 5826, 6637). There is no church within us unless the truths we have been taught are grounded in good actions from a caring heart, and therefore grounded in the way we live: 3310, 3963, 5826. There is no church in us if all we care about are the truths that we call matters of faith: 5826. How good the church would be if it put caring first and faith second (6269); and how evil the church is when it puts faith first (6272). In the ancient churches caring was the primary and essential focus of the church: 4680. If everyone were devoted to caring, the church would be like heaven: 2385, 2853. If goodness were the hallmark of the church and not truth apart from goodness—that is, if caring rather than faith alone played this role—then the church would be one and would attach no importance to differences in particular tenets of faith or outward forms of worship: 1285, 1316, 2982, 3267, 3445, 3451.

[5] Every church begins with a focus on caring, but in the course of time strays from it (494, 501, 1327, 3773, 4689), and turns instead toward falsities born of evil and eventually to evils themselves (1834, 1835,

2910, 4683, 4689). A comparison of the rise and fall of a church with the infancy and old age of an individual (10134) and also with sunrise and sunset (1837). A discussion of the successive states of the Christian church all the way to its last, including an explanation of the Lord's predictions in the twenty-fourth chapter of Matthew, from beginning to end, about the close of the age and his Coming: 3353–3356, 3486–3489, 3650–3655, 3751–3757, 3897–3901, 4057–4060, 4229–4231, 4332–4335, 4422–4424, 4635–4638, 4807–4810, 4954–4959, 5063–5071. The Christian church is now at its last days, because it has lost its faith as a result of losing its caring: 3489, 4689. The "Last Judgment" is the last time of a church: 2118, 3353, 4057, 4333, 4535. On the final devastation of the church: 407–411. The "close of the age" and the "Coming of the Lord" is the end of an old church and the beginning of a new one: 2243, 4535, 10622. Profound truths are revealed as an old church is undergoing its final devastation, for the service of the new church that is then being raised up: 3398, 3786. On the raising up of a church among non-Christians: 1366, 2986, 4747, 9256.

247   *The ancient churches.* The first and earliest church on this planet was the one described in the first chapters of Genesis; it was a heavenly church, the finest of them all: 607, 895, 920, 1121, 1122, 1123, 1124, 2896, 4493, 8891, 9942, 10545. What the people of the earliest church are like in heaven: 1114–1125. They live in the best light: 1116, 1117. There were several churches after the Flood, which are collectively referred to as "the ancient church": 1126, 1127, 1128, 1327, 10355 (which contain further discussion of these churches). The ancient church was spread across all the countries of the Middle East: 1238, 2385. What the people of the ancient church were like: 609, 895. The ancient church was a church of symbolism; the symbols it used had been gathered together by certain people of the earliest church: 519, 521, 2896. There was a Word in the ancient church, but it has been lost: 2897. What the ancient church was like when it began to go into decline: 1128. The difference between the earliest church and the ancient church: 597, 607, 640, 641, 765, 784, 895, 4493. The earliest and ancient churches were present in the land of Canaan, and this is the source of the symbolism of its particular places: 3686, 4447, 4454. On the church that began with Eber and was called "the Hebrew church": 1238, 1241, 1343, 4516, 4517. The difference between the ancient church and the Hebrew church: 1343, 4874. The Hebrew nation began the practice of ritual sacrifices, a practice utterly unknown to the ancient churches: 1343. The inward aspects of the ancient churches agree with those of the Christian church, but the outward aspects do not: 3478,

4489, 4772, 4904, 10149. In the earliest church, revelation was direct; in the ancient church it came through correspondences; in the Jewish church it came by audible speech; and in the Christian church it came through the Word: 10355. The Lord was the God of the earliest church and was known as Jehovah: 1343, 6846. The Lord is heaven, and the Lord is the church: 4766, 10125, 10151, 10157. On the fact that the Lord's divine nature makes heaven, see *Heaven and Hell* 7–12, 78–86; so it also makes the church, since what makes heaven for us also makes the church, as stated earlier in these teachings [§§60, 241].

The Jewish church and Jews. The statutes, judgments, and laws that were commanded in the Jewish church were somewhat like those of the ancient church: 4449, 4834. How the symbolic rites of the Jewish church differed from the symbolic rites of the ancient church: 4288, 10149. A symbolic church was established for the people of that nation, but there was no real church among them: 4899, 4912, 6304. So they had something that symbolized a church but not an actual church: 4281, 4288, 4311, 4500, 6304, 7048, 9320, 10396, 10526, 10531, 10698. Because of the stubborn insistence of their ancestors and Moses, the Israelite and Jewish people were accepted as a church, not because they actually were a chosen people but rather so that they would symbolize a church: 4290, 4293, 7051, 7439, 10430, 10535, 10632. Their worship was solely external, without any inner worship: 1200, 3147, 3479, 8871. They knew absolutely nothing about inner worship and did not want to know: 301, 302, 303, 3479, 4429, 4433, 4680, 4844, 4847, 10396, 10401, 10407, 10694, 10701, 10707. What they thought of the inner aspects of worship, the church, and the Word: 4865. Their inner natures were foul, full of their love for themselves and the world and of avarice: 3480, 9962, 10454–10457, 10462–10466, 10575. Therefore the inner teachings of the church were not disclosed to them, because otherwise they would have defiled them: 2520, 3398, 3480, 4289. The Word was completely closed to them: 3769. They saw the Word from the outside and not from the inside (10549, 10550, 10551), so their inner self was closed when they were engaged in worship (8788, 8806, 9320, 9377, 9380, 9962, 10396, 10401, 10407, 10492, 10498, 10500, 10575, 10629, 10692). All the same, this people was more capable than any other of being outwardly holy despite the fact that their inner self was closed: 4293, 4311, 4903, 9373, 9377, 9380. Their state at such times: 4311. That is also why they have been preserved to this day: 3479. Their holy outward behavior was miraculously raised up and exhibited to heaven by the Lord, and as a result deeper levels of worship, the church, and the Word were perceived there: 3480, 4307, 4311, 6304, 8588, 10499, 10500, 10602. So that this could happen, they were driven by external pressures to a strict observance of their rituals in outward form: 3147, 4281, 8006. Because they could be outwardly holy without inner holiness, they were able to represent what is truly holy in the church and heaven: 3479, 3881, 4208, 6304, 8588, 9377, 10430, 10500, 10570. Nevertheless, they were not interested in what is truly holy: 3479. It does not matter what a person who symbolizes something is like, because symbolism focuses on the issue and not on the person: 665, 1097, 1361, 3147, 3881, 4208, 4281, 4288, 4292, 4500, 6304, 7048, 7439, 8588, 8788, 8806.

[2] Those people were worse than other peoples; a description of what they were like, including material from the Word of both Testaments: 4314, 4316, 4317, 4444, 4503, 4750, 4751, 4815, 4820, 4832, 5057, 5998, 7248, 8819, 9320, 10454–10457, 10462–10466. The tribe of Judah strayed more than the other tribes: 4815. How they took pleasure in cruelly treating other peoples: 5057, 7248, 9320. That people was idolatrous at heart and worshiped other gods more than other peoples did: 3732, 4208, 4281, 4825, 5998, 6877, 7401, 8301, 8871, 8882. Even their worship, seen in the context of that people, was idolatrous, since it was superficial, with no inner substance: 4281, 4825, 8871, 8882. They worshiped Jehovah in name only (6877, 10559, 10560, 10561, 10566), and only because of the miracles he did (4299). It is incorrect to think that the Jews are going to be converted at the end of the church and brought back into the land of Canaan: 4847, 7051, 8301. A copious selection of passages from the Word on this subject—passages that are, however, to be understood in their inner meaning and therefore not taken literally: 7051. The Word was changed in its outer meaning because of that people, but not in its inner meaning: 10453, 10461, 10603, 10604. The way Jehovah appeared to them on Mount Sinai was shaped by their own nature, so he appeared in devouring fire, thick cloud, and smoke like that of a furnace: 1861, 6832, 8814, 8819, 9434. The way the Lord appears to each of us depends on what we ourselves are really like—as a life-giving and creative fire if we are devoted to doing good, but as a devouring fire if we are bent on doing evil: 934, 1861, 6832, 8814, 8819, 9434, 10551. One lineage of that people was of Canaanite ancestry and two others were the result of fornication with a daughter-in-law: 1167, 4818, 4820, 4874, 4899, 4913. Those stories represent the nature of their relationship with the inner truth of the church, namely, that it was like that of union with a Canaanite or fornication with a daughter-in-law: 4868, 4874, 4899, 4913. Their state in the other life: 939, 940, 5057.

[3] Because despite all this that people symbolized the church, and because the Word was composed among and about them, their names—for example, Reuben, Simeon, Levi, Judah, Ephraim, Joseph, and the rest—have divine and heavenly meanings. In its inner meaning, "Judah" means the Lord in respect to his heavenly love and his heavenly kingdom: 3654, 3881, 5583, 5603, 5782, 6363. An explanation of Israel's prophecy concerning Judah in Genesis 49:8–12, which is about the Lord: 6362–6381. Both the tribe of Judah and Judea mean the heavenly church: 3654, 6364. The twelve tribes represented and meant all the aspects of love and faith taken together (3858, 3926, 4060, 6335), and therefore heaven and the church as well (6337, 6637, 7836, 7891). Their meanings depend on the order in which they are named: 3862, 3926, 3939, 4603 and following, 6337, 6640. The twelve tribes were divided into two kingdoms so that the Judeans could represent the heavenly kingdom and the Israelites could represent the spiritual kingdom: 3654, 8770. The seed of Abraham, Isaac, and Jacob means the goodness and truth that belong to the church: 3373, 10445.

Sacred Scripture, or the Word

249 WITHOUT revelation from the Divine, we cannot know anything about eternal life or even about God, and even less about love for God and faith in God. This is because we are born into utter ignorance and have to learn from worldly sources everything that gives form to our understanding. It is also because by heredity we are born with evils of every kind, which come from love for ourselves and for the world. These loves give rise to pleasures that retain constant control over us and prompt us to think things that are diametrically opposed to the Divine. This, then, is why we know nothing about eternal life; so there must of necessity be some revelation that makes it possible for us to know.

250 If we consider people in the church, we can see very clearly that the evils of love for ourselves and for the world bring about this kind of ignorance about eternal life. Even though people in the church are informed from revelation that God exists, that heaven and hell are real, that there is an eternal life, and that this eternal life is gained by doing good things that are inspired by love and faith, still they fall into denial; and the educated are as prone to this denial as the uneducated.

This shows how great the ignorance would be if there were no revelation.

251 So since we live after death and our life after death is eternal, and since the particular life that lies ahead for us is based on the state of our love and faith, it follows that the Divine, out of love for the whole human race, has revealed the kinds of things that will guide us toward that life and be beneficial to our salvation.

In the Christian world, what the Divine has revealed for us is the Word.

252 Since the Word is a revelation from the Divine, it is divine in every detail. This is because whatever comes from the Divine cannot be otherwise.

Whatever comes from the Divine comes down to us through the heavens, so in the heavens it is adapted to the wisdom of the angels who live there, and on earth it is adapted to the grasp of the people who live here. Consequently, the Word has an inner meaning, which is spiritual and intended for angels, and an outer meaning, which is earthly and intended for us. For this reason it is the Word that joins heaven and us together.

The true meaning of the Word is understood only by those who are **253** enlightened, and we are enlightened only when we are devoted to loving the Lord and having faith in him. In that case our inner levels are lifted into the light of heaven by the Lord.

The Word in its letter cannot be understood properly except by **254** means of a body of teaching drawn from the Word by an enlightened person. Its literal meaning has been accommodated so that it is possible even for those with no education to comprehend it; therefore [to find their way to a truer understanding] they need a body of teaching drawn from the Word to serve as a lamp.

From *Secrets of Heaven*

*T*HE *necessity and excellence of the Word.* From earthly light, we know **255** nothing about the Lord, heaven and hell, our life after death, or the divine truths that are essential for our spiritual and eternal life: 8944, 10318, 10319, 10320. Evidence for this is the fact that many people, including scholars, do not believe in these things even though they were born where the Word is present and have been taught from it about these matters: 10319. That is why it became necessary for there to be some revelation from heaven, since we are born for heaven: 1775. For this reason there has been a revelation in every era: 2895. Information about the various kinds of revelation in this world over time: 10355, 10632. The earliest people, the ones who lived before the Flood, whose era was called the Golden Age, had direct revelation and therefore had divine truth written on their hearts: 2896. The ancient churches that existed after the Flood had a Word containing both historical and prophetic material: 2686, 2897. (On these churches, see §247 above.) Its historical materials were called *The Wars of Jehovah* and its prophetic materials were called *Pronouncements:* 2897. This Word was like our own Word as far as its inspiration was concerned: 2897. It was mentioned by Moses: 2686, 2897. However, this Word has been lost: 2897. There were also prophetic revelations among other peoples, as we can see from Balaam's prophecies [Numbers 23–24]: 2898.

[2] The Word is divine throughout and in every detail: 639, 3305, 10321, 10637. The Word is divine and holy down to the smallest letters and the tip of every letter: 9349 (which includes evidence from eyewitness experience). How people nowadays explain the claim that the Word is inspired down to the smallest letters: 1886.

[3] The church takes a particular form where the Word exists and the Lord is known by means of it, and therefore where divine truths have been revealed: 3857, 10761. Still, though, this does not mean that people are part of the church by merely being born where the Word exists and the Lord is known by means of it; people are part of the church only if they are being regenerated by the Lord by means of truths from the Word—that is, they are living lives of love and faith: 6637, 10143, 10153, 10578, 10645, 10829.

256   *The Word is understood only by people who are enlightened.* Our rational capacity cannot grasp things that are divine; it cannot even grasp things that are spiritual unless it is enlightened by the Lord: 2196, 2203, 2209, 2654. This means that only enlightened people can understand the Word: 10323. The Lord makes it possible for people who are enlightened to understand what is true and to sort out things in the Word that seem contradictory: 9382, 10659. Understood on a literal level, the Word is not consistent and often seems self-contradictory (9025); therefore people who are not enlightened can interpret it and constrain it to support all kinds of opinions and heresies and to favor all kinds of worldly and bodily loves (4783, 10330, 10400). We gain enlightenment from the Word if we read it out of a love for what is true and good, but not if we read it out of a love for fame, profit, or prestige, and therefore out of a love for ourselves: 9382, 10548, 10549, 10550. We are enlightened if we are committed to living good lives and therefore are affected by what is true: 8694. We are enlightened if our inner self has been opened—that is, if our inner self is capable of being raised into heaven's light: 10400, 10402, 10691, 10694. Enlightenment is an actual opening of the deeper reaches of our minds as well as a raising of them into heaven's light: 10330. If we regard the Word as holy, then without our knowing it something holy flows in from within us—that is, through our inner self from the Lord: 6789. We are enlightened and see truths in the Word if we are being led by the Lord, but not if we are leading ourselves: 10638. We are being led by the Lord when we love what is true because it is true; that is, when we love to live by divine truths: 10578,

10645, 10829. The Word is brought to life for us depending on the amount of life there is in our love and faith: 1776. The products of a self-oriented intelligence have no life in them, because nothing good comes from our self-centeredness: 8941, 8944. We cannot be enlightened if we have thoroughly convinced ourselves of false teachings: 10640.

[2] It is our understanding that is enlightened (6608, 9300), because it is our understanding that receives truth (6222, 6608, 10659). For every teaching of the church, how well we understand it depends on the nature of the concepts we have of it: 3310, 3825. As long as we are living in this world, our concepts are earthly because we are thinking on an earthly level. However, there are spiritual concepts hidden within them if we are passionately interested in the truth for its own sake: 10236, 10240, 10551. If we cannot conceive of something, we cannot comprehend it, either: 3825. Our concepts of matters of faith are disclosed in the other life, and angels there see what our concepts are like: 1869, 3310, 5510, 6200, 6201, 8885. This means that the Word is understood only by rational people, since without some concept of a subject and some rational insight, "believing" is only keeping in our memory some statement that we do not comprehend or love. This is not believing: 2533. It is the literal meaning of the Word that is enlightened for us: 3436, 9824, 9905, 10548.

The Word is understood only by means of a body of teaching drawn from the Word. The church's body of teaching must be drawn from the Word: 3464, 5402, 5432, 10763, 10765. Without a body of teaching, the Word is not intelligible: 9025, 9409, 9424, 9430, 10324, 10431, 10582. A true body of teaching is a lamp for us when we read the Word: 10400. Any authentic body of teaching must come from people who are enlightened by the Lord: 2510, 2516, 2519, 9424, 10105. The Word is to be understood by means of a body of teaching constructed by someone who is enlightened: 10324. People in a state of enlightenment construct a body of teaching for themselves from the Word: 9382, 10659. The nature of the difference between people who teach and learn on the basis of the church's body of teaching and those who do so solely on the basis of the literal meaning: 9025. People who are focused on the literal meaning without having a body of teaching do not arrive at any understanding of divine truths: 9409, 9410, 10582. They fall into many errors: 10431. When people who have a passionate interest in the truth for its own sake reach adulthood and can see things with their own understanding, they do not simply rest in the theological tenets of their church but check them carefully against the Word to see whether they are true: 5402, 5432, 6047. Otherwise, what

257

everyone believes could be declared true merely because someone else said so or because it was the religion of the person's native soil, whether that person was born Jewish or Greek: 6047. Nevertheless, principles that have become matters of faith on the basis of the Word's literal meaning should not be eliminated unless they have been fully examined: 9039.

[2] The church's true body of teaching is made up of teachings focused on caring and faith: 2417, 4766, 10763, 10764. What makes a church is not a body of teaching about faith but living according to faith, which means caring: 809, 1798, 1799, 1834, 4468, 4672, 4766, 5826, 6637. A body of teaching is nothing unless its teachings are lived: 1515, 2049, 2116. In today's churches there is a body of teaching focused on faith and not on caring, and the body of teaching focused on caring has been consigned to the discipline known as moral theology: 2417. The church would be united if individuals were recognized as members of the church on the basis of their lives and therefore of their caring: 1285, 1316, 2982, 3267, 3445, 3451, 3452. How much more valid a body of teaching focused on caring is than a body of teaching focused on faith separated from caring: 4844. If we know nothing about caring, then we know nothing about heaven: 4783. How many errors people fall into if they have a body of teaching focused only on faith and not on caring at the same time: 2383, 2417, 3146, 3325, 3412, 3413, 3416, 3773, 4672, 4730, 4783, 4925, 5351, 7623–7627, 7752–7762, 7790, 8094, 8313, 8530, 8765, 9186, 9224, 10555. [In the ancient church,] people who were devoted to teachings on faith but not to living according to faith, which means caring, were called "the uncircumcised" or "Philistines": 3412, 3413, 8093. The early people had a body of teaching focused on love for the Lord and caring about their neighbor, and their teachings about faith were subsidiary to it: 2417, 3419, 4844, 4955.

[3] Once a body of teaching has been constructed by someone who is enlightened, it can then be supported by rational means; in this way it is more fully understood, and this strengthens it: 2553, 2719, 3052, 3310, 6047. (For more on this subject, see §51 above.) People who are committed to faith separated from caring want the church's body of teaching simply to be believed without any rational inquiry: 3394.

[4] The practice of wisdom is not to support a dogma blindly but to see whether or not the dogma is true before convincing ourselves of its truth; this is what people do when they enjoy enlightenment: 1017, 4741, 7012, 7680, 7950. The light that is shed by convincing ourselves is an earthly light, not a spiritual one, and it is accessible even to evil people: 8780. We can convince ourselves of anything, even something false, in such a way that it seems to be true: 2477, 5033, 6865, 8521.

There is a spiritual meaning in the Word that is known as "the inner meaning." No one who does not know what correspondence is can know what the inner meaning of the Word is: 2895, 4322. Absolutely everything in the earthly world, right down to the smallest details, corresponds to and therefore means something spiritual: 2987–3003, 3213–3227. The spiritual realities to which earthly things correspond take on different guises on the earthly level and therefore are not recognized: 1887, 3632, 8920. Hardly anyone nowadays knows where in the Word its divine quality resides, when in fact it is in its inner or spiritual meaning—and people nowadays do not even know that this meaning exists: 4989, 9280. The mystical dimension of the Word is precisely that the contents of its inner or spiritual meaning deal with the Lord, his kingdom, and the church, and not with earthly things that take place in this world: 4923. In many passages the statements of the prophets are unintelligible and therefore of no use apart from their inner meaning: 2608, 8020, 8398 (which provide some examples). For example, the meaning of the white horse in the Book of Revelation (2760 and following); the meaning of the keys of the kingdom of the heavens that were given to Peter (preface to Genesis 22, §9410); the meaning of flesh, blood, bread, and wine in the Holy Supper, and therefore why it was instituted by the Lord (8682); the meaning of Jacob's prophecies about his sons in Genesis 49 (6306, 6333–6465); the meanings of many of the prophecies about Judah and Israel, prophecies that in their literal meaning contradict each other and do not square with [the actual history of] that people (6333, 6361, 6415, 6438, 6444); and countless other passages (2608).

An overview of the inner or spiritual meaning of the Word: 1767–1777, 1869–1879. There is deeper meaning throughout the Word and in every detail of it: 1143, 1984, 2135, 2333, 2395, 2495, 2619. These meanings are not visible in the literal meaning, but they are there within: 4442.

The inner meaning is primarily for angels, but it is also for us. To explain what the inner meaning of the Word is, what its nature is, and what its source is, I need to offer the following overview.

People think and speak differently in heaven than in this world—those in heaven think and speak in a spiritual way, and those in this world think and speak in an earthly way. As a result, when we are reading the Word, the angels who are with us take spiritually what we are taking in an earthly way. This means that angels are focused on the Word's inner meaning while we are focused on its outer meaning. However, the two make a single meaning because of their correspondence.

258

259

[2] The Word is understood differently by angels in the heavens than by us on earth; the meaning accessible to angels is an inner or spiritual one, while the meaning accessible to us is outer or earthly: 1887, 2395. Angels are aware of the inner meaning of the Word and not its outer meaning: 1769, 1770, 1771, 1772 (which include evidence from personal experience with angels who spoke with me from heaven while I was reading the Word). Angelic concepts and angelic speech are both spiritual, while our concepts and speech are earthly, so the inner meaning, being spiritual, is for angels: 2333 (which includes evidence from eyewitness experience). Even so, the literal meaning of the Word serves as a support for the spiritual concepts of angels, much the way the words of our language carry the meaning of a subject for us: 2143. Matters of the Word's inner meaning fall under the kinds of things visible in heaven's light and therefore are suited to angelic perception: 2618, 2619, 2629, 3086. As a result, what angels get from the Word is very precious to them: 2540, 2541, 2545, 2551. Angels do not understand even a single word of the literal meaning of the Word: 64, 65, 1434, 1929. They do not know the names of people or places in the Word, either: 1434, 1888, 4442, 4480. Names cannot enter heaven or be pronounced there: 1876, 1888. All the names in the Word denote actual things, and are changed into concepts of those things in heaven: 768, 1888, 4310, 4442, 5225, 5287, 10329. Further, angels think in terms of qualities without reference to individuals: 5287, 8343, 8985, 9007. Examples from the Word showing the elegance of its inner meaning even when it consists of nothing but names: 1224, 1888, 5095. Further, a long list of names sometimes expresses just one topic in its inner meaning: 5095. All numbers in the Word have definable meanings as well: 482, 487, 647, 648, 755, 813, 1963, 1988, 2075, 2252, 3252, 4264, 6175, 9488, 9659, 10217, 10253. To the extent that their inner reaches are opened into heaven, spirits as well perceive the inner meaning of the Word: 1771. The literal meaning of the Word, which is earthly, is transformed instantly into spiritual meaning for angels because there is a correspondence (5648); and this happens apart from any hearing or awareness on their part of the content of the literal or outer meaning (10215). So the literal or outer meaning exists only on our level and does not reach beyond it: 2015.

[3] There is an inner meaning of the Word and also an inmost or highest meaning: 9407, 10604, 10614, 10627 (which include some discussion). Spiritual angels (that is, angels from the Lord's spiritual kingdom) perceive the inner meaning of the Word, and heavenly angels (that is,

angels from the Lord's heavenly kingdom) perceive its inmost meaning: 2157, 2275.

[4] The Word is for us and is also for angels; it has been accommodated to each: 7381, 8862, 10322. The Word is what unites heaven and earth: 2310, 2895, 9212, 9216, 9357. The joining of heaven to us is brought about by means of the Word: 9396, 9400, 9401, 10452. That is why the Word is called "a covenant": 9396. In fact, "covenant" means a joining together: 665, 666, 1023, 1038, 1864, 1996, 2003, 2021, 6804, 8767, 8778, 9396, 10632. There is an inner meaning in the Word because the Word came down to us from the Lord through the three heavens (2310, 6597); and in this way it was adapted to the angels of the three heavens and also to us (7381, 8862). This is why the Word is divine (4989, 9280), and is holy (10276), and spiritual (4480), and is inspired by the Divine (9094). This is what inspiration is: 9094.

[5] People who have been regenerated, too, are effectively engaged with the Word's inner meaning even though they do not realize it, since their inner self is open, and this self has spiritual perception: 10400. However, the spiritual content of the Word flows into earthly concepts for them and therefore presents itself in earthly terms, because as long as we are living in this world, we do our thinking in the earthly self: 5614. This means that for people who are enlightened, the light of truth comes from within, that is, through their inner selves from the Lord: 10691, 10694. Something holy also flows in by this path for people who regard the Word as holy: 6789. Since regenerate people are (without knowing it) effectively engaged with the Word's inner meaning and with its holiness, after death they come into that meaning spontaneously and are no longer engaged with the literal meaning: 3226, 3342, 3343.

There are countless treasures hidden in the inner or spiritual meaning. In its inner meaning, the Word contains countless things that are beyond our grasp: 3085, 3086. They also cannot be explained: 1955. They are manifest only to angels and are understood only by them: 167. The inner meaning of the Word contains hidden treasures of heaven that have to do with the Lord and his kingdom in the heavens and on earth: 1, 2, 3, 4, 937. These treasures are not visible in the literal meaning: 937, 1502, 2161. Many of the things in the prophets that seem random come together coherently in a beautiful sequence in the inner meaning: 7153, 9022. There is not a single word in the literal meaning of the Word—not even the smallest letter—that can be lost without causing a break in the inner meaning, so this is why, in the Lord's divine providence, the Word

260

has been so completely preserved, right down to every word and the tip of every letter: 7933. There are countless things within the details of the Word (6617, 6620, 8920), and in every word (1869). There are countless things in the Lord's Prayer and in its details (6619), and in the Ten Commandments, though their outer meaning contains things that were known to every people quite apart from any revelation (8862, 8902).

[2] In the Word, especially in the prophetic books, there are what seem to be paired expressions of the same idea, but one refers to what is good and the other to what is true—to what is heavenly, then, and to what is spiritual: 683, 707, 2516, 8339. Teachings about truth and teachings about goodness are wondrously joined to each other in the Word, but this joining is visible only to people who know about its inner meaning: 10554. Therefore in the Word as a whole and in its details there is a divine marriage and a heavenly marriage: 683, 793, 801, 2173, 2516, 2712, 5138, 7022. The divine marriage is the marriage of divine goodness and divine truth and is therefore the Lord, in whom alone this marriage exists: 3004, 3005, 3009, 4137, 5194, 5502, 6343, 7945, 8339, 9263, 9314. "Jesus" means divine goodness and "Christ" means divine truth, and together they mean the divine marriage in heaven, which is the marriage of divine goodness and divine truth: 3004, 3005, 3009. This marriage is in the details of the Word in its inner meaning, so the Lord is there with his divine goodness and divine truth: 5502. What is called the heavenly marriage is the marriage of goodness and truth that comes from the Lord in heaven and in the church: 2508, 2618, 2803, 3004, 3211, 3952, 6179. So in this respect the Word is a kind of heaven: 2173, 10126. Heaven is compared to a marriage in the Word because of the marriage of goodness and truth there: 2758, 3132, 4434, 4835.

[3] The inner meaning contains the genuine teachings of the church: 9025, 9430, 10400. People who understand the Word in its inner meaning know the true teachings of the church, because the inner meaning contains them: 9025, 9430, 10400. The inner reality of the Word is also the inner reality of the church, as well as the inner reality of worship: 10460. The Word is a body of teaching focused on love for the Lord and caring about our neighbor: 3419, 3420.

[4] The Word in its literal sense is like a cloud, while in its inner meaning it is glory (preface to Genesis 18, §§5922, 6343, in explanation of the statement that "the Lord is going to come in the clouds of heaven, with glory" [Matthew 24:30; Mark 13:26; Luke 21:27]). Further, "clouds" in the Word means the Word in its literal meaning, and "glory"

means the Word in its inner meaning: preface to Genesis 18, §§4060, 4391, 5922, 6343, 6752, 8106, 8781, 9430, 10551, 10574. Compared to the contents of the inner meaning, the contents of the literal meaning are like the distorted images around a polished optical cylinder that actually present a beautiful image of a person on the cylinder: 1871. People who want and acknowledge only the literal meaning of the Word are represented in the other life by misshapen old women, while people who want and acknowledge the inner meaning as well are represented by beautifully dressed young women: 1774. The Word in its fullness is an image of heaven because the Word is divine truth, and divine truth is what makes heaven; and since heaven is like one individual, the Word is in this respect like an image of a person: 1871. (On the fact that heaven taken as a whole is like one individual, see §§59–67 of the book *Heaven and Hell,* and on the fact that it is divine truth emanating from the Lord that makes heaven, see §§7–12, 126–140, 200–212.) The inner meaning of the Word is presented to angels' view in a beautiful and pleasing way: 1767, 1768. The literal meaning is like a body, and the inner meaning is like the soul of that body: 8943. The life of the Word therefore comes from its inner meaning: 1405, 4857. The Word is pure in its inner meaning, although it does not seem to be so in its literal meaning: 2362, 2395. The contents of the Word's literal meaning are holy as a result of their inner meaning: 10126, 10276.

[5] There is also an inner meaning in the historical books of the Word, but it is deep within them: 4989. So just like the prophetic books, the historical books contain hidden treasures of heaven: 755, 1659, 1709, 2310, 2333. Angels take them spiritually rather than as history: 6884. Why the deep treasures in the historical books are less visible to us than the ones in the prophetic books: 2176, 6597.

[6] Further discussion of the nature of the inner meaning of the Word (1756, 1984, 2004, 2663, 3035, 7089, 10604, 10614), illustrated with an example (1873).

The Word was composed using correspondences and therefore representa- **261** *tions.* In its literal meaning, the Word was composed entirely by means of correspondences, that is, by means of things that represent and symbolize spiritual realities that have to do with heaven and the church: 1404, 1408, 1409, 1540, 1619, 1659, 1709, 1783, 2179, 2763, 2899. This was done so that there would be an inner meaning in the details (2899); so it was done for the sake of heaven, because the inhabitants of heaven do not understand the Word in its literal meaning, which is earthly; they understand it in its inner meaning, which is spiritual (2899). The Lord spoke using correspondences, representations, and symbolic language because he spoke from his divine nature: 9049, 9063, 9086, 10126, 10276. This means that the Lord spoke to the world and at the same time to heaven: 2533, 4807, 9049, 9063, 9086. What the Lord said spread through the whole of heaven: 4637.

The historical events recounted in the Word are representative and the individual words used are symbolic: 1540, 1659, 1709, 1783, 2686. The Word could not have been composed in any other style if it was to serve as a means of communication and connection with the heavens: 2899, 6943, 9481. It is an immense mistake for people to belittle the Word because of its seemingly simple and inelegant style and to think that they would accept it if it had been written in a different style: 8783. Indeed, the style and standard mode of writing among the earliest people in general was to use representative imagery and symbolism: 605, 1756, 9942. The early sages enjoyed the Word because of its representative imagery and symbolism: 2592, 2593 (which include evidence from eyewitness experience). If people of the earliest church had read the Word they would have seen what is in its inner meaning clearly and what is in its outer meaning dimly: 4493. Jacob's descendants were led into the land of Canaan because all the places in that land had been given symbolic meaning from the earliest times (1585, 3686, 4447, 5136, 6516), and so that a Word could be composed there in which places would be mentioned because of their inner meaning (3686, 4447, 5136, 6516). All the same, the Word was changed in its outer meaning because of that people, although it was not changed in its inner meaning: 10453, 10461, 10603, 10604.

[2] To show the nature and characteristics of correspondences and of the representative imagery in the Word, I need to say something further about them. Everything that corresponds to something also represents and therefore means that something, in such a way that the correspondence and the representation unite: 2896, 2899, 2973, 2987, 2989, 2990, 3002, 3225. What correspondence and representation are: 2763, 2987–3002, 3213–3226, 3337–3352, 3472–3485, 4218–4228, 9280 (which include evidence from eyewitness experience and examples). For the early people, the most highly prized body of knowledge was knowledge of correspondences and representative imagery (3021, 3419, 4280, 4748, 4844, 4964, 4966, 6004, 7729, 10252); especially among the people of the Near East (5702, 6692, 7097, 7779, 9391, 10252, 10407); in Egypt more than any other region (5702, 6692, 7097, 7779, 9391, 10407); but also in other

nations, such as Greece and elsewhere (2762, 7729). Today, though, it is one of the lost bodies of knowledge, especially in Europe: 2894, 2895, 2995, 3630, 3632, 3747, 3748, 3749, 4581, 4966, 10252. Nevertheless, this body of knowledge truly does transcend all others, since without it we cannot understand the Word, or the meaning of the rituals of the Jewish church that are described in the Word, or what heaven is like, or what spiritual reality is, or how the inflow of what is spiritual into what is earthly happens, or a great many other matters: 4280, *and the references cited just above.* All the things that are visible to angels and spirits represent matters of love and faith through correspondences: 1971, 3213–3226, 3475, 3485, 9457, 9481, 9576, 9577. The heavens are full of representative imagery: 1521, 1532, 1619. The deeper you go into the heavens, the more beautiful and perfect are the images that arise: 3475. What these images show you is real because they come from the light of heaven, which is divine truth; and this is the very essential reality from which everything arises: 3485.

[3] The reason absolutely everything that exists in the spiritual world is represented in the earthly world is that the inner reality clothes itself with suitable materials from the outer world as a means of taking on visible form: 6275, 6284, 6299. Just so, a purpose takes on suitable clothing in order to manifest itself as a means in a lower realm and then to manifest itself as something that results on a still lower level; and when a purpose becomes a result through its means it becomes visible, or takes form before our eyes: 5711. This is illustrated by the inflow of the soul into the body. That is, the soul is clothed with a body that allows those things the soul is thinking and intending to become visible and evident, so when a thought flows down into the body it is represented there by whatever motions and actions correspond to it: 2988. Our minds' emotions are represented so clearly by the various expressions of our faces that they can actually be read there: 4791–4805, 5695. We can see, then, that within absolutely everything in the material world there lie more deeply hidden some means and some purpose from the spiritual world (3562, 5711), because the things that exist in the material world are the final effects into which prior realities are flowing (4240, 4939, 5651, 6275, 6284, 6299, 9216). It is inner realities that are represented and outer ones that do the representing: 4292.

[4] Because everything in the material world is symbolic of spiritual and heavenly realities, there were churches in the early times in which all the outer, ritual practices were symbolic. Because of this, these churches

were called "symbolic churches": 920, 1361, 2896. The church established among the children of Israel was a symbolic church: 1003, 2179, 10149. All its rituals were outward practices that symbolized inner realities, aspects of heaven and the church: 4288, 4874. The symbolic practices of the church and its worship came to an end when the Lord came into the world, since the Lord opened the inner reaches of the church and since, in the highest sense, everything about that church focused on him: 4835.

262   *The literal meaning or outer form of the Word.* The literal meaning of the Word is in keeping with the outward appearance of things in this world (589, 926, 1832, 1874, 2242, 2520, 2533, 2719), and is suited to the comprehension of ordinary people (2533, 9049, 9063, 9086). In its literal meaning, the Word is earthly: 8783. This is because the earthly level is the outermost level to which spiritual and heavenly realities descend and on which they rest, the way a house rests on its foundation; otherwise, the inner meaning without the outer would be like a house without a foundation: 9360, 9430, 9433, 9824, 10044, 10436. Because this is the nature of the Word, it is a vessel that contains spiritual and heavenly meanings (9407); and because this is its nature, there is something holy and divine in absolutely every bit of its literal meaning, right down to the smallest letter (639, 680, 1869, 1870, 9198, 10321, 10637). Even though some laws given for the children of Israel have been annulled, they are still the holy Word because of the inner meaning they contain: 9211, 9259, 9349. Of the laws, judgments, and statutes established for the Israelite or Jewish church (which was a symbolic church), there are some that are still valid in both senses, inner and outer; there are some that are still absolutely mandatory in their literal sense; there are some that can be helpful at our own discretion; and there are some that have been completely annulled: 9349 (which gives details). The Word is divine even in respect to the laws that have been annulled: 10637.

What the Word is like in its literal meaning if it is not understood in its inner meaning as well, or what amounts to the same thing, understood according to a true body of teaching drawn from the Word: 10402. A vast number of heresies comes into existence from reading the literal meaning without the inner meaning or without a genuine body of teaching drawn from the Word: 10400. People whose interest lies solely in the outer level of the Word apart from what lies within cannot bear the deeper messages of the Word: 10694. That is what the Jews were like, and they still are today: 301, 302, 303, 3479, 4429, 4433, 4680, 4844, 4847, 10396, 10401, 10407, 10694, 10701, 10707.

The Lord is the Word. The sole subject of the deepest meaning of the **263** Word is the Lord, and it describes all the phases of the glorification of his human nature (that is, of its union with the divine nature itself), as well as all the phases of his taking control of the hells and setting in order everything there and in the heavens: 2249, 7014. So in this meaning there is a description of the Lord's whole life in our world, and by means of this there is a constant presence of the Lord with the angels: 2523. At the very center of the Word there is only the Lord, and this is the source of what is divine and holy in the Word: 1873, 9357. The Lord's saying that the Scripture about him was fulfilled [Luke 18:31; 24:44] was referring to everything in the deepest meaning of the Word: 7933.

"The Word" means divine truth: 4692, 5075, 9987. The Lord is the Word because he is divine truth: 2533. The Lord is the Word also because the Word comes from him and is about him (2859); and in its deepest meaning is about no one but the Lord, so the Lord himself is there (1873, 9357); and also because there is a marriage of divine goodness and divine truth throughout the Word and in its every detail (3004, 5502). "Jesus" means divine goodness and "Christ" means divine truth: 3004, 3005, 3009. Divine truth coming from divine goodness is the sole reality, and only what it dwells in—which comes from what is divine—is substantial: 5272, 6880, 7004, 8200. And because divine truth emanating from the Lord is heaven's light and divine goodness is its warmth, and because everything there comes into being from that light and warmth, and because this earthly world as a whole comes into being by means of heaven or the spiritual world, we can see that everything that has been created has been created from divine truth—that is, from the Word, just as it says in John: "In the beginning was the Word, and the Word was with God, and the Word was God. All things that were made were made through him. *And the Word became flesh*" [John 1:1, 3, 14]: 2803, 2894, 5272, 7678. For more on the creation of everything by divine truth and therefore by the Lord, see §137 of the book *Heaven and Hell*. A fuller picture can be drawn from two of its chapters: §§116–125 ["The Sun in Heaven"] and 126–140 ["Light and Warmth in Heaven"].

A joining together of the Lord and us is accomplished through the Word, by means of its inner meaning: 10375. Absolutely everything in the Word is a means to this joining together, and this is why the Word is more wondrous than anything else that has been written: 10632, 10633, 10634. Now that the Word has been written, the Lord speaks to us through it: 10290.

264   *People who are hostile to the Word.* People who belittle, ridicule, blaspheme, and profane the Word: 1878. What they are like in the other life: 1761, 9222. They are like blood disorders: 5719. How dangerous it is to profane the Word: 571, 582. How much harm is done by using the Word to justify premises that are false, especially if they are in support of a love for oneself and for the world: 589. People who do not care about truth for the sake of truth flatly reject whatever has to do with the inner meaning of the Word and are nauseated by it: 5702 (which includes evidence from eyewitness experience). About some people in the other life who rejected the deeper contents of the Word and went berserk: 1879.

265   *More on the Word.* In Hebrew, the term "word" has various meanings—speech, a thought of the mind, anything that actually comes into being, and some particular thing: 9987. "The Word" means divine truth and the Lord: 4692, 5075, 9987. "Words" means truths: 4692, 5075. "Words" also means a whole body of teaching: 1288. The phrase "The Ten Words" means all divine truths: 10688. "Words" also means the things that exist in reality: 1785, 5075, 5272.

[2] Especially in the prophetic books of the Word, there are paired expressions of the same idea, one that refers to goodness and one that refers to truth, which are joined together in this manner: 683, 707, 2173, 8339. The only way to tell which expression refers to goodness and which to truth is from the Word's inner meaning, because there are words that properly express things that are good and words that properly express things that are true: 793, 801. These meanings are so consistent that we can tell just from what the words generally refer to whether that passage has to do with goodness or with truth: 2712. In some instances, too, one expression involves a generalization and the other some particular thing defined by that generalization: 2212. Sometimes in the Word there occurs an alternation in pairs of meanings: 2240 (which includes some discussion). Many things in the Word also have an opposite meaning: 4816. The inner meaning of a statement is in accord with what is being said about the subject: 4502.

[3] In the other life, people who have taken delight in the Word are open to heaven's warmth—which bears heavenly love within itself—in proportion to the nature and extent of their delight in and love for the Word: 1773.

266   *The books that are books of the Word.* The books of the Word are all the Bible books that have an inner meaning. The other Bible books are not the Word. In the Old Testament, the books of the Word are the following: the five books of Moses, the Book of Joshua, the Book of Judges, the two books of Samuel, the two books of Kings, the Psalms of David, and the prophets—Isaiah, Jeremiah, Lamentations, Ezekiel, Daniel, Hosea, Joel, Amos, Obadiah, Jonah, Micah, Nahum, Habakkuk, Zephaniah, Haggai, Zechariah, and Malachi. In the New Testament: the four Gospels—Matthew, Mark, Luke, and John—and the Book of Revelation. The others do not have an inner meaning: 10325.

Providence

267 PROVIDENCE is the name for the Lord's governance in the heavens and on earth. Since all the goodness that comes from love and all the truth that leads to faith—the things that are required for our salvation—come from him and none whatever comes from us, we can see that the Lord's divine providence is involved in absolutely everything that contributes to the salvation of the human race. As the Lord teaches in John:

> I am the way, the truth, and the life. (John 14:6)

And again,

> As a branch cannot bear fruit on its own unless it abides on the vine, the same goes for you unless you abide in me. Without me you cannot do anything. (John 15:4, 5)

268 The Lord's divine providence is operative in the smallest details of our lives; there is only one source of life, who is the Lord, and in him we live and move and have our being [Acts 17:28].

269 People who think about divine providence in worldly terms come to the conclusion that it applies only on the largest scale, but that the details are left to us. But people who think this way do not know the mysteries of heaven. They draw their conclusions solely on the basis of self-love, love for the world, and the things that give pleasure to these loves. So when they see evil people raised to high rank, making more money than good people, and skillfully and successfully accomplishing evil things, they say in their hearts that none of this would be happening if divine providence were operative in all the details. They fail to take into account, though, that the goal of divine providence does not concern what is momentary and transient, what comes to an end when our lives in this world cease. Rather, its goal concerns what lasts to eternity, what therefore does not have an end. Whatever has no end is real, while what comes to an end is relatively unreal. Consider, if you will, whether a hundred thousand years are anything next to eternity, and you will see that they are not. What then are the few years of our lives in this world?

270 Anyone who weighs the matter properly can know that eminence and wealth in this world are not genuine divine blessings, even though we call them that because we enjoy them so much. They come to an end for us; and they also lead many of us astray and turn us away from heaven. No, the real blessings that come from the Divine are eternal life and the happiness it brings. This is what the Lord is teaching us in Luke:

> Provide yourselves a treasure in the heavens that does not fail, where no thief approaches and no moth destroys; because where your treasure is, there your heart will be also. (Luke 12:33, 34)

The reason the skills of evil people bring them success is that by the divine design, whatever we do, we do on the basis of our own reasoning and our own free will. If we did not have the freedom to act on the basis of our own reasoning, and if our consequent skills never accomplished anything, we could not even begin being prepared to receive eternal life. Eternal life is instilled in us only when we are in a state of freedom and when our powers of reason are enlightened. This is because no one can be compelled by outside forces to become a good person, since nothing that is done under compulsion is of lasting effect. The goodness under that circumstance would not become ours. What is ours is what we do freely according to our own reasoning, and what we do freely is what we do because we will it and love it; our will or our love is our true self. If we are compelled to do something that we do not want to do, then our mind is constantly turning to what we would rather do instead. Not only that, everyone is drawn to what is forbidden because of the hidden pull of freedom. So we can see that if we were not kept in a state of freedom we could not be provided with any goodness.

God's allowing us the freedom to think, intend, and (within the limits of the law) even do what is evil is called "permission."

When our skills bring us happiness in this world, it seems as though this were being done by our own prudence; in actuality, however, divine providence is always with us, permitting what is evil but also constantly leading us away from it. As for happiness in heaven, people know and understand that our being led in this direction is not something accomplished by our own prudence; heavenly happiness comes from the Lord and is brought about by his divine providence preparing us for goodness and constantly guiding us in that direction.

We cannot grasp the truth of this from the light of the physical world, because this light does not reveal to us the laws of the divine design.

It is important to know that there is divine providence and there is also divine foresight. Goodness is what the Lord provides, and evil is what the Lord foresees. Both foresight and providence are necessary, because what comes from us is nothing but evil and what comes from the Lord is nothing but good.

From *Secrets of Heaven*

SINCE everything good that the Lord provides us flows in, I need to include in what follows citations from *Secrets of Heaven* concerning *inflow;* and since everything that the Lord provides he provides in accordance with the divine design, I need also to cite passages from the same source concerning *the divine design.*

276 *Providence.* Providence is the Lord's governance in the heavens and on earth: 10773. As part of his providence, the Lord governs everything in accord with the divine design, so providence is his governance in keeping with the divine design: 1755, 2447. All things that occur under his governance are things that he wills or things that he can accept or things that he has to allow; the differences depend on the nature of the individual involved: 1755, 2447, 9010, 9940. Providence works invisibly: 5508. Many things that happen because of providence seem to us to be coincidental: 5508. The reason providence works invisibly is so that we will not be compelled to believe by visible signs of providence's handiwork; so this is done to avoid harming our freedom, since without freedom we could not be reformed, which would mean that we could not be saved: 1937, 1947, 2876, 2881, 3854, 5508, 5982, 6477, 8209, 8987, 9588, 10409, 10777. Divine providence's aim is to supply not temporary blessings that will soon fade away but eternal ones: 5264, 8717, 10776. An illustration of this: 6491. People who do not grasp this think that wealth and eminence in the world are the only concerns of providence, so they call them "blessings from God"; yet the Lord does not see these as blessings but solely as means for our lives in this world. The Lord focuses instead on what will contribute to our eternal happiness: 10409, 10776. People who trust in the Lord's divine providence are at every moment moving forward toward a state of eternal happiness: 8478, 8480. People who give all the credit to material things and their own prudence and none to the Divine do not think this is true and do not even comprehend it: 6484, 10409, 10775.

[2] The Lord's divine providence does not deal solely with issues on a large scale, as people in the world think it does; that is, it does not leave all the small matters and details up to our own prudence: 8717, 10775. Nothing exists on a large scale unless it is composed of details and includes them, since it is the details taken all together that constitute the large scale, just as specifics taken all together constitute what is generally the case: 1919, 6159, 6338, 6482, 6483, 6484. The nature of anything on a large scale depends on the nature of the details that constitute it and that it includes: 917, 1040, 6483, 8858. The Lord's providence exists on the largest scale *because* it is in the smallest details: 1919, 2694, 4329, 5122, 5949, 6058, 6481–6486, 6490, 7004, 7007, 8717, 10774. Some support for this from heaven: 6486. If the Lord's divine providence were not made universal by being in the smallest details and building on them, nothing could continue to exist: 6338. This presence at the smallest level is what allows everything in the divine design to be set in order and kept in order, both generally and specifically: 6338. How this compares with a monarch on earth: 6482, 10800. Our own prudence is like a dust mote in the universe, while divine providence is like the universe itself in comparison: 6485. It is hard for us in this world to grasp this (8717, 10775, 10780) because many fallacies oppose it and blind us (6481). A man in the other life who had convinced himself during his life in this world to believe that everything that happened to him was a result of his own prudence and nothing was a result of divine providence; the qualities within him were revealed to be hellish: 6484.

The nature of the Lord's providence in regard to evils: 6481, 6495, 6574, 10777, 10779. The Lord governs evils through his laws of permission; evils are tolerated for the sake of the divine design as a whole: 8700, 10778. The Lord tolerates evil, but not because he wants it to happen; he does not want it to happen, but he cannot remedy it completely, because his overall goal, which is salvation, takes precedence: 7877. "Permission" means that God allows us the freedom to think, intend, and (as far as the law does not stop us) even do what is evil: 10778. Without freedom—and therefore without the permission of evil—we could not be reformed and therefore could not be saved; see §§141–149 above in this volume, in the teachings on freedom.

The Lord has providence and also has foresight, and the one does not exist without the other: 5195, 6489. The Lord provides what is good and foresees what is evil: 5155, 5195, 6489, 10781.

There is no predestination in the form of fate: 6487. All of us are predestined to heaven and none to hell: 6488. Providence does not impose absolute necessity on us, but instead we have full freedom: 6487 (which includes a comparison by way of illustration). "The chosen" in the Word means all people who lead a life devoted to goodness and truth: 3755, 3900, 5057, 5058. How to understand the statement in Exodus 21:13 that "God brought it unexpectedly to that person's hand": 9010.

"Luck," which in many instances in this world seems amazing, is the workings of divine providence on the lowest level of the divine design in accordance with the nature of our own states; this can serve to assure us that divine providence is involved in the very least details of everything: 5049, 5179, 6493, 6494. Luck comes from the spiritual world, and this accounts for the way that it changes: 5179, 6493, 6494 (which include evidence from personal experience).

277   *Inflow.* The inflow of heaven into the world and the inflow of the soul into all parts of the body: 6053–6058, 6189–6215, 6307–6327, 6466–6495, 6598–6626 (which include evidence from personal experience). Nothing comes into being from itself, but rather from something prior, so everything comes from one primary entity: 4523, 4524, 6040, 6056. Everything constantly continues to exist in the same way that it came into being, because continued existence is a perpetual coming into being: 2886, 2888, 3627, 3628, 3648, 4523, 4524, 6040, 6056. Inflow happens according to the divine design: 7270. This makes it possible for us to see that everything is continuing to exist from the primary and underlying reality, because it came into being from that underlying reality: 4523, 4524, 6040, 6056. Every bit of life flows in from that primary underlying reality because that is its source, so it flows in from the Lord: 3001, 3318, 3337, 3338, 3344, 3484, 3619, 3741, 3742, 3743, 4318, 4319, 4320, 4417, 4524, 4882, 5847, 5986, 6325, 6468, 6469, 6470, 6479, 9276, 10196. Every "coming into being" comes from an underlying reality, and nothing can come into being unless it has its own underlying reality within it: 4523, 4524, 6040, 6056.

All of our thinking and all of our willing flows into us: 904, 2886, 2887, 2888, 4151, 4319, 4320, 5846, 5848, 6189, 6191, 6194, 6197, 6198, 6199, 6213, 7147, 10219 (which include evidence from personal experience). Our ability to examine things, to think, and to reach conclusions as the result of analysis comes from an inflow: 2888, 4319, 4320. If the inflow from the spiritual world were taken away from us we could not survive for a single moment, and yet we are in a state of freedom: 2887, 5849, 5854, 6321 (which include evidence from eyewitness experience). The life that flows in from the Lord varies depending on our state and on our receptivity: 2069, 5986, 6472, 7343. In evil people the goodness that flows in from the Lord is turned into evil and the truth into falsity: 3643, 4632 (which include evidence from eyewitness experience). How much we receive of the goodness and truth that is constantly flowing in from the Lord depends on the extent to which evil and falsity in us have been moved out of the way: 2411, 3142, 3147, 5828.

Everything good flows in from the Lord and everything evil flows in from hell: 904, 4151. People nowadays believe that everything is in and from themselves even though it is all flowing in; and they ought to know this from the church's teaching that everything good comes from heaven and everything evil comes from hell: 4249, 6193, 6206. If people believed the way things actually are, they would not take evil into themselves, because they would throw it out of themselves and back into hell, and they would not claim that goodness was their own and therefore would not take any credit for it: 6206, 6324, 6325. How happy our state would be then—with the Lord's help we would have an inward perspective on both goodness and evil: 6325. People who deny the existence of heaven or who know nothing about it are unaware that there is any inflow coming from it: 4322, 5649, 6193, 6479. What inflow is: 6128, 6190, 9407 (which is illustrated by comparisons).

[2] Inflow is spiritual; it is not physical. It flows from the spiritual world into the physical world and not from the physical world into the spiritual world: 3219, 5119, 5259, 5427, 5428, 5478, 6322, 9109, 9110. Inflow flows through the inner self into the outer self and not the reverse: 1702, 1707, 1940, 1954, 5119, 5259, 5779, 6322, 9380. This is because the inner self is in the spiritual world and the outer self is in the physical world: 978, 1015, 3628, 4459, 4523, 4524, 6057, 6309, 9701–9709, 10156, 10472. The appearance that there is an inflow from outward things into inward ones is an illusion: 3721. Within us, inflow flows through our rational faculty into our factual knowledge and not the reverse: 1495, 1707, 1940. The nature of the pattern of inflow: 775, 880, 1096, 1495, 7270.

Inflow comes directly from the Lord and also indirectly through the spiritual world or heaven: 6063, 6307, 6472, 9682, 9683. The Lord flows directly into the tiniest details of everything: 6058, 6474–6478, 8717, 8728.

On the Lord's indirect inflow through heaven: 4067, 6982, 6985, 6996. It happens through the spirits and angels who are associated with us: 697, 5846–5866. The Lord flows through angels into the goals from and for which we think, intend, and act as we do (1317, 1645, 5846, 5854), and also into matters of conscience within us (6207, 6213); through spirits, he flows into our thoughts and from there into the contents of our memory (4186, 5858, 5864, 6192, 6193, 6198, 6199, 6319). It is hard for people to believe this: 6214. How the Lord flows into things that are highest and things that are lowest at the same time, or into what is inmost and what is outermost at the same time: 5147, 5150, 6473, 7004, 7007, 7270. The Lord flows into what is good in us and through that goodness into what is true, but not the reverse: 5482, 6027, 8685, 8701, 10153. Goodness gives us the ability to accept the inflow from the Lord; truth apart from goodness does not: 8321. Nothing that comes into our thoughts does us any harm, but what comes into our will does, because it becomes part of us: 6308. The Divine at the highest levels is quiet and peaceful, but as it comes down toward the lower levels within us it becomes unpeaceful and even tumultuous because of the disorder there: 8823. The effect of the Lord's inflow on the prophets: 6212.

There exists a kind of divine inflow that is general: 5850 (which includes some description of it). It is a constant force that causes things to act in keeping with the overall design: 6211. This is the kind of inflow that affects the lives of animals (5850), and also the members of the plant kingdom (3648). Even in us, thought descends into speech and will into behavior in accord with this general inflow: 5862, 5990, 6192, 6211.

278 *The inflow of life into human beings in particular.* There is only one source of life; from it comes the life found in everyone in heaven and everyone in the world: 1954, 2021, 2536, 2658, 2886–2889, 3001, 3484, 3742, 5847, 6467. That life comes from the Lord alone: 2886–2889, 3344, 3484, 4319, 4320, 4524, 4882, 5986, 6325, 6468, 6469, 6470, 9276, 10196 (which include various illustrations). The Lord is life itself: see John 1:1, 4; 5:26; 14:6. Life flows from the Lord into angels, spirits, and people in this world in a wondrous way: 2886–2889, 3337, 3338, 3484, 3742. The Lord flows in because of his divine love, the nature of which is to want what belongs to it to belong to others: 3742, 4320. All love is like that, so divine love is infinitely that way: 1820, 1865, 2253, 6872. As a result, our life seems to be within us and does not seem to be flowing in: 3742, 4320. Another reason our life seems to be within us is that the principal cause, which is life from the Lord, and the instrumental cause, which is we ourselves as a recipient form, act as a single cause and therefore we as the instrument perceive life as our own: 6325. The pinnacle of angels' wisdom and intelligence is to perceive and know that every bit of life comes from the Lord: 4318. I perceived a joy that angels were experiencing as a result of leading a life that comes from the Lord and not from themselves; things they said to me confirmed my perception: 6469. Evil people are unwilling to be persuaded that their life is flowing in: 3743. Doubts that our life flows in from the Lord cannot be removed as long as we are controlled by illusions, ignorance, and negativity: 6479. As all people in the church should know, everything good and true comes from heaven (that is, through heaven from the Lord) and everything evil and false comes from hell; in fact, every bit of life goes back to either goodness and truth or evil and falsity, and apart from these there can be no life at all: 2893, 4151. This is the clear message of the teachings of the church that have been drawn from the Word: 4249. Yet in spite of all this, people do not believe that life flows in: 4249. In reality, if our communication and connection with spirits and angels were taken away, we would die instantly: 2887. This also shows us that all life flows in from the primary reality underlying life. Nothing arises from itself; things arise only from other things that are prior (which means that absolutely everything arises from the primary underlying reality), and in all cases things maintain their existence in the same way that they arose, because continuing existence is constant coming into being: 4523, 4524. Angels, spirits, and people in this world have been created to receive life, so we are all simply forms that are receptive to life: 2021, 3001, 3318, 3344, 3484, 3742, 4151, 5114, 5986. The kind of forms we are depends on our receptivity: 2888, 3001, 3484, 5847, 5986, 6467, 6472. So the basic nature of people in this world, spirits, and angels depends on the basic nature of their forms for receiving life from the Lord: 2888, 5847, 5986, 6467, 6472. We have been created in such a way that in the inmost parts of ourselves, and therefore in other parts as well, we are capable of receiving what is divine and being raised up and joined to the Divine through the good things we love to do and the truths we believe; and therefore we, unlike animals, live forever: 5114.

[2] Life from the Lord also flows into evil people, so it flows into people in hell as well: 2706, 3743, 4417. However, they turn what is good into evil and what is true into falsity; so they turn life into spiritual death, since our nature is what determines how we accept the life that is flowing in: 4319, 4320, 4417. Goodness and truth are still constantly flowing into them from the Lord, but they reject or stifle or pervert them: 3743. The life that is in people who are devoted to evil and falsity is not genuine life; what the life they have is like: 726, 4623, 10284, 10286.

279   *The divine design.* The divine truth that emanates from the Lord is the origin of the divine design, and divine goodness is what constitutes its essence: 1728, 2258, 8700, 8988. The Lord himself, then, is the divine design, because divine goodness and divine truth come from the Lord and in fact are the Lord in the heavens and on earth: 1919, 2011, 5110, 5703, 10336, 10619. The laws of the design are divine truths: 2447, 7995. Where there is order the Lord is present; where there is no order the Lord is not present: 5703. Since divine truth is [the basis of] the design and divine goodness constitutes its essence, absolutely everything in the universe must go back to goodness and truth in order to be anything at all, for the very reason that everything goes back to the design: 2451, 3166, 4390, 4409, 5232, 7256, 10122, 10555. Since goodness is the essence of the design, it arranges the truths that form the design; the truths do not arrange the goodness: 3316, 3470, 4302, 5704, 5709, 6028, 6690. The entire heaven, with all its angelic communities, is arranged by the Lord according to his divine design, since the divine nature of the Lord in and among the angels is what constitutes heaven: 6338, 7211, 9338, 10125, 10151, 10157. So heaven's form is a form in keeping with the divine design: 4040–4043, 6607, 9877.

[2] To the extent that we live according to the design—that is, to the extent that we are devoted to doing what is good in response to the divine truths that are the laws of the design—to that extent we are human: 4839. The more we live this way, the more perfectly proportioned and beautiful we will look in the other life; the less we live this way, the more monstrous we will look: 4839, 6605, 6626. Clearly then, all the elements of the divine design have been gathered together in human beings; we have been created to be the divine design in form: 4219, 4220, 4223, 4523, 4524, 5114, 6013, 6057, 6605, 6626, 9706, 10156. Because angels are receptive to the divine design from the Lord, they are in the human form—and in a form that is more perfect and beautiful the more receptive they are: 322, 1880, 1881, 3633, 3804, 4622, 4735, 4797, 4985, 5199, 5530, 6054, 9879, 10177, 10594. Not only that, the angelic heaven, taken as a whole, is like a human being in respect to its form; and this is because the whole heaven, with all its angelic communities, is arranged by the Lord according to the divine design: 2996, 2998, 3624–3649, 3636–3643, 3741–3745, 4625. We can see from this that the Divine-Human Being is the source of all the above: 2996, 2998, 3624–3649, 3741–3745. It also follows from this that the Lord is the only human being, and that we are human only if we are receptive to what is divine from him: 1894. The more receptive we are, the more we become images of the Lord: 8547.

[3] We are born not with goodness and truth but with evil and falsity, so we are not born into the divine design but into something contrary to that design. That is why we are born in utter ignorance and why, in order to be brought into the divine design and thus become human, we must of necessity be born again—that is, regenerated—which is accomplished by means of divine truths from the Lord and by a life in accord with them: 1047, 2307, 2308, 3518, 3812, 8480, 8550, 10283, 10284, 10731. When the Lord is regenerating us, he arranges everything in us according to the divine design—that is, according to the form of heaven: 5700, 6690, 9931, 10303. Anyone who is being led by the Lord is being led according to the divine design: 8512. Those who are in the divine design have deeper levels of the mind that are opened into heaven all the way to the Lord; those who are not in the divine design have deeper levels of the mind that are closed: 8513. The more we live according to the divine design, the more intelligence and wisdom we have: 2592.

[4] The Lord governs everything from the inmost to the outermost elements of the design; he governs the inmost elements from the outermost and the outermost from the inmost, and this is how he keeps everything connected and coordinated: 3702, 3739, 6056, 9828. On sequential order and on the last stage of that order, in which sequential elements are all together and yet the order of their succession is preserved: 634, 3691, 4145, 5114, 5897, 6239, 6326, 6465, 8603, 9216, 9828, 9836, 10044, 10099, 10335.

[5] Things that are evil and false are contrary to the design, and yet the Lord still governs them, not according to the design but based on their opposition to it: 4839, 7877, 10778. Things that are evil and false are governed through the laws of permission, and this is done for the sake of the design: 7877, 8700, 10778. Some things are impossible because they are contrary to the divine design—for example, it is impossible for someone whose life is devoted to evil to be saved out of pure mercy, and it is impossible for evil people to be in the company of good people in the other life, among many other things: 8700.

The Lord

280 THERE is one God, who is both the Creator and the Sustainer of the universe, and who therefore is God of heaven and God of earth.

281 There are two things that make a life of heaven for us—the good that we do out of love and the truth we believe. This life is given to us by God, and nothing of it comes from ourselves. For this reason, the primary duty of a church is to acknowledge God, believe in God, and love him.

282 Those born within the Christian church should acknowledge the Lord, his divine nature, and his human nature and believe in him and love him, because all salvation comes from the Lord. That is what the Lord tells us in John:

> Those who believe in the Son have eternal life. Those who do not believe in the Son will not see life; instead, the wrath of God abides on them. (John 3:36)

And in the same Gospel,

> This is the will of the one who sent me, that all those who see the Son and believe in him will have eternal life, and I will raise them up on the last day. (John 6:40)

And again,

> Jesus said, "I am the resurrection and the life. Even if they die, those who believe in me will live; and anyone who lives and believes in me will never die." (John 11:25, 26)

283 This means that people within the church who do not acknowledge the Lord and his divine nature cannot be joined to God, and therefore their portion will not be among angels in heaven. You see, no one can be joined to God except by the Lord and in the Lord.

The Lord teaches in John that no one can be joined to God except by the Lord:

> No one has ever seen God. The only-begotten Son, who is close to the Father's heart, has made him visible. (John 1:18)

Again,

> You have never heard the Father's voice or seen what he looks like. (John 5:37)

Again,

> No one knows the Father except the Son, and those to whom the Son wills to reveal him. (Matthew 11:27)

And again,

> I am the way, the truth, and the life. No one comes to the Father except through me. (John 14:6)

The reason no one can be joined to God except in the Lord is that the Father is in him and they are one, as he teaches us, again in John:

> If you know me you also know my Father. Those who see me see the Father. Philip, do you not believe that I am in the Father and the Father is in me? Believe me that I am in the Father and the Father is in me. (John 14:7–11)

And again,

> The Father and I are one. . . . [Believe in my works,] so that you may know and believe that I am in the Father and the Father is in me. (John 10:30, 38)

Since the Father is in the Lord and the Father and the Lord are one, and since we are to believe in the Lord and whoever believes in him has eternal life, we can see that the Lord is God. The Word tells us that the Lord is God, as in John:

> In the beginning was the Word, and the Word was with God, and *the Word was God.* All things were made through him, and nothing that was made came about without him. And *the Word became flesh* and lived among us; and we saw his glory, glory like that of the only-begotten child of the Father. (John 1:1, 3, 14)

In Isaiah:

> A Child has been born to us; a Son has been given to us. Leadership will be upon his shoulder, and his name will be called *God,* Hero, *Father of Eternity,* Prince of Peace. (Isaiah 9:6)

Again:

> A virgin will conceive and give birth, and the [child's] name will be called "*God with us.*" (Isaiah 7:14; Matthew 1:23)

And in Jeremiah:

> Behold, the days are coming when I will raise up for David a righteous
> branch who will rule as king, and prosper. And this is his name: they
> will call him "*Jehovah our Righteousness.*" (Jeremiah 23:5, 6; 33:15, 16)

285   Everyone in the church who receives light from heaven sees divinity
in the Lord, but people who do not receive light from heaven see only
humanness in the Lord. Yet the divinity and the humanity in him are so
united that they are one, as he also tells us in another place in John:

> Father, all that is mine is yours, and all that is yours is mine. (John
> 17:10)

286   The church knows that the Lord was conceived by Jehovah the
Father and was therefore God from his conception. It also knows that he
rose with his whole body, since he left nothing in the tomb. He assured
his disciples of this later when he said, "See my hands and my feet—that
it is I myself. Touch me and see, because a spirit does not have flesh
and bones as you see I have" (Luke 24:39). And yet even though he was
human in having flesh and bones, he entered through closed doors and
vanished after he had revealed himself (John 20:19, 26; Luke 24:31).

It is different for everyone else. We rise again only in our spirits, not
in our bodies, so when he said that *he was not like a spirit,* he was saying
that he was not like anyone else.

We can see from this that even the human part of the Lord is divine.

287   We all get from our fathers the reality underlying our life that is called
our soul. The manifestation of life from that underlying reality is what
is called the body. So the body is an image of its soul, since the soul carries on its life through its body at will. That is why we are born looking
like our parents and why we can tell families apart. We can see from this
what the body or the human nature of the Lord was like—it was like the
Divine itself that was the reality underlying his life, that is, like the soul
from the Father. That is why he said, "Those who see me see the Father"
(John 14:9).

288   According to the statement of faith accepted throughout the whole
Christian world, the divinity and the humanity of the Lord together
make one person. That statement reads as follows:

> Although Christ is God and a human being, yet he is not two, but one
> Christ. Indeed, he is one altogether, one person. Therefore as the body

and the soul are one human being, so God and a human being are one Christ.

This is from the Athanasian Creed.

People whose concept of divinity is a concept of three persons can-not have a concept of one God. If they say "one" with their mouth, they still think "three." However, people whose concept of divinity is a con-cept of three aspects in one person can have a concept of one God. They can say "one God," and they can think "one God" as well. 289

Our concept of God is a concept of three aspects in one person when we think that the Father is in the Lord and that the Holy Spirit emanates from the Lord. In this case all three aspects are in the Lord: divinity itself, which is called the Father; the divine-human nature, which is the Son; and divinity emanating, which is the Holy Spirit. 290

Since all divinity is in the Lord, he has all power in heaven and on earth. This he himself tells us in John: "The Father has given all things into the hand of the Son" (John 3:35); again, "The Father has given the Son power over all flesh" (John 17:2); in Matthew, "All things have been delivered to me by the Father" (Matthew 11:27); and again, "All power has been given to me in heaven and on earth" (Matthew 28:18). Divinity is that kind of power. 291

People who suppose the Lord's human nature to be just like the human nature of anyone else are not taking into consideration that he was conceived by the Divine, nor are they pondering the fact that the body is for everyone an image of the soul. Nor are they considering that he was resurrected with his whole body, nor the way he appeared when he was transfigured, when his face shone like the sun. 292

Nor do they think about what the Lord said about believing in him, about his being one with the Father, about his glorification, and about his power over heaven and earth—that these are divine attributes and yet they are said of his human nature.

Nor do they bear in mind that the Lord is omnipresent even with respect to his human nature (Matthew 28:20), though this is the basis of belief in his omnipresence in the Holy Supper—omnipresence is a divine trait.

Perhaps people do not even consider that the divinity called the Holy Spirit emanates from the Lord's human nature, when in fact it does ema-nate from his glorified human nature; for it says, "There was not the Holy Spirit yet because Jesus was not yet glorified" (John 7:39).

The Lord came into the world to save the human race, which oth-erwise would have suffered eternal death. He saved it by gaining control 293 over the hells, which were assaulting everyone who entered this world and everyone who left it. He also saved the human race by glorifying his own human nature, because this gave him the power to keep the hells under his control forever.

His gaining control over the hells and the simultaneous glorification of his human nature were effected by allowing the human nature that he received from his mother to undergo spiritual crises and by continuous victories in those crises. His suffering on the cross was his last spiritual crisis; in it he made his victory complete.

294 The Lord tells us in John that he gained control over the hells: as his suffering on the cross was impending, Jesus said, "Now is the judgment of this world; *now the ruler of this world will be cast out*" (John 12:27, 28, 31); and again, "Take heart! *I have overcome the world*" (John 16:33); and in Isaiah, "'Who is this who is coming from Edom, approaching in the immensity of his strength, and having the power to save?' 'My own arm brought about salvation for me.' Therefore he became their Savior" (Isaiah 63:1–19; 59:16–21).

He also tells us in John that he glorified his human nature and that the suffering on the cross was his last crisis of the spirit and the complete victory that brought about his glorification:

> After Judas went out, Jesus said, "Now the Son of Humanity is glorified, and God will glorify him in himself and glorify him immediately." (John 13:31, 32)

And again,

> Father, the hour has come. Glorify your Son, so that your Son may also glorify you. (John 17:1, 5)

And again,

> "Now my soul is troubled. Father, glorify your name." And a voice came from heaven, saying, "I both have glorified it and will glorify it again." (John 12:27, 28)

Also in Luke,

> Was it not necessary for the Christ to suffer this and enter into his glory? (Luke 24:26)

He made these statements concerning his suffering on the cross. To "glorify" is to make divine.

This now shows that unless the Lord had come into the world and become human and in this way had freed from hell all who believe in him and love him, no human being could have been saved. That is how to understand the statement that there is no salvation apart from the Lord [Acts 4:12].

When the Lord fully glorified his human nature he divested himself of the human nature from his mother and put on a human nature from his Father, which is the divine-human nature. As a result, he was no longer the son of Mary. 295

The first and foremost duty of a church is to know and acknowledge its God, since without this knowledge and acknowledgment there can be no joining with God. In the Christian church, then, there is no joining with God without acknowledgment of the Lord. The Lord tells us this in John: 296

> Those who believe in the Son have eternal life. Those who do not believe in the Son will not see life; instead, the wrath of God abides on them. (John 3:36)

And elsewhere,

> If you do not believe that I am, you will die in your sins. (John 8:24)

The fact that the Trinity—divinity itself, the divine-human nature, and divinity emanating—exists within the Lord is a secret revealed by heaven for those people who will be in the holy Jerusalem. 297

From *Secrets of Heaven*

THE Lord had a divine nature from the very moment of his conception. The Lord had a divine nature from the Father: 4641, 4963, 5041, 5157, 6716, 10125. Only the Lord was born from divine seed: 1438. His soul was Jehovah: 1999, 2004, 2005, 2018, 2025. His inmost core was the 298

Divine itself; the covering over that came from his mother: 5041. The divine nature was the reality underlying the Lord's life; from it his human nature came forth and became the manifestation of that underlying reality: 3194, 3210, 10269, 10372.

299 *We are to acknowledge the divinity of the Lord.* Within the church, where the Word exists and the Lord is known by means of it, it is important that we not deny the divinity of the Lord or the holiness that emanates from him: 2359. People within the church who do not acknowledge the Lord cannot be joined with the Divine. It is different for people outside the church: 10205. The essence of the church is to acknowledge the Lord's divine nature and his oneness with the Father: 10083, 10112, 10370, 10738, 10730, 10816, 10817, 10818, 10820.

300 *In this world the Lord glorified his human nature.* Many places in the Word speak of the Lord's glorification (10828); in the Word's inner meaning it is the subject throughout (2249, 2523, 3245). The Lord glorified his human nature, not his divine nature, because that in and of itself was already glorious: 10057. The Lord came into the world to glorify his human nature: 3637, 4287, 9315. The Lord glorified his human nature by means of the divine nature that was within him from conception: 4727. We can get some idea of the glorification of the Lord's human nature from our idea of our own regeneration, since the Lord regenerates us in the same way that he glorified his human nature: 3043, 3138, 3212, 3296, 3490, 4402, 5688. Some of the mysteries involved in the glorification of the Lord's human nature: 10057. By glorifying his own human nature the Lord saved the human race: 1676, 4180. The Lord's state of glorification and his state of being humbled: 1785, 1999, 2159, 6866. When it has to do with the Lord, "glorification" in the Word means the union of his human nature with his divine nature, and "glorifying" means making divine: 1603, 10053, 10828.

301 *While the Lord was in the world, by means of his human nature he gained control over the hells.* While the Lord was in the world he gained control over all the hells and then brought everything in the heavens and the hells into order: 4075, 4287, 9937. At that time the Lord also freed the world of spirits from the [evil] people who lived before the Flood: 1266. What they were like: 310, 311, 560, 562, 563, 570, 581, 607, 660, 805, 808, 1034, 1120, 1265–1272. By gaining control over the hells and at the same time glorifying his human nature, the Lord saved the human race: 4180, 10019, 10152, 10655, 10659, 10828.

The glorification of the Lord's human nature and his gaining control 302
over the hells were accomplished by means of crises of the spirit. Beyond all
others, the Lord suffered the most severe spiritual crises: 1663, 1668, 1787,
2776, 2786, 2795, 2816, 4295, 9528. The Lord fought out of his divine love
for the human race: 1690, 1691, 1812, 1813, 1820. The Lord's love was a
love for the salvation of the human race: 1820. The hells fought against
the Lord's love: 1820. The Lord, alone and by his own power, fought
against the hells and conquered them: 1692, 1813, 2816, 4295, 8273, 9937.
As a result, the Lord alone became righteousness and merit: 1813, 2025,
2026, 2027, 9715, 9809, 10178. The Lord's last spiritual crisis was in Gethsemane and on the cross, followed by the complete victory through which
he gained control over the hells and at the same time glorified his human
nature: 2776, 2813, 2814, 10655, 10659, 10828. The Lord could not undergo
spiritual crisis with respect to his divine nature: 2795, 2813, 2814. That is
why he took on from his mother a weak human nature that was susceptible to spiritual crisis: 1414, 1444, 1573, 5041, 5157, 7193, 9315. Through
spiritual crises and victories he drove out everything he had inherited
from his mother and shed the human nature received from her so completely that finally he was no longer her son: 2159, 2574, 2649, 3036,
10830. Jehovah, who was within him, nevertheless seemed to be absent
during his spiritual crises to the extent that he was centered in the human
nature he had from his mother: 1815. This was the Lord's state of being
humbled: 1785, 1999, 2159, 6866. Through spiritual crises and victories
the Lord set everything in the heavens in order: 4287, 9528, 9715, 9937.
By the same means he also united his human nature to his divine nature—
that is, glorified his human nature: 1725, 1729, 1733, 1737, 3318, 3381, 3382,
4286, 4287, 9528, 9937.

When the Lord was in the world his human nature was divine truth. 303
When he was in the world, the Lord made his human nature divine truth
from the divine goodness that was in him: 2803, 3194, 3195, 3210, 6716,
6864, 7014, 7499, 8127, 8724, 9199. The Lord then arranged everything
within himself into the form of heaven in accord with divine truth: 1928,
3633. As a result, heaven was then in the Lord and the Lord was like
heaven: 911, 1900, 1928, 3624–3631, 3634, 3884, 4041, 4279, 4523, 4524,
4525, 6013, 6057, 6690, 9279, 9632, 9931, 10303. The Lord spoke from the
divine truth itself: 8127. So in the Word, the Lord used correspondences
when he spoke: 3131, 3472–3485, 8615, 10687. As a result, the Lord is the
Word and is called the Word, which is divine truth: 2533, 2813, 2859,

2894, 3393, 3712. In the Word, "the Son of Humanity" means divine truth and "the Father" means divine goodness: 2803, 3704, 7499, 8724, 9194. Since the Lord was divine truth, he was also divine wisdom: 2500, 3382. Only the Lord's perception and thinking came entirely from himself, and they transcended all angelic perception and thinking: 1904, 1914, 1919. His divine truth was susceptible to spiritual assault; his divine goodness was not: 2824.

304   *The Lord united divine truth to divine goodness; that is, he united his human nature to the divine nature itself.* The Lord was taught like anyone else: 1457, 1461, 2523, 3030. The Lord progressed step by step toward oneness with the Father: 1864, 2033, 2632, 3141, 4585, 7014, 10076. When the Lord was in a state of oneness with the Father he talked with him as identical with himself; in other states he spoke with him as someone other than himself: 1745, 1999, 7058. The Lord united his human nature to his divine nature by his own power: 1616, 1749, 1753, 1813, 1921, 2025, 2026, 2523, 3043, 5005, 5045, 6716. The Lord united divine truth, which was he himself, with the divine goodness that was within him: 10047, 10052, 10076. The uniting was reciprocal: 2004, 10067. When the Lord left the world he made his human nature divine goodness: 3194, 3210, 6864, 7499, 8724, 9199, 10076. So he came forth from the Father and returned to the Father: 3194, 3210. In this way he became one with the Father: 2751, 3704, 4766. The Lord's purpose in becoming one with the divine nature that was within him was to be joined to the human race: 2034. Ever since this oneness became complete, divine truth has emanated from the Lord: 3704, 3712, 3969, 4577, 5704, 7499, 8127, 8241, 9199, 9398. A description of how divine truth emanates: 7270, 9407.

Unless the divine nature had been within the Lord's human nature from conception, his human nature could not have become one with his divine nature, because of the intensity of infinite love in which divinity itself resides: 6849. So there is no way for any angel to become one with the Divine itself except remotely and by means of veiling; otherwise the angel would be consumed: 6849. This is what divine love is like: 8644. This shows that the Lord's human nature was not like that of anyone else: 10125, 10826. His oneness with the Father, the source of his soul, was not like a uniting of two but like a uniting of a soul and a body: 3737, 10824. The relationship of the Lord's human nature with the Divine is called "oneness," while our relationship with the Divine is called "a joining together": 2021.

In this way the Lord made his human nature divine. The Lord's human 305
nature is divine because it came from the underlying reality of the Father
that was the Lord's soul (10269, 10372, 10823, which use as an illustration
the way children resemble their fathers) and because it came from the
divine love that is within him (6872). The nature of every individual is
determined by the nature of his or her love; we are all our own love: 6872,
10177, 10284. The Lord was divine love: 2077, 2253. The Lord made every
aspect of his human nature divine, both inner aspects and outer ones:
1603, 1815, 1902, 1926, 2093, 2803. So unlike anyone else, he rose from
the dead with his whole body: 1729, 2083, 5078, 10825. The fact that the
Lord's human nature is divine can be recognized from the omnipresence
of that human nature in the Holy Supper (2343, 10826) and from his
transfiguration in the presence of three of his disciples (3212) as well as
from various statements in the Word (10154), particularly his being called
"Jehovah" in it (1603, 1736, 1815, 1902, 2921, 3035, 5110, 6303, 6281, 8864,
9194, 9315). A distinction is maintained between the Father and the Son
or between Jehovah and the Lord in the literal meaning, but not in the
inner meaning of the Word, which the angels have: 3035. The Christian
world does not recognize the Lord's human nature as divine; the view
that his divinity and his humanity are separate was arrived at in a council
to support recognition of the pope as the Lord's vicar (as I learned from
conversation with members of that council in the other life): 4738.

[2] The divine-human nature has existed from eternity, in the form
of divine truth in heaven and therefore as the manifestation of divine
presence; later, in the Lord, though, the divine-human nature became
the divine underlying reality, the source of the manifestation of divine
presence in heaven: 3061, 6280, 6880, 10579. What the state of heaven
was like before the Lord came into the world: 6371, 6372, 6373. What was
divine could not be perceived then and therefore could not be accepted
unless it had passed through heaven: 6982, 6996, 7004. The Lord from
eternity was the divine truth in heaven: 2803, 3195, 3704. This is "the Son
of God born from eternity": 2628, 2798.

[3] The only divinity they perceive in heaven is the divine humanity:
6475, 9303, 9356, 10067. The earliest people were not able to worship the
infinite underlying reality but they were able to worship the infinite manifestation of it, which is the divine humanity: 4687, 4692. The ancients
acknowledged the Divine because it appeared in a human form, and this
was the divine humanity: 5110, 5663, 6846, 10737. The inhabitants of

all planets worship the Divine in a human form; they rejoice when they hear that God actually became a human being: 6700, 8541–8547, 9361, 10736, 10737, 10738. See my booklet *Worlds in Our Solar System, and in the Starry Heavens.* If we do not think of God as being in a human form, we can have no definite idea of God, because what is incomprehensible does not take shape in the mind: 9359, 9972. We can worship only something of which we have some concept; we cannot worship something of which we have no concept: 4733, 5110, 5663, 7211, 9356, 10067. So most people throughout the world worship the Divine in a human form, and this happens because of an inflow from heaven: 10159. When people who are devoted to living good lives think about the Lord, they all think about him as having a divine-human nature and not as having a human nature separate from a divine one: 2326, 4724, 4731, 4766, 8878, 9193, 9198. Why the people in today's church who are consumed with leading an evil life, as well as the people who are devoted to faith apart from caring, think about the Lord's human nature as not being divine, and why they do not understand what the divine-human nature is: 3212, 3241, 4689, 4692, 4724, 4731, 5321, 6371, 8878, 9193, 9198.

306 *The trinity exists within the Lord.* Christians in the other life have been examined to see what kind of concept of the oneness of God they had, and it has been found that they have a concept of three gods: 2329, 5256, 10736, 10737, 10738, 10821. It is possible for us to form a concept of a divine trinity within one person and therefore an idea that there is one God; if we are thinking there are three persons, though, it is not possible for us to form an idea of one God: 10738, 10821, 10824. The trinity within one person (therefore within the Lord) consists of the divinity itself that is called the Father, the divine-human nature that is called the Son, and the emanating divine influence that is called the Holy Spirit; the trinity is therefore a unity: 2149, 2156, 2288, 2321, 2329, 2447, 3704, 6993, 7182, 10738, 10822, 10823. The divine trinity that exists within the Lord is acknowledged in heaven: 14, 15, 1729, 2004, 5256, 9303. The Lord is one with the Father, so he is both the divinity itself and the divine humanity: 1729, 2004, 2005, 2018, 2025, 2751, 3704, 3736, 4766. His emanating divine influence is also his divinity in heaven, which is called the Holy Spirit: 3969, 4673, 6788, 6993, 7499, 8127, 8302, 9199, 9229, 9407, 9818, 9820, 10330. So the Lord is the one and only God: 1607, 2149, 2156, 2329, 2447, 2751, 3194, 3704, 3712, 3938, 4577, 4687, 5321, 6280, 6371, 6849, 6993, 7014, 7091, 7182, 7209, 8241, 8724, 8760, 8864, 8865, 9194, 9303.

The Lord in heaven. The Lord is seen in heaven as a sun or a moon— 307
as a sun by people in the heavenly kingdom and as a moon by people in
the spiritual kingdom: 1053, 1521, 1529, 1530, 1531, 3636, 3641, 4321, 5097,
7078, 7083, 7173, 7270, 8812, 10809. The light that radiates from the Lord
as the sun is divine truth, the source of all intelligence and wisdom for
angels: 1053, 1521–1533, 2776, 3138, 3195, 3222, 3223, 3225, 3339, 3341, 3636,
3643, 3993, 4180, 4302, 4415, 5400, 9399, 9407, 9548, 9571, 9684. The
warmth that radiates from the Lord as the sun is divine goodness, the
source of the love that angels have: 3338, 3636, 3643, 5215. The Lord's
divinity as it is in itself is far above his divinity as it is present in heaven:
7270, 8760. Divine truth is not in the Lord but emanates from him,
just as light is not in the sun but emanates from it: 3969. The underlying reality exists within the Lord, and the manifestation of it comes
from the Lord: 3938. The Lord is the one center toward which all the
angels in heaven turn: 3633, 9828, 10130, 10189. Still, angels do not turn
themselves toward the Lord; rather, the Lord turns them toward himself
(10189), because angels do not make themselves present with the Lord;
the Lord makes himself present with the angels (9415). The Lord's presence with angels depends on how receptive they are to the goodness of
love and of caring that come from him: 904, 4198, 4206, 4211, 4320, 6832,
7042, 8819, 9680, 9682, 9683, 10106. The Lord is present with everyone
in heaven and also everyone in hell: 2706. Because of his divine love, the
Lord wants to lead everyone toward himself in heaven: 6645. The Lord
is constantly engaged in an effort to join with us, but his inflowing and
his joining with us are impeded by our own loves: 2041, 2053, 2411, 5696.

[2] The Lord's divine humanity flows into heaven and constitutes
it; those in heaven are joined not to the divinity itself but to the divine
humanity: 3038, 4211, 4724, 5663. Further, the divine humanity flows
through and out of heaven to be with us: 9706. The Lord is everything to
heaven and is the life of heaven: 7211, 9128. The Lord dwells with angels
in what is his own: 9338, 10125, 10151, 10157. Therefore those who are in
heaven are in the Lord: 3637, 3638. Heaven corresponds to the Lord's
divine humanity, and a human being in every detail corresponds to
heaven, so heaven taken as a whole is like one individual and is therefore
called "the universal human": 2988, 2996, 3624–3649, 3741–3745, 4625.
The Lord is the only true human being, and we become human only if
we become receptive to what is divine from him: 1894. The more receptive we are to the Lord, the more we become images of the Lord: 8547.

Angels are embodiments of love and caring in human form, a quality that they get from the Lord: 3804, 4735, 4797, 4985, 5199, 5530, 9879, 10177.

308   *All goodness and truth come from the Lord.* The Lord is goodness itself and truth itself: 2011, 5110, 10336, 10619. All goodness and truth come from the Lord, so all peace, innocence, love, caring, and faith do as well (1614, 2016, 2751, 2882, 2883, 2891, 2892, 2904), as do all wisdom and intelligence (109, 112, 121, 124). Nothing but what is good comes from the Lord, but evil people turn the goodness from the Lord into evil: 7643, 7679, 7710, 8632. Angels know that all goodness and truth come from the Lord; evil people do not want to know this: 6193, 9128. The [increased] presence of the Lord causes angels to move further into goodness but hellish spirits to move further into evil: 7989. Evil people throw themselves into hell solely because of the Lord's presence: 8137, 8265. The Lord judges all people from his own goodness: 2335. The Lord looks at everyone out of mercy: 223. The Lord is never angry at anyone, never does anyone harm, and never consigns anyone to hell: 245, 1683, 2335, 8632. How to understand the fact that it says in the Word that Jehovah or the Lord is angry, kills, casts into hell, and many similar things: 592, 696, 1093, 1874, 1875, 2395, 2447, 3605, 3607, 3614, 6071, 6997.

309   *The Lord has all power in heaven and on earth.* The whole heaven is the Lord's (2751, 7086); he has power in the heavens and on earth (1607, 10089, 10827). Because the Lord governs the whole heaven, he also governs everything that depends on it, so he governs everything in this world: 2026, 2027, 4523, 4524. He also governs the hells: 3642. The Lord governs all things from his divinity and through his divine humanity: 8864, 8865. The Lord governs all things in accord with the divine design; the divine design covers things that he wills, things that he can accept, and things that he has to allow: 1755, 2447, 6574, 9940. On the divine design, see §279 above. The Lord governs the outermost elements from the inmost and the inmost elements from the outermost, and this is why he is called the First and the Last: 3702, 6040, 6056. Only the Lord has the power to move the hells away from us, restrain us from evils, and keep us in goodness, and therefore to save us: 10019. Judgment belongs to the Lord: 2319, 2320, 2321, 10810, 10811. What the Lord's priestly function is, and what his royal function is: 1728, 2015.

310   *How to understand various statements about the Lord that are found in the Word.* What "the seed of the woman" means in the prophecy about the Lord: 256. The meaning of "the Son of Humanity" and "the Son of God" in the Word: 2159, 2813. What the two names "Jesus" and "Christ" mean: 3004–3011. What it means when the Lord is described as "sent by the Father": 2397, 6831, 10561. What the Word means when it says that the Lord carried the iniquities of us all (9937), that the Lord redeemed us through his blood (10152), that the Lord fulfilled everything of the law (10239), that the Lord intercedes for us (2250, 8573, 8705), and that there is no salvation apart from the Lord (10828). Salvation did not come about through the Father's contemplation of the suffering of the Son, and it does not come about by our praying to the Father to have mercy on us for the sake of his Son. After all, the Lord said, "I am the way, the truth, and the life. No one comes to the Father except through me" (John 14:6): 2854. The irrational ideas implicit in the widely accepted belief that the Lord reconciled the human race to the Father by means of his suffering on the cross: 10659. The Lord's Coming means his presence in the Word: 3900, 4060. The Lord wants glory from us not for his own sake but for the sake of our salvation: 5957, 10646. Where the Lord is called "the Lord" in the Word, it means divine goodness (4973, 9167, 9194); where he is called "Christ," it means divine truth (3004, 3005, 3008, 3009).

True acknowledgment and true worship of the Lord is to do his commandments: 10143, 10153, 10578, 10645, 10829 (which include supporting material from the Word).

Ecclesiastical and Civil Governance

311 IN human society, there need to be two arenas of governmental order—one that is concerned with heavenly matters, and another that is concerned with worldly matters. The governance concerned with heavenly matters is called "ecclesiastical," and the governance concerned with worldly matters is called "civil."

312 Good order cannot be maintained in the world without officials who are required to observe everything that is orderly and everything that is disorderly and to reward people who live properly and penalize people who live improperly. If this is not done, the human race will perish, since everyone has by heredity an innate desire to rule over others and to gain possession of their goods, which gives rise to hostility, envy, hatred, vengefulness, guile, cruelty, and any number of other evils. So we need to be kept under restraint by laws. Those of us who do what is good need to receive rewards that accord with our love of honors and of financial gain. Those of us who do what is evil need to receive punishments that affect those same loves (namely, loss of honor, wealth, and life). Otherwise the human race would perish.

313 So there need to be officials to keep society in order—people who are skilled in the law, wise, and God-fearing. The officials also need their own organizational structure to prevent any of them, on some whim or out of ignorance, from allowing evils to occur that violate and therefore destroy proper order. This is guarded against when there are higher and lower officials in a hierarchical structure.

314 The officials overseeing the arena of our lives that concerns heavenly matters, the ecclesiastical arena, are called priests, and their function is priesthood. The officials overseeing the arena of our lives that concerns worldly matters, the civil arena, are called magistrates, and the highest of them, where such a form of government exists, is the monarch.

315 As for priests, they are to teach people the way to heaven and are also to lead them on that path. They are to teach them according to the body of teaching of their church drawn from the Word and are to lead them to live by that teaching. Priests who teach what is true and who by means of truths lead people to practice goodness in their lives and therefore lead

them to the Lord are good shepherds of their sheep; priests who teach but
do not lead people to practice goodness in their lives and therefore do not
lead them to the Lord are bad shepherds.

Priests must not claim to have power over people's souls, because in
actuality they do not know the state of people's inner selves. It is even
more important for priests not to claim the power to open and close
heaven, since that power belongs to the Lord alone.

316

Priests should be accorded dignity and honor because of the holy
functions they perform; but if they are wise, they ascribe the honor not to
themselves but to the Lord, who is the source of what is holy. If they are
not wise, they ascribe the honor to themselves—and take it away from
the Lord.

317

Priests who ascribe honor to themselves because of the holy functions they perform place honor and financial gain above the salvation of
souls, which should be their primary concern. In contrast, priests who
ascribe honor to the Lord and not to themselves place the salvation of
souls above honor and financial gain.

None of the honor that goes with any function belongs to the individual performing it. Rather, it is appended to the individual in accord
with the importance of the function being performed; and anything that
is appended does not belong to the individual and is taken away from her
or him when the position passes to another. The only honor that remains
ours is honor we receive for our wisdom and fear of the Lord.

Priests are to teach the people and to lead them by means of truths to
practice goodness in their lives. Priests are not to compel anyone, though,
because people cannot be compelled to believe anything that contradicts
what they think in their hearts to be true. People whose beliefs differ
from those of the priest but who do not cause disturbances should be left
in peace; but if they do cause disturbances, they should be removed [from
the church]. This is part of the priesthood's responsibility to maintain
order.

318

As priests are officials in charge of matters of divine law and worship,
so monarchs and magistrates are in charge of matters of civil law and
judgment.

319

Since the monarch cannot administer everything alone, there need to
be officials under him or her, each with a particular area of responsibility
that the monarch does not have the skills or the ability to manage. These
officials, taken as a whole, are the royal government, but the monarch is
the highest among them.

320

321 Royal majesty does not belong to the individual but is appended to her or him. Kings and queens who believe that royal majesty is intrinsic to themselves, and officials who believe that the dignity of their rank is intrinsic to themselves, are lacking in wisdom.

322 Royal governance consists in conducting administration according to the laws of the realm and in delivering judgments in accord with those laws with an eye toward justice. Monarchs who regard the laws as higher than themselves are wise; monarchs who regard themselves as above the law are not. Monarchs who regard the laws as higher than themselves ascribe the royal governing to the law, and allow the law to rule over themselves. They know that the law is justice and all justice that is truly just is divine. Monarchs who see themselves as above the law, though, ascribe the royal governing to themselves. They believe either that they themselves are the law or that the law that is justice comes from them. So they claim for themselves something that is divine, when they should be subject to it.

323 The law that is justice should be enacted in the realm by individuals who are skilled in the law, wise, and God-fearing, and thereafter the monarch and subjects should live by that law. Monarchs who live by the duly enacted law set an example for their subjects by doing so. They are true monarchs.

324 There are monarchs with absolute power, who regard their subjects as slaves, so much so that they as monarchs have a right to their subjects' possessions and even lives. If they exercise this right, they are not monarchs but tyrants.

325 A monarch is to be obeyed as the laws of the realm prescribe and is not to be harmed in any way by deed or word. The security of the nation depends on this.

THE END

BIOGRAPHICAL NOTE

Biographical Note

E MANUEL SWEDENBORG (1688–1772) was born Emanuel Swedberg (or Svedberg) in Stockholm, Sweden, on January 29, 1688 (Julian calendar). He was the third of the nine children of Jesper Swedberg (1653–1735) and Sara Behm (1666–1696). At the age of eight he lost his mother. After the death of his only older brother ten days later, he became the oldest living son. In 1697 his father married Sara Bergia (1666–1720), who developed great affection for Emanuel and left him a significant inheritance. His father, a Lutheran clergyman, later became a celebrated and controversial bishop, whose diocese included the Swedish churches in Pennsylvania and in London, England.

After studying at the University of Uppsala (1699–1709), Emanuel journeyed to England, the Netherlands, France, and Germany (1710–1715) to study and work with leading scientists in western Europe. Upon his return he apprenticed as an engineer under the brilliant Swedish inventor Christopher Polhem (1661–1751). He gained favor with Sweden's King Charles XII (1682–1718), who gave him a salaried position as an overseer of Sweden's mining industry (1716–1747). Although Emanuel was engaged, he never married.

After the death of Charles XII, Emanuel was ennobled by Queen Ulrika Eleonora (1688–1741), and his last name was changed to Swedenborg (or Svedenborg). This change in status gave him a seat in the Swedish House of Nobles, where he remained an active participant in the Swedish government throughout his life.

A member of the Royal Swedish Academy of Sciences, he devoted himself to studies that culminated in a number of publications, most notably a comprehensive three-volume work on natural philosophy and metallurgy (1734) that brought him recognition across Europe as a scientist. After 1734 he redirected his research and publishing to a study of anatomy in search of the interface between the soul and body, making several significant discoveries in physiology.

From 1743 to 1745 he entered a transitional phase that resulted in a shift of his main focus from science to theology. Throughout the rest of his life he maintained that this shift was brought about by Jesus Christ, who appeared to him, called him to a new mission, and opened his perception to a permanent dual consciousness of this life and the life after death.

He devoted the last decades of his life to studying Scripture and publishing eighteen theological titles that draw on the Bible, reasoning, and his own spiritual experiences. These works present a Christian theology with unique perspectives on the nature of God, the spiritual world, the Bible, the human mind, and the path to salvation.

Swedenborg died in London on March 29, 1772 (Gregorian calendar), at the age of eighty-four.